W9-ATH-245

FIVE GOSPELS

An Account of How the Good News Came to Be

John C. Meagher

BR
129
.M43
1983

WINSTON PRESS

205541

Cover art: "I Saw the Figure 5 in Gold" by Charles Henry Demuth (1883-1935), courtesy of the Metropolitan Museum of Art, New York.

Copyright © 1983 by John C. Meagher.
All rights reserved. No part of this book may be reproduced in any form without written permission of Winston Press, Inc.

Library of Congress Catalog Card Number: 82-51163

ISBN (hardcover): 0-86683-731-0
ISBN (paperback): 0-86683-691-8

Printed in the United States of America.

5 4 3 2 1

Winston Press, Inc.
430 Oak Grove
Minneapolis, Minnesota 55403

Five Gospels is dedicated to five persons
who have been to me
good news
beyond my telling:

Eleanor Meagher
Don Costello
Christine Costello
Ardis Collins
Lynn York

Acknowledgments

This book has been longer and harder in the making than is likely to be apparent. As it passed through its various metamorphoses—expanding and contracting, undergoing alterations and reorganization, enduring accidental losses and deliberate cuts and detailed rewritings and periods of discouraged abandonment—it was gradually helped along far more than I can recount by students, research assistants, colleagues, and friends who offered reactions, advice, criticism, help, and encouragement of various kinds, as well as by financial support from the Institute of Christian Thought, the Social Sciences and Humanities Research Council of Canada, the University of Toronto, and the Faculty of Theology of the University of St. Michael's College. I offer my particular gratitude to Steve Wilson and John Kloppenborg for their special generosities, and my sincerely apologetic thanks to Cy Reilly for his patient and devoted labors in the final stages. But to all whose efforts have touched these pages, I send the hope that your own work will always be as free of setbacks as I wish this had been and as free of deficiencies as I wish this were.

Toronto
Epiphany, 1983

Contents

Introduction

"It is one of those cases where the art of the reasoner should be used rather for the sifting of details than for the acquiring of fresh evidence. The tragedy has been so uncommon, so complete, and of such personal importance to so many people that we are suffering from a plethora of surmise, conjecture, and hypothesis. The difficulty is to detach the framework of fact—of absolute, undeniable fact—from the embellishments of theorists and reporters. Then, having established ourselves upon this sound basis, it is our duty to see what inferences may be drawn, and which are the special points upon which the whole mystery turns. . . . See the value of imagination," said Holmes. "It is the one quality which Gregory lacks. We imagined what might have happened, acted upon the supposition, and find ourselves justified. Let us proceed."

—*The Memoirs of Sherlock Holmes*

FACT AND SURMISE

It is not only the private investigator who is plagued by a plethora of surmise and who dreams of discovering and building upon absolute, undeniable fact. This is also the plague and the dream of the scientist, the judge—and the historian of the Christian gospel. The plague is unsettling and the dream is seductive: one is always trying to enlist new facts into the enterprise, and always trying to commission as many as possible in the bold uniform of Absolute and Undeniable. It is small wonder that new facts are constantly being conscripted for lack of volunteers, and that able-bodied surmises are constantly being promoted into the honored rank of facts. The Christian gospel is "so uncommon, so complete, and of such personal importance to so many people" that we want a settlement to which we are not entitled, and try to lean on frail supports.

There are no absolute, undeniable facts strong enough to provide a framework that will explain how the Christian good news came to be. For facts are not solid truths, irreducible realities, inescapable givens: they are constructs which the mind has made. Some are made with enough care and procedural agreement that they go uncontested. Because they are undenied, they seem undeniable; because they have no competition, they appear absolute. But they are nonetheless provisional constructs, and the questions they seem to close are always subject to being reopened. One of the most eminent of New Testament scholars wrote in 1932, and republished in 1953, that "the criticism of the Gospels has achieved at least one secure result. Scarcely anyone now doubts that Mark is our primary Gospel."[1] Since 1953, there has been an increasing body of scholarship that registers doubt about this one speciously secure result and argues cogently against retaining it.[2] That which we call a fact is a conjecture with the appearance of stability; but that appearance often fades under closer scrutiny.

The study of Christian origins has undergone enormous shifts over the last few generations, in the course of which an unprecedented number of previously uncontested "facts" have been dismantled and discharged. The resulting uncertainties plead for resolution. The compelling dream inevitably resurfaces: some of those who find these matters important try to reassert absolute, undeniable facts; others, more in tune with the sophistications of procedure, promote candidates for absolute, undeniable methodologies.

This book proposes neither. It begins with the conviction that it is desirable to attempt to reconstruct the origins and early development of Christian gospelling as accurately as possible, and it proceeds by trying to discern what is plausible in such a reconstruction. But this book will appeal neither to undeniable facts nor to absolute methods of investigation, because neither is readily available, and pursuing them is not a realistic way of dealing with a subject of this size and complexity. The virtually unquestionable facts are of trivial importance, and the more important surmises are usually seriously questionable, whether or not they are in fact normally questioned. The most watertight methods can encompass only small matters and necessarily produce small results; the larger questions are not themselves accessible through strictly scientific procedures. The task at hand is to discern the special points on which the whole mystery turns, as Holmes would put it. As for the procedure, he was half right. It does not have to do with isolating undeniable fact—for there is virtually no such thing—but it has a great deal to do with the way imagination deals with the whole body of evidence. It is the evidence itself that finally counts. But to see how it counts, one can rely neither on religious faith nor on the most rigorous techniques of modern scholarship, for neither is comprehensive or versatile enough to handle the job. *We must imagine what might have happened, act upon the supposition, and see whether we may find ourselves justified.*

SPIRAL STAIRCASES

At one point during my schooldays, one of my classmates pointedly asked me to tell him what a spiral staircase was. It was obviously a test of some sort, but I had no idea what might constitute passing or failing. I therefore fell back on vulgar instinct: I said that it was a staircase constructed like this, and I made the inevitable gesture, outlining a spiral from bottom to top. He chuckled triumphantly, announced that I was one more victim who had fallen into the trap by using my hands in the course of a definition, and sauntered away, no doubt looking for a new conquest.

I smarted for a couple of minutes, not liking to be caught that way. Then I thought about it; and as I thought about it, it became increasingly obvious to me that in fact I had done what any sensible person would do to communicate the meaning he had asked for. If he had thought that I had been somehow caught, he was playing by odd rules.

Some people play by odd rules, in a becoming and responsible way. I have just learned about the fellow who could thwart that prank: a nuclear physicist who, offered the same question, "answered with the sine and cosine equations for a helix, without moving his hands, but this is not a common response."[3]

Nuclear physicists are used to playing by rules that seem odd when transferred to an ordinary situation like defining a spiral staircase. They are the right rules for nuclear physics, and must be followed if any good work is to be done in that field. But they are not the right rules for communicating the nature of a spiral staircase to people like me, whose knowledge of even good high-school-level mathemetics is too limited and too rusty to grasp sine and cosine equations readily enough to see their implications.

Modern New Testament scholarship has reached a high level of technical sophistication. It now has its own equivalents of sine and cosine equations for analyzing scriptural texts. It is normally in this sort of language that scholarly discussion is carried on in professional journals and graduate seminars—the way such things are discussed among the perfect, as the Apostle Paul would put it (1 Cor 2:6), as contrasted with the ways intelligible to those whose technical sophistication is not so advanced. Such language is usually more precise than the nearest non-technical equivalents, more nuanced and efficient. It is normally accompanied by an expositional and argumentative procedure that takes explicit footnoted account of the previous scholarly literature bearing on the subject under discussion. That is the most effective way of dealing with a manageable and continuous scholarly conversation. This book will proceed differently, for three reasons.

First, I wish to enlarge the conversation beyond scholarly boundaries. I do not wish to evade the notice or judgment of my scholarly colleagues; this book is intended especially for them, since it is their thinking that I most want to affect, and it is their evaluation that most interests me. But the matters I discuss are of concern to many people whose intelligent interest is much stronger than their technical training, and I wish to speak to them as well. I think that it is desirable, and I believe that it is possible, to address both groups at once, whether or not I have succeeded in doing so. This book at least makes that attempt, and accordingly adopts a policy of exposition and argument that is deliberately more sketchy than the usual professional standard. I have, under advice, considerably shortened the text in the process of revision to concentrate on the main points at the expense of qualifications, nuances, and substantive additional questions that deserve a hearing but are not indispensable to the presentation of my principal views. I have, in short, oversimplified, cut corners, and reduced the scope of what the book attempts. This is therefore a designer's sketch, not an architect's finished set of drawings; it is my hope that the scholarly reader will find the result helpfully suggestive, however incomplete, and that the less scholarly reader will find it readable and illuminating.

Second, in order to make the project more manageable I have written the book in dialogue with the primary evidence rather than with the secondary scholarly discussion. It is the evidence of the New Testament that we are trying to explain, and it is the history which this evidence both conceals and reveals that we are attempting to reconstruct. I cite representative selections of my primary evidence in the text; scholarly and non-scholarly readers alike will be able to see why I think as I do. I have not tried to make consistently clear why I do not think otherwise. More than a thousand relevant articles, monographs, and books appear every year to propose changes and refinements in the way we think about various aspects of the New Testament; and while I have dutifully consulted what is available, I have not tried to record that process in footnotes or in detailed argumentation. Scholarly readers will recognize that nearly every page of this book could be expanded into forty or fifty pages if I were to deal with the present range of professional discussion, and dozens of notes could be appended at nearly every turn of argument to indicate my agreements and disagreements with those who have gone before me. A fully finished set of drawings might require that. I do not think that this book does. I regret that my relatively skimpy annotation does not register my respect and gratitude properly: I am deeply in the debt of scholars from whose work I have learned, including those who did not persuade me but forced me to think more clearly why they did not. I have tried to write from within the scholarly conversation, but not about it.

Third, this book is in some ways not in direct continuity with the main scholarly conversation. There are various challenges within it to relatively settled scholarly opinions and surmises, and there are novel suggestions that cut across the usual discussion at oblique angles. The reader will be able to see in general how my study of the primary evidence has led me to these things, and this book is intended to invite readers to entertain that evidence in these ways, if only as an experiment, to see the kind of sense it makes to do so. I have not tried to prove my right to challenge or deviate by arguing with or against others, only by appealing to the evidence we all share and offering a way of reading it that seems to me to make satisfactory and potentially fruitful sense. The most efficient way of going about my task is to present my reconstruction directly. The result is sketchy, incomplete, admittedly oversimplified, often questionable. It will be easy to find fault with this book. But I hope that the unconventionality of it will not be found annoying or disappointing or misleading. Or, indeed, all that unconventional—for, to revert once more to the architectural metaphor: modern scholarship is agreed that the New Testament does not always tell it like it was. The original building-stones have been substantially rearranged, including various instances in which stones rejected by the original builders have been made the head of the corner. It is generally agreed among scholars that to get at the historical truth we must deconstruct the New Testament and reconstruct something other than what it apparently offers.

I have come to think that it is illuminating to see the origins of the Christian good news in terms of five distinct but interrelated stages of proclamation. To show you how and why I think that, I mean to reorganize the surviving stones in the way I suppose they were originally placed, so that you may see how they fit. I do not intend to argue one by one why I think they fit better my way than in the other configurations that have been proposed for them. I rather try to imagine what might have happened, act upon the supposition by building in the light of the surviving texts, and invite the reader to see if the result is not faithful both to historical likelihood and to the historical evidence. That is, I will draw the clumsy spiral, and let the mathematics wait.

SKEPTICISM AND HOSPITALITY

All attempts to deal with Christian origins have to face a set of difficulties that must give pause to the bold, and may freeze the blood of the timid. One of the most formidable is to determine how reliable the evidence is. One must travel uncertain and unsteady distances in moving from the elementary and uncontested facts (e.g., most surviving manuscripts of Mark quote Jesus as saying "I am" at 14:62; Acts represents

Paul, just before his conversion, as going from Jerusalem to Damascus with letters of authority to persecute Christians) to the facts we really want to know (e.g., what *did* Jesus say at his trial? how *did* Paul wind up in Damascus?). There was a time when virtually all writers on this subject assumed that everything in the New Testament was historically reliable. But a century and more of searching criticism has made most informed and experienced scholars instinctively suspicious about the historical reliability of New Testament reports. This skepticism, a useful corrective to the naive trust that once obtained, has settled in especially around the reconstruction of what we most want to know about—the deeds and message of Jesus. Scholars seem to have considerably more confidence in reports concerning John the Baptist or Peter than in reports dealing with the central figure in the story. This is understandable, since there is more motivation for early tradition to tamper with the central figure than with one who is more marginal. It is also a bit strange, in that there is also more motivation for preserving more accurate memories of the central figure than of the marginal ones, and it is usually harder to get by with misrepresentations of what is most important. But be that as it may, it is the scholarly fashion to be highly skeptical about the reliability of New Testament representations, especially about Jesus.

There are good reasons for this scholarly agnosticism. But I have nevertheless chosen in this book to proceed somewhat differently. I would like briefly to explain why, and how.

First, although there are good reasons for the customary agnosticism, the reasons do not seem to me nearly as strong and compelling as they have usually been regarded. The New Testament contains unreliable surmises, but so does the work of its critics, which requires as ready a skepticism as those surmises which criticism has dismantled. Let me cite one fairly typical and significant example, from the opening page of the first chapter of Norman Perrin's important and influential book, *Rediscovering the Teaching of Jesus*. Perrin gives his reasons why teaching ascribed to Jesus is likely to be rather a teaching that stems from the early Church, not from Jesus himself. I quote the first three reasons: "The early Church made no attempt to distinguish between the words the earthly Jesus had spoken and those spoken by the risen Lord through a prophet in the community. . . ." "The early Church absolutely and completely identified the risen Lord of her experience with the earthly Jesus of Nazareth. . . ." "Further, the gospel form was created to serve the purposes of the early Church, but historical reminiscence was not one of those purposes."[4]

It is not difficult to see that these considerations would make a serious difference in how we read the remarks attributed to Jesus and how we reconstruct their historical origins. It is difficult, however, to see how these three surmises come to be presented so boldly, as if they were facts, givens, achieved truths that require neither evidence nor argument, that need not be cushioned by "apparently" or "probably" or "in my opinion"—in short, that lay such claim to absolute and undeniable status. Perrin's statements are founded on surprisingly little evidence. They are reasonable surmises, often found in contemporary scholarship, but they are not facts. Actually, they are rather easy to call into question, not only by means of alternative surmises but even on the basis of fairly firm evidence. For example, the opening verses of the Book of Revelation attempt to distinguish between the words of the earthly Jesus and words spoken by the risen Lord through a prophet in the community; 2 Cor 5:16 offers a voice from the early Church claiming that the risen Lord is not to be identified absolutely and completely with the earthly Jesus;[5] and the opening verses of the Gospel of Luke, taken together with the opening verses of Acts, obviously imply that historical reminiscence was one of the purposes that informed not only the work of Luke but that of some of his predecessors. I do not say that Perrin's claims are nonsense: I merely observe that they are quite exaggerated, and although they seem to be presented as a set of Holmesian absolute, undeniable facts, they are no such matter. Perrin's confidence about them was widely shared by other scholars, but it was, and is, nonetheless ill-founded and misplaced.

A second ground for being less skeptical about the historical reliability of New Testament evidence than is usual in current scholarly circles—a ground which initially must seem paradoxical—is that the surviving evidence is so incomplete. That is a sobering truth, and has generally been taken to indicate that relatively little can be reconstructed on a solid scientific basis. I agree that this is so. But this leaves not one course of action, but two. One may concentrate on what is scientifically controllable—or one may be experimentally speculative, and measure the evidence against hypotheses that, although they cannot be scientifically established, may indeed sketch what was the case. We imagine what might have happened, and act upon the supposition. Such imaginings are not evidence, but only a conjectural context in which one may reread the evidence experimentally. But such experiments are worth undertaking, especially when the evidence is scanty, ambiguous, and uprooted:

> There are some interpretations that are *compelled* by texts: we are driven to them because the text simply refuses to cooperate until its will is done. Other interpretations are *invited,* still others *suggested,* and others yet are *allowed.* But the most elusive, and often the most interesting, are the interpretations for which the text secretly longs—and we can tell only by the way it beams when the gift is finally made.[6]

A third reason for using a less skeptical procedure is that there is an intrinsic likelihood in supposing a general reliability. I do not deny that there are various instances in the Gospels in which Jesus is made to say things that he almost certainly did not say. But I think that the probability on the whole is that most of the sayings attributed to him, especially when they complement one another in larger consistent patterns, are rooted in actual reminiscence, to a considerable degree. I think this for two reasons. On the one hand, it would in principle be far easier and more natural for Jesus' followers to preserve and build upon reminiscences of what they heard and saw than to make up a whole body of artificial recollections. On the other hand, the first three Gospels not only evidently propose actual reminiscences of Jesus but are also strikingly limited in their attempts to make him say what we know the post-resurrection Church came to believe. Even in the Fourth Gospel, which offers a paradigmatic case of how far one could go in revising memories of Jesus' message, there are (as I will argue in the last chapter of this book) grounds for supposing that real recollections generally underlie the further developments there grafted to his teaching. In the first three Gospels, where the recollections of Jesus are certainly infiltrated by post-Easter understandings, it is hardly right to say that they are altogether conquered and occupied by them, though such is a common scholarly assumption. For instance, at the end of the Gospel of Matthew, Jesus charges his followers to make and baptize disciples in the name of the Father, the Son, and the Holy Spirit. This charge comes as a climactic summary of the new Church's divine and universal commission, and surely represents a supremely important element of post-Easter self-understanding in Matthew's community. But it is nowhere anticipated in the rest of the Gospel. It would presumably have been easy enough to make Matthew's Jesus thematize it well before the crucifixion, if the beliefs and purposes of the Church had completely dominated the formation of Gospel materials. But, significantly, it did not happen. In fact, the Synoptic Gospels give to Jesus various emphatic themes that the Church does not appear to have used in its own preaching (e.g., the place of the Son of Man), and they subdue others that were clearly important in the preaching of the Church (e.g., Jesus' Messiahship). It is not unreasonable to suppose that the Synoptics report it that way because it happened that way.

On balance, then, there is surely at least as much ground for supposing a generally accurate remembrance of Jesus in the Synoptic tradition as for supposing that such a remembrance has been, as Norman Perrin put it, "overlaid and almost drowned out" by the consideration of the risen Lord or the needs of the Church.[7]

Accordingly, my attempt at reconstruction will proceed from the assumption, admittedly risky, that the transmissional distortion and editorial overlay in the Synoptic Gospels is not so great as to prevent the voice of Jesus from coming through in the main, in the general patterns. I do not presume that in any given instance we are offered the exact words of Jesus, or a literal translation of them into the Greek of the received texts, though I suppose it likely enough that in some cases this is exactly what we have. I agree that it is best not to rely on any specific quotation, even though some seem to me to capture the probable meaning and intention more adequately than others. But I will attempt to show what happens if we take attributed sayings of Jesus as representing at least roughly what Jesus said, presuming them more or less reliable and authentic unless there is good ground for believing otherwise—that is, unless there is a probability of falsification, not merely a possibility.

Here and there I will qualify my statements to show special tentativeness. That should not be taken to imply that I am utterly confident of my unqualified statements: everything in this reconstruction should be understood as if prefaced by "in the light of the evidence and of historical plausibility, it seems to me likely that. . . ." Similarly, while I sometimes say "Matthew's Jesus" rather than simply "Jesus," when I wish to register doubt about the accuracy of Matthew's reporting, this does not mean that when I write without that qualification I believe that Jesus spoke precisely as reported. A thorough representation of my felt caution would call for a circumlocution more like this: "Jesus, according to the text of Matthew as represented in what appears in this case to be the best manuscript tradition, says. . . ." or "Matthew, or the final editor of the Gospel associated with that name, or the group that produced it, or possibly a written or oral source used in the composition of that Gospel, apparently believed—or at least wanted us to suppose—that Jesus said. . . ." I do not consider that a useful way to proceed. It is all true enough, but it is pointlessly overcautious to postpone decision indefinitely and fatuous to forgo it altogether. Consequently, I have felt it my obligation to make up my mind as well and responsibly as I can about when there is some fair ground for thinking that we are getting approximately what Jesus (or John the Baptist, or Peter) actually said, and to set aside the protective scholarly hedging, technically appropriate though it may be. I will proceed in that way even in cases in which I do not think the saying in its received form is entirely authentic; if it seems to me to be at least a generally successful imitation of what on other grounds we have reason to think Jesus (or Peter, or Stephen) said, or to harbor a significant and probably authentic element or two, I consider it reasonable to bring it into consideration, at least in a gingerly way.

In the last few paragraphs I have concentrated on the case of Jesus, because that is the most disputed and cautiously handled area of investigation in contemporary New Testament scholarship, and requires the most explicit acknowledgment and apologia. But the principles by which I proceed in this case are my principles throughout this book. Paul Ricoeur has introduced the useful distinction between the hermeneutics of trust (which was characteristic of critical reconstructions a century ago, interpreting the Gospels as if they are quite reliable at face value) and the hermeneutics of suspicion (which is characteristic of more contemporary scholarship, interpreting on the assumption that things are probably not as the texts would have them seen). I am here trying to mingle the two into what might be called a hermeneutics of hospitality. This is a procedure that takes two cues from Holmes. The first is corrective: I do not dream of absolute, undeniable fact, but

I try to remember what facts really are and try not to ask of them what they cannot give. The second is more directly accepting: I imagine what might have happened, act upon that supposition in my reading of the texts, and try to see what configurations and patterns suggest themselves as making most sense of the whole body of evidence. These particular strategies of interpretation seem to me to justify, and probably to require, an unconventional argumentative and presentational procedure. I must accordingly ask for the reader's patience, tolerance, and (if possible) hospitality as my account unfolds without the usual demonstrations of why I am entitled to read as I do.

ADDITIONAL PRELIMINARIES

Various practical matters concerning my procedure should be cleared up in advance. Rather than trying to manufacture the illusion of coherence, I present them in no particular order.

1. By now, almost everyone knows that the word *gospel* is an early English word whose appropriate meaning was "good news." It is now a fossil, having come into the language so long ago that the language has outgrown it; but its meaning was once lively and clear, and almost exactly the meaning of the Greek original of the New Testament—*euaggelion.* The Greek word *euaggelion* had a longer and more cosmopolitan history than anything in early English had a chance to have, and in various of its occurrences in the ancient world, it could be roughly but rather accurately translated into modern English as "proclamation" (in which the news was usually but not always good), or even, still more roughly, as "press release." It fossilized in Greek and Latin just as it did in English: the traditional titles of the first four books of the New Testament accordingly came to mean, in all three languages, something like "the story about what Jesus taught and did"

(see Acts 1:1). The fossilization took place very early. The Latin translators simply transliterated the Greek original as *evangelium,* making no attempt to recover its livelier meanings, and most of the European languages quietly followed suit: French settled on *évangile,* Italian held to *vangelo,* and even German, despite its usual verbal inventiveness and its unindebtedness to Latin ancestry, wound up with *Evangelium.*

But the earliest English translators were clever and hopeful. The English language, unlike the others, attempted to recapture the pre-technical flavor of the original meaning, and its homespun state of development at the time offered nothing more sophisticated than *gospel* (cf. *good spiel*)—"good news." The most important sense of the word is this lively one. I am grateful that the founders of English usage tried to go beyond the fossil to get the original meaning. Hence the title of this book. "Five gospels" uses the word *gospel* in its original sense of proclamation, big news, message, preachment, press release. Throughout the book, when I use the word *gospel* without a capital letter, that is what I mean. But when I speak of Gospels, with a capital *G* (except in the book title and in headings), I am following the conventional modern way of referring to the New Testament books of Matthew, Mark, Luke, and John.

2. My renderings of scriptural texts will be unfamiliar. All the quotations from the New Testament are my own translations, designed to bring out the shades of meaning that are most relevant. Anyone experienced with any second language will recognize that this is desirable, and that it is in fact often rather lazy to use a standard translation. Translation is always an interpretive and a moral decision. The original text, carefully scrutinized, means this or that, and frequently this plus that. A standard translation must stay in the optimum middle of the road, but a spot translation should bring out what is specifically relevant. I have tried to be fair, accurate, and appropriately helpful.

MAGNETS AND CROCODILES: SOME FINAL OBSERVATIONS

I have been fascinated by magnets for as long as I can remember. I have played with nearly all kinds: the old horseshoe variety that dominated my earliest magnet memories, the light-metal ones on which little dogs were mounted, round and square and rectangular ceramic ones, electromagnets of my own devising. I still remember the thrill and wonderment that came over me the first time I did the standard routine of putting a piece of paper over a magnet and sprinkling iron filings: suddenly there it was, the invisible pattern made visible. I admit that I have had a similar experience writing this book, and it is not a bad analogy to the way I have written it. I am reporting how my mental iron filings were arranged when I interposed this paper on which I write between me and another study of the magnetic New Testament. When I started, I inevitably and appropriately had some ideas about what the results would be, some provisional theses that guided my study. Nearly all of those ideas have been altered or scuttled in the course of my writing: the evidence would have its own way with me; it forbade me to sustain the opinions I had thought would hold true, and dictated a different pattern, one I had not anticipated, one that now rings far truer to my ear than any of the many alternatives I have read, held, or taught. I am undoubtedly self-deceived in many particulars, and have varying degrees of confidence in the accuracy of the judgments I have provisionally made in this book. But my experience was that the pattern was not of my own devising, and was certainly not what I expected to find when I set out. I think it to be close to the pattern that is really there, hidden under the surface of the evidence, just waiting for the filings to get relaxed enough to submit and conform.

The mind acts much like a magnet, especially when important matters are at stake. More precisely, it acts like a magnet dealing with a magnet. If the poles are set one way, it clamps down hard and readily. If they are set the other way, it refuses to submit: it shies away powerfully, and if it gets a chance, it spins around and locks in its favorite position. I have done that many times over the years with this very material, and I have watched my students do it. This opinion or that reading may in fact be more comprehensive, more in tune with the evidence, more generally adequate than the alternative that happens to possess one's mind at the moment, but the mind nevertheless repulses it, backs off firmly, spins, and settles into its favorite position. If that were the only way the mind could work, homing in on what it is used to, then there would of course be no point at all to discussing these things with one another. Fortunately, that is not the only way it works. But it works that way often, almost constantly, with a regularity that is sometimes infuriating. Much of the story that will be told in this book involves the story of magnets snapping back into familiar postures, unable or unwilling to do otherwise, despite a worthy invitation to change. And many of the misunderstandings, contentions, animosities, and other failures in the history of the gospel's development were precisely of this kind. I think the matter to be so important that I feel a frustration when I observe some of the unhappy turns in that history, or failures to turn: but I myself have done such things so often and in so many ways that I know the right response to be compassionate pity, not annoyance.

But the magnet of the mind has another property. The whole idea of gospel is predicated on it. We do not spontaneously seek the truth; we rather long to be reassured that our favorite positions are the right ones to be in. But the magnet of the mind has a deeper hunger than this, although it is not as strong. That deeper hunger makes us rest uneasy until everything clicks into place. Everything. What we deeply want is not a conformity to what we are used to, or to what is fashionable, or to what is avant garde, but to what is true, what finally makes sense of everything. A gospel is an invitation to change, a call to leave our favorite positions and conform to what is really true. Whether the gospeller in question is really in better touch with the truth than those to whom the gospel is addressed is, of course, always a moot point. Unfortunately, when the mind snaps into a new position, there is no sure way of telling whether this is a click to what is more likely true, or only a diverting novelty. And there is no sure way of telling, when the mind snaps back from an interesting invitation into a familiar position, whether this is from lack of enlightening imagination or from a genuine loyalty to what makes more sense. The people in the story told by this book were often perplexed, and often not perplexed enough, by this ambiguity.

Some readers of this book—I hope all of them—will have a similar struggle, and will wonder about why they resist what I say, or give ready assent to it, why their minds are changed or unchanged. For my part, I assure you that I thought a great deal about magnets as I wrote, and questioned myself often about the unexpected spins and clicking into new places that I experienced. As the filings gathered into an unanticipated pattern, I wondered whether this was only what I somehow unconsciously hoped would be the eventual result. I can only say that I have tried not to let my hopes interfere with my process of learning, that most of this book came as a surprise to me, and that I consistently felt and thought that my mental filings were falling into the places where the true pattern lay. That, at any rate, was my ambition: to find what was really there.

We naturally presume that the truth will probably be very much like what we are used to thinking, and anything that deviates substantially from this is automatically odd and suspect in its appearance, and does not taste like truth. Matthew and Luke, and various anonymous others whose writings mediate between the original happenings and us, suffered from the same disability—sometimes overcoming old habits heroically, sometimes resisting new temptations heroically, but sometimes settling lazily back in a way that obscures what really took place. The matter is further complicated for the

Gospel writers and for us by the fact that these things mattered, and matter, importantly: not only habits, but loyalties too are involved in how these things are to be understood. That makes it more difficult to detach oneself from familiar assumptions so as to be ready to make appropriate changes. But sometimes the familiar assumptions, though readily validated by what one sees all around, will not do as the groundwork for sound repentance or for reconstructing earlier history. Anyone can plainly see that the distance between Africa and South America is sufficient to prevent any important interaction between the animals of the one and the animals of the other. But if we confine ourselves to thinking within the boundaries of this observable truth, then we cannot understand the development of alligators and crocodiles, because their evolutionary prehistory goes back to an earlier time, before the major continental shifts, when what we now know as Africa and South America were joined together. Christendom's thinking has been relatively stable and constant for so many centuries that it takes unhabitual imagination to grasp the kind of massive continental shifting that went on in the earliest and most volatile days, before the stabilities set in. Those are the days with which this book deals, and it is impossible to deal with them adequately without being ready to face strange and unfamiliar shapes and movements beneath the surface of the texts we are used to and the ways of reading that we are used to applying to them.

I do not ask that anyone take my word for it that the reconstruction I offer is more satisfactory, and closer to the truth, than the patterns and places our mental magnets have got used to. I have no independent authority. I merely try, as carefully and responsibly as I can, to help the surviving evidence tell its own story—not the story its authors wanted to tell, nor the one I, or you, may have wanted to hear; but the story of what really happened, whether they liked it or not, whether they understood it or not, and no matter where you or I stand on such issues.

1

The Gospel of John the Baptist

JOHN AS THE BEGINNING OF THE GOOD NEWS

Just when did the Good News begin? There are various legitimate answers. The "man-on-the-street" (and certainly the child-on-the-street) would probably pick the birth of Jesus, though some would take it back a step earlier, to the annunciation made to Mary. Those who are more theologically cautious might rather say that it began with the crucifixion, or with the resurrection, or perhaps with the pentecostal outpouring of spirit and fervor that initiated the Church's active preaching. Some might take it farther back in history, to the prophets' predictions of Jesus' coming; or to the promise God made to Abraham; or to the hope offered to the fallen Adam and Eve; or even to a time before time itself, when the preexistent Logos dwelt in the beginning with, and as, God.

All these are reasonable answers, each with its own justification. But there is still another that has a special claim to being heard. For if one looks carefully at the Gospels themselves to discover either their own sense of Christian beginnings or the sense that a modern historian should form according to their evidence, it is clear that the Christian good news really began with John the Baptist.

Mark is altogether explicit about it: his first verse is "The beginning of the gospel of Jesus Christ," and the words immediately following turn to John the Baptist, the voice in the wilderness. All four Gospels share this view. All four introduce the adult Jesus only after dealing with John, and all four place their introduction of Jesus in the context of John's baptism. Behind the Gospels lies a general common understanding that John was the basic point of departure for the new gospel. When Judas's defection left an opening, the Acts of the Apostles reports that it was decided that only a privileged few would be eligible to take his place. The condition of eligibility was not extended to everyone who could claim to be a witness of the resurrection, or a witness of Jesus' teaching, but was rather confined to those who had participated in the movement from the very start—who had been associated with Jesus "beginning from the baptism of John" (Acts 1:22). That was the true beginning of the word of salvation. As an early commentator succinctly put it, "John is the beginning of the gospel."[1]

THE IMPORTANCE OF JOHN'S GOSPEL

On the surface, it may appear that it was John's baptismal rite, and especially Jesus' reception of it, that constituted the true Christian beginning in John the Baptist. But a closer look reveals that it is not so much the baptism of Jesus that was the radical point of departure for the early Christian imagination, but John's general baptizing mission, and above all, the good news that accompanied and defined it. John's baptism was remembered not merely with reference to Jesus, but in itself—and not just in itself, but in relation to John's proclamation. John the Baptizer was first John the Voice. When Paul is portrayed as offering the gospel to Pisidian Antioch, Luke has him specify that God raised a savior for Israel, "John having proclaimed before his [Jesus'] entry a baptism of repentance" (Acts 13:24). Proclaimed, rather than performed. Peter in Caesarea similarly is made to speak of the Christian word that went forth from its Galilean beginnings "after the baptism which John preached" (Acts 10:37). Mark introduces

John not as a baptizer but as a voice proclaiming, and then mentions his baptizing only in conjunction with his preaching of a baptism of repentance for the forgiveness of sins (Mk 1:3-4). Matthew introduces John as a preacher of repentance, and mentions his baptism only some verses later (Mt 3:1,6). The Fourth Gospel consistently presents John as a preacher who bears witness, eventually mentioning his baptism only to characterize it as a form of witnessing (Jn 1:7, 15, 26, 31). Luke's Gospel not only introduces John's ministry with the coming of the word of God upon him, whereby he preaches a baptism of repentance (Lk 3:2-3), but in addition says in summarizing John's ministry that in exhorting many and different things, John "gospelled" (*euēggelizeto*) the people (Lk 3:18).

At the beginning of the Christian story, as the Gospel traditions understood it, lay the work, but especially the gospel, of John the Baptist.[2]

THE INDEPENDENCE OF JOHN'S GOSPEL

Why is the gospel of John the Baptist given so important a place in the Christian memories of that time of beginning? The question may seem naive. After nearly two thousand years of Christian culture, it may even seem foolish. Christian thought and art and story have accepted John's place of privilege and have elaborated it like an ornament. John has the role of introducing the star of the show, and whatever is known or imagined about his life is understood to be a preparation for this helpful but preliminary task. Artists depict John and Jesus playing together as children, John already deferential to his much greater cousin. Consistently, from very early days, John has been portrayed as aware that his task is only to prepare Jesus' way, instruct the Jews about him, deliberately (if somewhat self-apologetically) usher him into the public view, and then, his life's work finished, retire decorously and willingly from the scene as the last martyr of Christian preparations. When the career of John is elaborated and understood in this way, it seems a graceful and appropriate prologue to the ministry of Jesus. The well-acculturated Christian reader may look through the beginnings of the Gospels without any sense of awkwardness, admiring the dramatic strategies of Providence in electing John to play so perfectly his minor role.

That smooth sense of the coherence between John and Jesus is, however, a later development which the acculturated Christian reader imposes on the Gospel texts, not what the texts themselves imply. It is the product of inventive imagination and comfortable habit, not of an attentive and critical reading of the gospels. Closer scrutiny reveals the awkwardness of John's position, the grain of sand within the pearl. The story of John and his gospel as actually registered in the texts themselves is not the perfect prologue to the career of Jesus. It is, in fact, from a traditional Christian point of view, a rather inconvenient prologue.

The inconvenience was already felt by the evangelist. We can see in Matthew's version of Jesus' baptism that Matthew detected an awkwardness in having Jesus submit to John's rite; hence he has John try to decline the privilege, on the grounds of his unworthiness, and has Jesus assure him that in some mysterious way the baptism is fitting (Mt 3:14-15). Luke's opening chapter subordinates John to Jesus when they are still unborn (Lk 1:41-44), and sidesteps the problem of Jesus' baptism by removing John to prison before it takes place, leaving it entirely unclear by whom Jesus was baptized, if indeed by anyone but himself (Lk 3:20-21). The Fourth Gospel takes elaborate pains to have John assure both his followers and Jesus that his entire mission is merely to pave the way for this greater one (Jn 1:15, 26-27, 29-31; 3:27-30)—and in the Fourth Gospel, Jesus' own baptism is not even mentioned. The task of smoothing-out has already begun; the evangelists want us to see John in as conveniently Christian a way as can be readily arranged.

The rearrangements in the Fourth Gospel are extensive enough to cover up the problem almost entirely, but the first three evangelists leave more readily visible awkwardnesses. The portrait of John that appears in their work, despite corrective touches here and there, is not conveniently Christian. The work of John is not devoted to paving the way for Jesus. His public message does not point specifically to Jesus, or predict the features of his career; there is no mention of later teachings or healings, nothing about crucifixion or resurrection, nothing at all that would lead John's audiences to think of Jesus either at the time or subsequently. What it points to, if read carefully, is in fact very different from Jesus. And that, of course, is why the first three Gospels may be more or less trusted in their depiction of John: for despite the fact that their authors evidently wanted Jesus to be seen as the continuation and fulfillment of John's mission, their description of that mission works toward the opposite effect. They do not give us a Christian John the Baptist. The one they give us does not serve their Christian purposes but interferes with them.

Why then did they offer such an inconvenient version of John's work and gospel? There is only one likely answer: because that is approximately the way it happened, the way it was.

John was evidently well known in his own time, and for some time afterward. A full two generations after John's death, the Jewish historian Josephus includes a brief account of him in his history of those times.[3] Josephus does not mention John out of necessity, as if John were an indispensable link in an explanation of some major historical event. On the contrary, his account of John comes as an aside, digressing needlessly from his main account of events. Evidently, Josephus refers to John simply because John was remembered to have been a personage important enough to be catalogued by the historian. The Gospel accounts suggest the same thing: even if Matthew (3:5) and Mark (1:5) exaggerate in claiming that all the people of Jerusalem and Judea came to John, it is clear that in their received remembrance he attracted large numbers and was well known. His gospel was preached openly and heard widely, and its fame (or notoriety) was broadly bruited about. When the Synoptic evangelists came to record it, its main content was still remembered. Having decided to begin their stories with John, they quite naturally supposed that they must next report what John in fact said, whether or not it was convenient for Christian purposes.

Why then did they choose to begin with John at all? Again, the only plausible answer is that that is the way it was. The public career of Jesus was known to have begun in the context of John's mission, so much so that Jesus' mission appeared here and there to be little more than an extension and continuation of John's; and it was also understood that the impetus to Jesus' mission was his reception of John's baptism (combined with John's subsequent arrest and imprisonment). Jesus always speaks respectfully of John in the received Gospel texts, and sometimes refers to him as the initiator of the good news which Jesus himself preached. In short, the reason why the Gospels see John as the beginning of the good news is probably because that is the way Jesus himself saw him, and because that is the way it would have appeared to almost anyone who knew about John.

Jesus recognized John as an important new beginning; but there is no reason to suppose that John recognized Jesus. Neither Mark nor Luke records any public or private acknowledgment of Jesus by John (apart from Luke's undoubtedly fanciful story of the infant John leaping in his mother's womb), and Matthew's acknowledgment is confined to two verses of private conversation between John and Jesus (Mt 3:14-15) which are generally conceded to be an invention rather than a remembrance. Obviously, if John had been known to have accorded Jesus any such recognition, either publicly or privately, early Christian tradition would have celebrated and exploited it. Mark and Luke, and the rest of Matthew, undoubtedly show us the basic truth: that no such thing happened. Matthew's two verses and the Fourth Gospel's extensive testimony are clearly pious inventions, designed to remove the awkwardness of the historical non-happening and establish a self-subordination of John to Jesus that did not in fact occur. However advantageous it may have been to early Christians to see John as the forerunner of Jesus, John did not see himself that way. He believed himself to be preparing the way, but not for Christianity.

THE EVIDENCE FOR JOHN'S GOSPEL

For what, then, *was* John preparing the way? What good news was John preaching, if not the good news about Jesus? To discover the content of the gospel of John the Baptist, we must attend carefully to the few pieces of evidence we have. The primary evidences are those which apparently derive from followers and admirers of John the Baptist, and they fall into three or four main groups.

The first is the body of tradition that forms the basic information about John in the Synoptic Gospels and—in a significantly altered form—in the Fourth Gospel as well. These purport to be direct recollections of what John said and did, as observed by witnesses and passed down among those who saw John as the center of a religious reawakening and as the initiator of a gospel of a new kind.

The second is the smaller set of materials incorporated by Luke into the first chapter of his Gospel, reporting the annunciation, birth, and early childhood of John. There we find, cast back into a story of John's own ultimate beginnings, predictions of what he was to become and what he was to accomplish. These predictions differ in some significant ways from the characterizations that form the first group, and most probably derive from a different group of John's followers, who recast their memories of John in accordance with their experience within the movement he began and concentrated not so much on his gospel as on his general importance and the results of his mission. This picture of John is more muted and more concordant with the Hebrew Scriptures than is the view offered by the first group, and it most likely represents a later rethinking that provides less evidence for the historical John but more about what his movement later became among some of his faithful followers.

The third body of evidence is a passage in Josephus's *Jewish War,* giving a brief description of John's message and work. This description, I will argue presently, seems to derive from still another set of John's followers, a group more Hellenized in their religious ways than the others. It represents a still later rethinking of John; it blurs historical beginnings by conforming them to the thoughts and practices of the group responsible for Josephus's information—a group who maintained a baptist ritual but reinterpreted it to suit a changed setting and a changed theological view.

A fourth set of traditions about John may be seen in some of the materials present in the initial chapters of the Fourth Gospel. These are of tenuous value for reconstructing the historical John, though useful for understanding how the transformation of his message by still another group of disciples eventually entered into the transformation of the Christian gospel in its final stages. I will return to this evidence in the last chapter of this book.

I believe that when these evidences are properly appreciated, situated, and weighed, a roughly accurate reconstruction of the gospel of John the Baptist can be accomplished. And the balance of evidence suggests that his gospel had two major interrelated motifs: the proclamation of a baptism of repentance, and the proclamation of an imminent Coming One through whom a decisive judgment would take place.

THE CONTENT OF JOHN'S GOSPEL

THE BAPTISM OF REPENTANCE

John is sometimes remembered essentially as the Baptizer, but the surviving evidence suggests that he was, in the early days, remembered primarily as a *proclaimer* who preached a baptism (specifically, a baptism of repentance), and secondarily as one who also administered it. Mark's account separates the two, although transposing them: "John was baptizing in the desert and proclaiming a baptism of repentance for the forgiveness of sins" (Mk 1:4).[4] John's gospel evidently defined the meaning of his baptism. But just what *was* that meaning?

THE FORGIVENESS OF SINS

Is Mark right in describing John's baptism as a "baptism of repentance for the forgiveness of sins"? Luke follows this phrase exactly in 3:3, and repeats the first half of it through Paul in Acts 13:24. But Matthew's phrase is slightly different in that he represents the baptism as being *for* repentance (rather than *of*) and does not directly mention the forgiveness of sins. The difference is significant, having to do with the power and authority of John, of his baptism, and of his gospel. Matthew is dissociating the baptism from actual forgiveness, and making for it only the more modest claim of having a connection with repentance. The account of Josephus shows an even more extreme version of the same dissociation, insisting on the separation of baptism from forgiveness and reducing baptism to a symbolic act of no sacramental significance. Josephus says that John invited Jews to join in baptism, and to do so frequently—but he adds that those who do so "must not employ it to gain pardon for whatever sins they committed, but as a consecration of the body implying that the soul was already thoroughly cleansed by right behavior." On the other hand, the lost Gospel of the Hebrews, as reported by Jerome,[5] seems to have leaned in the other direction, characterizing John's baptism as being for the forgiveness of sins (*in remissionem peccatorum*), with no mention of repentance. The Fourth Gospel offers no description of the baptism, other than saying that it is in water and that its ultimate purpose is to assist in manifesting to Israel the one who comes after John—nothing is said of either repentance or forgiveness.

The silence of the Fourth Gospel can be discounted. Its description of the baptism is manifestly inadequate to account for the crowds that gathered at the Jordan: something is clearly being withheld in this characterization. The motivation for the withholding is evident in the rest of the Fourth Gospel, which consistently reduces John's role to that of preparing for and witnessing to Jesus and consistently claims that forgiveness of sin comes through Jesus alone. The suggestion that John's baptism might have independent power or even significance could not be hospitably received within the Fourth Gospel. Any direct association of it with the forgiveness of sins would be intolerable. The Fourth Gospel simply deliberately ignores what was obviously otherwise well known: John's baptism had some immediate connection with repentance and perhaps with the forgiveness of sins.

The connection with repentance is clear in the other Gospels, whether one adopts the Markan and Lucan "baptism *of* repentance" or the Matthean "*for*." Matthew and Mark agree that those receiving the baptism confess their sins as they do so, and Matthew's John not only begins his proclamation with the imperative "Repent!" but also describes his baptism as "for repentance" (3:11). But the connection with forgiveness is more obscure; Matthew shies away from it entirely, and Luke and Mark leave it indefinite: forgiveness is what the baptism is *for,* but nothing is said about how and when such forgiveness is to come about.

This is, of course, a delicate matter. The Gospels show that to announce that forgiveness of sins is in fact taking place could give great scandal. It was too bold a claim, bordering on a blasphemously arrogant pretension to know or command the mind of God or to effect what God alone can bring about. Yet Jesus maintained that sins were forgiven, and that he could announce the fact. Had John the Baptist done this before him? Josephus is at pains to deny it, and Matthew seems deliberately to avoid it, as if to protect John's reputation from the charge of claiming to accomplish more that Matthew thought it was possible to claim, at least at that stage of the unrolling of salvation. John may have characterized his baptism merely as an instrument for bringing about, or perhaps only for confirming, true repentance. But he may have claimed much more. At least some of those who submitted repentantly to John's baptism believed that their sins were forgiven—not *would be* but *already were*. For in addition to the traditions about John's public ministry, Luke gathered into his Gospel some other materials that must have derived from the followers of John the Baptist, and preserved them in his account of John's conception and birth. There we find confirmation of the general association between John's mission and repentance when the angel Gabriel tells Zechariah that John will "turn many of the sons of Israel to the Lord their God" and, like Elijah, will turn hearts "to make ready for the Lord a prepared people" (1:16-17). But we also find, at the conclusion of the Benedictus, that John will "give knowledge of salvation to his people, in forgiveness of their sins" (1:77). Not promise, but knowledge: the most obvious reading (even if not the only possible one) suggests that through John's ministrations, people actually understood themselves to have been forgiven "on account of tender mercies of our God, in which he has visited [not "will visit"] us" (1:78).

"The baptism of John was from where—from heaven, or from men?" (Mt 21:25). Jesus' question was very likely on the lips of many of John's contemporaries during the course of his ministry. Is this proclamation of a baptism of repentance authentic, or not? Does it have divine authority and show the hand of God, or is it nothing but an invention of John's own, with no more authority than the scribes possess? The phrase "from men" is neither contemptuous nor trivializing: it is simply a semi-technical term by which to distinguish humanly invented rules and practices of piety from those enjoined by God himself (cf. Jn 7:17). The issue is not whether the proclamation of John is inspired or insane, holy or demonic, but whether it is authentically divine or merely edifyingly human. At its root, the question is about the ultimate source of the authority of John's preaching. If it is merely John's own invention, it may be disregarded with impunity. But if it was sent by God through John, then John's summons is the summons of God, and ought to be obeyed. And when obeyed, it must be effectual for forgiveness.

John appears to have claimed that a true repentance in conjunction with his baptism, at least when accompanied by an amendment of life that brings forth fruit worthy of repentance, was sufficient. Against those who supposed that their membership in Israel was enough to ensure their salvation—a position probably held widely by the pious, and notably by the Pharisees, as a corollary of God's gracious fidelity to his people Israel[6]—John maintained that descent from Abraham was not in itself sufficient: nothing short of true repentance would do. That was scandalous enough, from the perspective of a believer in universal Israelite salvation. If John extended it still further to announce the eligibility of repentant Gentiles (as may be indicated by his claim that God can raise up sons of Abraham from stones, or by Luke's inclusion of soldiers among John's followers in 3:14), the effect would be still more startling. The scandal among both Pharisees and Sadducees would have been still greater if John was in fact as indifferent to the value of both traditional pious practices and the official Temple cultus as the balance of evidence seems to imply. Forgiveness of sins, according to the

Scriptures (e.g., Lev 4-5), was contingent on prescribed animal sacrifices; John seems to have offered an alternative way that bypassed the Temple. Proper righteousness, according to the Pharisees—and it must be remembered that their views were popular with the Jewish people in general[7]—entailed observing the prescriptions of the Law with rigor and care, ideally along with the other religious customs developed by traditional piety. John's gospel seems to have appealed to those whom the Pharisees regarded as sinners or religiously unobservant, and there is no indication either in the direct evidence about John's gospel or in the behavior of his admirers that the reformation which he enjoined upon them to secure their repentance included their adoption of Pharisaic ways. In short, the indications are that both the excitement and the scandal of the gospel of John the Baptist arose because his gospel offered forgiveness and salvation through true repentance in conjunction with his baptism, and because it also offered the assurance that this was both sufficient and available to all who would leave their sins and turn to God.

JOSEPHUS AS WITNESS TO REINTERPRETERS OF JOHN

It remains to consider the one piece of evidence that seems to call into question this general reconstruction of John's gospel of the baptism of repentance—Josephus's account, which not only makes John emphatically reject any attempt to use baptism as a route to the forgiveness of sins, but even fails to use the word *repentance* in connection with either the baptism or the gospel of John.[8]

John's gospel, according to Josephus, was essentially an exhortation to virtue, justice, and piety (*aretē, dikaiosunē, eusebeia*); but Josephus concludes by acknowledging that John enjoined the Jews who followed this good way to practise baptism. The decidedly Greek list of virtues does not on the surface resemble the Gospels' accounts of John's preaching, but those virtues are in fact a nearly perfect translation into Hellenistic ethical categories of what a Jew would understand by "fruits worthy of repentance"; and Josephus's linking of these with John's baptism faithfully mirrors the pattern that emerges from the Synoptic Gospels. Baptism, says Josephus (still apparently speaking for John), is only in this way made acceptable to God—i.e., as an act that signifies a righteous life already entered into; or, to recast it in more traditional Jewish terms, as a sign of an achieved repentance.

It is at this point that Josephus deviates most sharply from the common tendency of the other texts (allowance made for Matthew's silence on this part of the subject): "for only thus does baptism appear acceptable to God—not undertaken to gain pardon for whatever sins were committed, but as a consecration of the body, implying that the soul was already cleansed by justice [righteousness]." The way in which the subsequent sentence continues makes it seem fairly clear that Josephus thinks he is describing John's views on baptism, not inserting his own editorial aside. John's gospel of the baptism of repentance thus becomes, as refracted through Josephus, the teaching of a ritual washing that is pleasing to God because it is undertaken not as a means of obtaining righteous standing, but as a bodily symbol and analogue of a righteousness already lived out.

Why does Josephus insist on making this distinction? At first it may appear that Josephus is protecting John by offering his own, probably fanciful, explanation in order to make the rude baptism of repentance palatable to cultivated Gentile taste, and that he is accordingly sidestepping the un-Greek notion of repentance or conversion and expressly denying that feature (the forgiveness of sins) that would seem most crudely superstitious to his audience. This explanation has a superficial attractiveness but is ultimately weak on two grounds. The first is historiographical plausibility. Why should Josephus attempt to rescue the reputation of a man probably quite unknown to his readers, by implicitly denying allegations which those readers would know only if Josephus suggests them? And why would he bother to distort the truth in behalf of such a relatively minor and incidental figure in his story, whom he did not even need to mention? The second ground is even more telling. Josephus elsewhere shows little shyness about reporting to the Greeks such radically Jewish notions as repentance, confession of sins, and divine forgiveness as a response. He readily tells of the repentance of David, Ahab, Johaz, and records that God relented as a result (*Antiquities* 7.153, 8.362, 9.176); he represents the confession of sins by Rohaboam and his people, as well as by David and Ahab, and observes that God accordingly held back his punishment (*Antiquities* 8.256-7, 7.153, 8.362); and he reports Huldah's assurance that long transgression without repentance will bring about the destructive wrath of God (*Antiquities* 10.60). Moreover, when he offers a portrait of himself confronting the Jews in an attempt to bring them to surrender to the Romans, he concludes his exhortation by assuring his hearers that a way of salvation (*sōtērias hodos*) is still left to them and that the deity is readily reconciled with those confessing and repenting (*exomologoumenois kai metanoousin*).[9] It is surely incredible that Josephus would feel any delicacy about reporting as part of John's gospel what he unhesitatingly records as part of his own!

These evidences considered, it seems quite clear that Josephus would have been ready to pass on, unchanged, the Synoptic representation of John's gospel of repentance if that is what he had known. Apparently that is not what he knew: what Josephus gives us is what he himself had received, and it was already thus clarified and adjusted.

Where does Josephus' information come from? The obvious general answer is that it comes from disciples of John the Baptist. Josephus was born too late to have known John at first hand, and was thus dependent upon others; but it is clear that the information in this case comes from highly sympathetic others. Its picture of John is neither detached nor critical, but firmly approving. Moreover—and this is the strongest indication of its derivation from disciples of John—it is corrective and apologetic in ways irrelevant to Josephus's purposes.

Josephus has just reported Herod's defeat by Aretas. Technically, he has no need to mention John the Baptist at all; but in a brief digression, he reports that "some of the Jews" thought the defeat was providential retribution for the execution of John "called the Baptist." Once he has identified John in that way, it is appropriate enough for Josephus to add that John had baptized, thus explaining the name, and then move on. But this is not what Josephus does. He does not say that John baptized—only that he urged virtuous Jews to come together for baptism. Nor does he get back promptly to his main point: he rather digresses further, to explain how John thought baptism did and did not work. For Josephus's purposes, it is entirely irrelevant what John thought about baptism. For the purposes of those whose information he uses, it was apparently important to be clear that John had no magical ideas about baptism, but that it was to him merely the appropriate hygienic bodily correlative of a gospel about virtue, piety, and righteousness towards one another.

This is, of course, a gospel very different from the one that can be reconstructed from the Synoptic accounts of John the Baptist. I suggest that the passage arises from followers of John close to Josephus's own time, reporting as John's views what is really an *apologia* for their own. This is what the gospel of John the Baptist had become in the tradition of one group of his disciples years after his death.

Josephus does not say that John baptized, but rather that he urged those Jews who were righteous toward one another and pious toward God to come together for baptism. This would make good sense if the baptism were intrinsically efficacious, but Josephus's text denies that it was: it has essentially symbolic value. Now, why would the righteous and pious think it a good idea to come together for this kind of baptism? It is hardly credible that this is what John's immediate followers thought was going on in his baptism—but the Josephus account makes good sense in the context of later followers. John no longer baptizes; but they come together in baptism because they do it in memory of him. Apart from the ritual recollection of John's founding actions, there would be relatively little point in doing so; but if they are reenacting exactly what they believe John exhorted them to do, then it becomes a intelligible rite.

If some such ritual recollection of John's original baptism lies at the foundation of Josephus's text, then it is also understandable how the baptism has been reinterpreted. In both the Josephus and the Synoptic versions, John's gospel was promoting righteousness, and it demanded the works of righteousness as the condition of eligibility for the proper reception of baptism. Evidently, some of John's first disciples believed that his baptism brought about the forgiveness of sins; apparently, other admirers of John thought that such a claim was extravagant and inaccurate, and insisted on a more modest formula like the one used by Matthew: a baptism for repentance, leaving the place of forgiveness much more indeterminate. Josephus's text comes from a style of thought much more Hellenized than both Matthew's and his own. The terms used, as I have remarked, are a nearly perfect translation, into Greek ethical language, of the state in which one would be after having repented and brought forth fruits worthy of repentance. But the passage only describes this final state; it does not attempt to say anything about the process of repentance, and it certainly does not undertake to make repentance part of John's gospel or to link his baptism with it. What is the significance of this strange silence about what other sources suggest was near to the heart of the gospel of the historical John the Baptist?

The readiest explanation again lies with later followers of John, who had preserved a baptismal rite and a reverent memory of John, but who had tailored their recollections to the shape of their religious life and practice. For them, the baptism does not accomplish anything except the physical washing that serves as a symbol of righteousness lived out. That is because it is no longer a one-time baptism for new converts, but a more modest ritual—and very likely a repeated ritual—for those who are already living the righteous life. If the Baptist group in question remembers John as encouraging baptism among the pious faithful, that is probably because this is their own way. They are not missionaries, not proselytizers; they are the pious faithful. Conversion is no longer an issue for them, because decisive conversion lies well back in their history. Hence John's demand for conversion, repentance, is no longer so important for them to remember. It is more important to remember that there is no magic in baptism, that the work of achieving piety and righteousness is their own responsibility and the only way to become acceptable to God. There is probably in this revised emphasis a relic of a dissension with another version of John's baptism. We know that at least some of the followers of Jesus thought that baptism in Jesus' name conferred a form of righteousness. It is highly likely that some of the followers of John believed similarly about the power of John's baptism, and continued to make such claims about it as they administered it. Thus the polemical resistance against such a view in Josephus's text comes from followers who reacted against such an understanding of John's baptism and sought in its place a steady and enduring piety. They make John speak to them—and to do so, he has to be divested of his gospel and given their cult in its place.

The absence of gospel from Josephus's account therefore need not be considered odd or irregular. The message that remains is just what one might expect to be remembered, cherished, and enacted within a group of later admirers of John who preserved only a decorously Hellenized way of sustaining his tradition. It was a development that was likely to take place even if John had in fact preached what the Synoptic tradition suggests.

I think there are good grounds for supposing that John did preach much as the Synoptic Gospels claim he did, and that his gospel of the baptism of repentance can be roughly approximated thus: I baptize as a summons to repentance, as a prophetic sign of the necessity of repentance and the divine summons; all, without exception, can be saved only through repentance. I therefore charge you to repent, to leave your sinful ways and turn to God, to amend your lives into lives of righteousness, and to be baptized in water as a sign of that repentant change and a submission to God—knowing that God forgives those who truly and effectively repent, whatever they have done or have failed to do. This gospel of the baptism of repentance was the dimension of John's gospel that was most consistently heard and remembered, it seems: and its reverberations are to be found throughout the foundations of Christianity, which saw in this gospel of the baptism of repentance its own beginning.

THE COMING ONE

John's gospel of the baptism of repentance seems to have been the heart of his mission and message, and it was a good news of offered salvation. But salvation from what? From sin, of course, and the effects of sin; but that much was hardly novel. The Jews had lived with the Law and the Prophets for centuries, and both Law and Prophets are rich with reminders of sin and assurances that God has provided a way of forgiveness. John's baptism appears to have been offered as a partially unprecedented way, by which effective repentance, leading to the forgiveness of sins, might be achieved even by the religiously marginal Jew—the despised, the sinner, the religiously unobservant who was avoided and condemned by strict Pharisees.[10]

This is enough to account for the excitement in the land over John's ministry: both the positive response by those who flocked to his baptism and the negative response by those who challenged its, and his, authenticity. But there was more. John's gospel framed his baptism within a context of urgency. His message was not the perennial reminder of God's displeasure at sin and God's call to righteousness, but a summons to act now or never: there was a wrath to come, and it was coming soon.

THE WRATH TO COME

Matthew and Luke preserve a remembrance of John's gospel in which the urgency is explicit. Luke's John addresses his message to the crowds coming for baptism; Matthew John addresses it specifically to the Pharisees and Sadducees. Since the two Gospels share John's message word for word but differ in their specifications of the addressees, we may conclude that they received in common only the words of John, not the setting, and that each composed a specific scene out of his own imagination. John's words define their own context: "Broods of vipers, who told you to flee from the coming wrath? . . . Yes, and now the axe is laid at the root of the trees; and thus every tree not bearing good fruit is cut down and cast into the fire" (Mt 3:7-10, Lk 3:7-9). I think it likely that both Matthew and Luke are wrong in supposing that this is the message addressed by John to those who came to receive his baptism, whether Pharisees and Sadducees or undifferentiated crowds. This is surely the message John preached to those who came to *decide,* not to receive; it is that part of John's proclamation that told the curious why and how his gospel mattered. The time is almost up: a terrible judgment will begin soon. Those who fail to make themselves ready will be doomed. Therefore, says Matthew's John, "Repent! for the kingdom of the heavens is at hand" (Mt 3:2).

THE BAPTIZER TO COME

John's gospel does not, however, confine itself merely to a general reference to an impending judgment. The evidences are almost all agreed (with one exception, for which I will account later) that John compared and contrasted his baptizing in water for repentance with the work of an analogous but superior baptizer who would administer a definitive baptism of judgment. Mark's truncated account contains only two verses that purport to be a direct quotation from John's gospel, and they are entirely given over to this message—"And he proclaimed, saying 'The one mightier than I comes after, of whom I am not worthy, bowed down, to untie the thong of his sandals. I baptized you in water; but he will baptize you in holy spirit'" (Mk 1:7-8). The substance of these verses appears also, nearly verbatim, in Matthew and Luke (who however include *fire* as part of the medium of this coming baptism). John's pointing to another is echoed as well in abbreviated form in Acts, in various setting and manners. Paul informs his audience in Pisidian Antioch that John pointed away from himself to one coming after him, whose sandals he was not worthy to untie (Acts 13:25), Paul informs a group in Ephesus that John had called for belief in the one coming after him (Acts 19:4). Before the ascension, Luke has the risen Jesus charge his followers to wait for the promise "which you heard from me: that while John baptized in water, you will be baptized in holy spirit" (Acts 1:5). After Peter experiences the conversion of Cornelius and his company, he remembers "the word of the Lord, how he said . . . ," then quotes verbatim the same saying (Acts 11:16). The Fourth Gospel, despite its differences from the Synoptics on the subject of John's gospel of the baptism of repentance, is at one with them on the gospel of the baptizer to come. John proclaims, "I baptize in water" but adds by contrast a reference to "the one coming after me, of whom I am not worthy to untie the thong of his sandal . . . , the one baptizing in holy spirit" (Jn 1:27, 33), and twice refers to "the one coming after me, who becomes before me, because he is prior to me" (Jn 1:15, 30). Of all the witnesses to John's gospel, Josephus alone is silent concerning this coming superior baptizer; the Gospels and Acts are unusually consistent with one another concerning the main outlines of this part of the gospel of John the Baptist.

Mark's account is the simplest. It reduces this portion of John's gospel to four elements: (a) John proclaims that someone is coming after him (*opisō mou*) who is (b) mightier than he (*ischeroteros mou*) and (c) so much more worthy that John is not fit to untie the thong of his sandals; and (d) while John baptizes in water as a preparation, the coming baptizer will baptize with (or in) holy spirit. All these elements are honored in the other three Gospels, with minor differences. Each has John proclaim a later baptizer of greater status, whose sandals John is not worthy to handle, who will baptize in (or with) holy spirit. The coincidence is striking, especially given the differences in outlook (particularly between the Fourth Gospel and the Synoptics) and the oddity of some of the details. The chances are that all preserve authentic elements of John's gospel, too well known to dodge or manipulate.

One striking element these texts have in common is the vagueness of the reference to the future baptizer. He is given no title of the expected and usual kind: he is not referred to as Messiah, or judge, or prophet, nor is it specified whether he is a man, an angel, a spirit of some other sort, or God himself. Was John in fact as vague as this? The Fourth Gospel is again the exception that proves the rule: it clearly intends to see in Jesus the fulfillment of John's predictions. Accordingly (although it repeats all four elements of the standard characterization) it specifies the coming baptizer as a man (*anēr*) who was in fact before (i.e., earlier: *prōtos*) John, even if his mission will manifest itself only later to human eyes. The Fourth Gospel is trying to bring its understanding of Jesus into line with its remembrance of the gospel preached by John. Its remembrance of John's gospel fudges a little to make this possible. The other early witnesses neither invite this nor permit it. John did not specifically predict Jesus, however much early Christians may have wanted him to have done so. His message was too well remembered to make it easy for them to pretend otherwise. He preached a coming baptizer of judgment who would complete the work which John himself had only initiated, and his references to this coming baptizer were evidently oblique.

Matthew's account may preserve a title actually used by John, however untraditional it may be: The Coming One (*ho erchomenos*). Even the Fourth Gospel repeats this title; and although Luke does not use it in his account of John's preaching, he puts it into the mouth of Paul in Ephesus when he writes the Acts of the Apostles: John baptized, saying that people should believe in the Coming One (*ton erchomenon*) after him (Acts 19:4). In addition, Luke preserves, along with Matthew, the story in which John sends to ask Jesus explicitly whether he is the Coming One (*ho erchomenos*) or whether we should wait for another (Mt 11:2-6, Lk 7:18-23). The question makes the most sense if we assume that John was widely known to have used the vague title "The Coming One" (*ho erchomenos*) for the definitive baptizer whom he proclaimed.

The oddity of the vagueness of this title is substantially resolved by a glance at Psalm 118:26, which reads "blessed is he who comes [*ho erchomenos* in Greek, the inevitable translation of the Hebrew *ha-ba*] in the name of the Lord." There is still controversy about the original meaning of this verse. It may have been meant to confer a blessing on the king, or on the worshipers who came to the Temple, or on both. But be that as it may, what counts much more is the meaning it was thought to have around the time of John the Baptist: it appears that by that time it had acquired a sense of special reference to an unusual agent of the divine purposes. All four Gospels claim that this verse was used to greet the triumphal entry of Jesus into Jerusalem on the eve of his crucifixion (Mt 21:9, Mk 11:9, Lk 19:38, Jn 12:13), obviously intending to see

Jesus as the One Who Comes in The Name of The Lord. Indeed, it is not unlikely that this verse was on the lips of the crowd entering Jerusalem, for they were coming for the feast of Passover, and this verse belongs to one of the traditional psalms sung in the course of the Passover festivities.[11] It is not likely that the singers, except perhaps for his closest followers, had Jesus in mind, but the Gospels' suggestion that they did is significant in another way: it implies that this verse, as well as the vague title embedded in it, was understood around that time as having a more dramatic meaning than the psalm requires or invites. It was thought to point to a special agent of God's plan. One can imagine that this special interpretation derived from the gospel of John the Baptist, but it is far more likely that John merely gave distinctive application to an interpretation that he too had received from previous tradition.[12] At any rate, John adopted the Coming One as a principal mode of reference to the Baptizer whose work would fulfill his own. This eschatological use of the title is importantly different from the Messianic use attributed by the Gospels to the Passover pilgrims. Such a Messianic interpretation may have been more popular at the time than John's non-Messianic eschatological one. But it is striking that John's interpretation is echoed by Jesus, who quoted the verse as an appropriate greeting for the eschatological figure who is to come at the very end, to bring in the Kingdom (Mt 23:39, Lk 13:35).

It is not necessary to assume that John used only this one title in reference to the coming Baptizer. Mark (1:7) and Luke (3:16) have him refer to "the one mightier than I" (*ho ischeroteros mou*; Matthew has the same expression without the definite article in 3:11; the Fourth Gospel's *hos emprosthen mou*—i.e., "the one who takes precedence over me"—is probably a deliberately adjusted version of the same, as I will argue in the final chapter). At first glance, this may seem an insignificant title; the second glance reveals not only that it is again disappointingly vague, but also that it could have been used by John only if he acknowledged his own strength. It would be pointless to refer to the Baptizer to come as "stronger" unless John the Baptist himself took account of the fact that his audiences regarded him as a powerful presence. There is nothing unlikely in this. John proclaimed a baptism of repentance toward the forgiveness of sins, and this proclamation was evidently thought presumptuous and bold by some of his contemporaries. The chances are that he admitted its boldness and denied its presumptuousness, by pointing to the Coming One who would fulfill the work of his baptizing and gospelling mission by a power as much greater than John's as spirit is than water, as salvation is than repentance. "The One More Powerful Than I" may well have been another way in which the gospel of John the Baptist referred to his fulfilling successor.

The Gospel accounts agree on the curious detail that John described himself as unfit (or unworthy) even to deal with the sandals of the Baptizer who was to come (Mt 3:11, Mk 1:7, Lk 3:16, Jn 1:27). Nothing is ever made of this odd saying, which suggests that it was preserved not because it served the purposes of the evangelists but despite their inability to do anything with it—that is, because it was simply something that John was known to have said. The different Gospels' variations on the wording of the quotation are minor, and commentators have not found much of significance in them. The common denominator is the description of a menial task: the job of dealing with another's sandals was a duty suitable only to a servant or a poor disciple. The net result is not so much a registration of John's humility, for the characterization of the Coming One as "more powerful than I" would have little point if John were self-effacing. It is rather an emphasis upon the remarkable greatness of the Coming One, as if the essential message is something like this: "Yes, I preach with authority, and baptize with a baptism that has power; but if you are impressed with all this, then just wait until you see what and who comes next!"

The detail that the Baptizer with holy spirit comes after John (*opisō mou*) is also slightly odd on the surface. Anything in the future can be so described. John probably used it with the sense of "My Successor," the agent who would grandly fulfill what John had initiated in a large but elementary way. But the persistence of this detail in the Christian memory of John's preaching is curious. The explanation probably lies in part in another meaning which the phrase may bear: "following me" in the sense of discipleship. The Synoptic tradition casually assumes that Jesus was in some sense a follower, a disciple, of John; the Fourth Gospel's attempts to deny this further indicate how generally it was supposed. The authority of John's gospel made it useful for early Christian belief to see Jesus as its fulfillment, and useful for early Christian proclamation to find ways of persuading others that John somehow pointed toward Jesus. Jesus was accordingly identified with the coming Baptizer preached by John, and thus Acts and the Fourth Gospel have the risen Jesus baptize his followers with holy spirit, fulfilling John's prediction. The entry into Jerusalem sees Jesus greeted as the Coming One. Similarly, the odd detail "after me" was seized upon and held because it could be applied to Jesus, as a follower of John in both senses.

But to characterize Jesus as a follower of John was not unqualifiedly handy. It helped make the case that Jesus was the one John proclaimed, but it raised difficulties in suggesting the subordination of discipleship. Luke evidently appreciated both factors. He exploits the advantage in Acts by having Paul evangelize Pisidian Antioch with a reference to John's claim that one would come "after him" (Acts 13:25), and similarly by having Paul inform a group in Ephesus that John had called his followers to believe in one coming "after him" (Acts 19:4). Obviously, Luke's Paul supposes that Jesus is the one who fulfills these predictions. But at the same time, Luke sidesteps the hint of discipleship. In his Gospel he never has John refer to one "following" him; and when he allows this part of the tradition to slip back into his account in Acts, he renders "following" by the preposition *meta* instead of *opiso,* thus signifying temporal succession without any overtones of subordination (Acts 13:25, 19:4). This is probably an adjustment in the same spirit as Luke's omission of any reference to Jesus' following of John—for although Luke admits that Jesus was baptized, he does not name John as baptizer, and he places the event just after his account of John's imprisonment (Lk 3:20-21). The likelihood is that the detail "after me" in the accounts of John's gospel survived in the early evidence mainly because it was a phrase that John in fact used; and that Jesus' reception of John's baptism seemed at first to make it convenient to adapt the phrase to him but then seemed to have too many awkward overtones of discipleship. Matthew struggles with this problem in one way, by having John attempt to beg off from baptizing Jesus (Mt 3:14); Luke does so in another way, by modifying the remembered phrase and dissociating Jesus from direct contact with John; the Fourth Gospel omits the baptism of Jesus altogether, and can afford to keep the remembered *opisō mou* by giving John ample room to insist that the one coming after him was already before him and has precedence over him, thus dispatching any hint of a discipleship or subordination of Jesus to John.

But these are special problems arising from special adaptations of the gospel of John the Baptist. They arose only when Christian interpreters wished to equate John's coming Baptizer with Jesus. John himself had no such thing in mind. He did not claim to know the identity of the Baptizer to come, only to know that he would be much mightier and worthier than himself, and that he would come after, to fulfill in a baptism of spirit what John had started with a baptism of water. Even the Fourth Gospel retains hints of the historical truth. It admits that John preached a greater successor to come but did not know his identity (1:31), and it remembers that the baptism of John was understood by John himself to be in part a way of gospelling not just a greater successor, but a greater baptism to come (1:31; cf. 26, 33). That coming baptism was the event for which John's gospel, along with his baptism, was preparing the way. What was it to be?

Matthew (3:11) and Luke (3:16) report that John expected a future baptism in holy spirit and in fire. Mark and the Fourth Gospel omit any reference to fire. The weight of probability lies with Matthew and Luke. There is small reason for a reference to fire to insinuate itself into the remembrances of John's gospel if it had not originally been there. But it is not difficult to imagine how it might have come to be omitted from Mark and from the Fourth Gospel. Early Christianity wanted to see in Jesus the fulfillment of John's promises. Early Christianity knew a baptism in spirit, and made Jesus the agent of it. The Fourth Gospel is variously explicit about this (20:22 represents one way of asserting it; another way is to be found in 1:33, and still another in 15:26). Luke has an oblique reference at the end of his Gospel (24:49), and has Jesus speak still more directly about it at the beginning of Acts (1:5, 8), and offers an account of its occurrence in his tale of the first Christian Pentecost (Acts 2). The gift of the Spirit is to be found repeatedly in the rest of Acts and throughout the letters of Paul; it is evidently one of the commonplace realizations of earliest Christianity. To the extent that John had predicted an outpouring of holy spirit, his gospel could be claimed to have been fulfilled among the followers of Jesus, and Jesus could be claimed, or hinted, to be the one who had poured it out. But the same was not true of fire. Luke's depiction of Pentecost represents an outpouring of holy spirit in conjunction with tongues of fire, and to that extent offers an answer to a gospel of John that foresaw both. But that is a rather feeble and fancy use of a baptism of fire, and is not otherwise echoed in the accounts of early Christian life. The spirit had come, and had come in abundance. The fire had not. Anyone wishing to report John's gospel in such a way as to maximize the chances of seeing it fulfilled in the Christian events would obviously be convenienced by mentioning the baptism of spirit and forgetting the baptism of fire. John's gospel probably spoke of both.

In doing so, it undoubtedly offered both good news and bad news. It proclaimed the spirit and fire of judgment. Fire, in scriptural texts, is an image of double weight: fire cleanses the lips of Isaiah (Is 6:6-7) and refines the valuable metal (Zech 13:9); but it also destroys Sodom and Gomorrah, and burns dross into oblivion (Is 1:25). Malachi's vision of the coming judgment sees it in terms of fire, both refining (3:2-3) and destroying (3:18-19). In the recorded remembrances of John's gospel, there can be little doubt which of these is the more prominent. The tree not bearing fruit is to be cut down and cast into the fire (Mt 3:10, Lk 3:9); the chaff, once the good grain has been separated from it, will be consumed with inextinguishable fire (Mt 3:12, Lk 3:17). The fire of judgment may refine those who are to be saved, or leave them unharmed, or bypass them altogether. They are not mentioned in direct connection with fire. But those who are found in their sins will clearly be consumed by the fire of righteous judgment, according to John's gospel.

Baptism by fire may traditionally save or destroy, according to the state of readiness. John seems to have concentrated on destruction. The same is evidently the case with baptism by spirit. The role of spirit in such sorts of ultimate testing is not as frequent a scriptural image as that of fire, but it is firmly registered—most strikingly in Isaiah's threat that God will sift his enemies with a tongue like fire, his spirit (or breath) like a flooded river, up to the neck (Is 30:27-30). The reports of John's gospel make it clear that he understood the coming baptism of spirit to function in that way. The baptizer who is to come is depicted as a thresher—that itself being a common enough image of judgment in both Old Testament and New—whose fan is in his hand to deal with his threshing-floor. The threshing technique in question is simple and decisive. The unthreshed grain is beaten with flails or trampled by feet or crushed by sledges until the husks are loosened; then it is tossed into the air while the thresher's fan blows the chaff to the side and lets the heavier grain fall clear. The grain is then gathered into the barn and the chaff consigned to the fire. In the language in which John preached, the image was inescapable: the Hebrew and Aramaic words for *spirit* and for *wind* (as well as *breath*) are identical. The baptism with holy spirit is one that will separate the grain from the chaff. Like the baptism of fire, it is an act of definitive judgment.

After centuries of Christian life, the word *baptism* has become almost exclusively associated with cleansing and initiation—strictly good news. In earlier days, the news of baptism was not so unequivocally good. The early alternative sense of terrible trial is clearly present when Jesus speaks of the baptism he is to undergo (Lk 12:50), and when he asks James and John whether they are capable of enduring a baptism like it (Mk 10:38). Baptism in this sense of threatening trial may have entered into the ritual of baptism administered by John in the waters of the Jordan: it has a great deal to do with the baptism which he maintained would be administered soon by the Coming One.

John's own baptism probably was not the joyful cleansing immersion of Christian ritual tradition, but rather had more in common with Isaiah's trial in a flooded river, up to the neck (Is 30:28), which in turn very likely derives from an ancient ritual of trial by water, mentioned twice in the code of Hammurabi. It is not unlikely that the representation in the *Vita Adae et Evae,* composed in the first century A.D., gives us a glimpse (though undoubtedly exaggerated and stylized) of the kind of ritual prescribed by Hammurabi for purposes of judicial trial. This ritual was adapted by John the Baptist to a ritual of penitence, in anticipation of the great baptismal trial to come:

> And Eve said to Adam: "What is penitence? Tell me, what sort of penitence am I to do?"...And Adam said to Eve: "Thou canst not do so much as I, but do only so much as

> thou hast strength for. For I will spend forty days fasting...and I will spend forty days in the water of Jordan, perchance the Lord God will take pity on us"....Adam walked to the river Jordan and stood on a stone up to his neck in water. And Adam said: "I tell thee, water of Jordan, grieve with me, and assemble to me all swimming [creatures], which are in thee, and let them surround me and mourn in company with me. Nor for themselves let them lament, but for me; for it is not they that have sinned, but I."[13]

John baptized in water, and in doing so gave the penitent a foretaste of the baptism of spirit and fire that would be much harder to endure. Isaiah and Malachi provided a precedent for seeing the ultimate divine visitation of judgment in such terms, but there had been in the meantime further reinforcement available through the Persian doctrine of a forthcoming eschatological trial by a river of molten metal, which the righteous would experience as a mild bath, while the unrighteous would be utterly consumed. It was from the Persians that the Jews acquired the main outlines of the doctrine of resurrection, as well as a variety of other religious ideas and customs. There may well be an ultimate link with Persian expectations in that aspect of the gospel of John the Baptist that proclaimed a final baptism in fire. This baptism in fire was sure to come in the wake of his water baptism that prepared the way of the Lord.

And there can be no question about its coming soon. The thresher's fan is already in the hand of the Coming One, just as the axe is already laid at the foot of the unworthy tree. Hence the urgency of John's gospel: the wrath to come is imminent. The agent of this judgment, depicted not only as the baptizer with spirit and fire but also as the wielder of the axe and the threshing fan, is left regrettably vague. It is not the Satan who, in Luke's account, asks permission to sift Simon like wheat (Lk 22:31), for when the good grain is sifted from the chaff in this larger threshing, the Coming One will himself burn the chaff—and will gather *his* wheat (Mt 3:12) into *his* storehouse (Lk 3:17). Who is he?

John apparently did not claim to know. The Coming One is unusually powerful and is God's agent in the great threshing judgment to come. Beyond that, his identity is shrouded in obscure titles—not the titles which later Christian voices have wanted to use (for he is never called Messiah, nor is he identified with Jesus either explicitly or implicitly in the Synoptic Gospels) but only the shadowy names which early tradition has passed down to us, probably from John himself. All we can fairly guess is that he is less than God (for otherwise John's language about him would be too feeble) and more than a human. Angels are frequently associated with the work of the great judgment in early Christian and pre-Christian times, especially the Archangel Michael,[14] and John's Coming One has something of the stature of such an avenging angel. But the record of John's gospel will not take us even as far as that. He did not say, and we therefore cannot know, precisely whom or what he expected as the ultimate fulfillment of his gospel of baptism and repentance, his gospel of imminent wrath and destruction and salvation. We can know only what he expected, and proclaimed: all this is coming, and coming soon; all are invited to salvation; the moment of decision is now.

POSTSCRIPT: THE SILENCE OF JOSEPHUS AND OF LUKE'S BENEDICTUS

Before leaving this phase of John's gospel, we must turn once more to Josephus, precisely because he seems to know nothing about the baptizer to come. His report of John says nothing about any special Coming One. The legacy of John, according to Josephus, was a symbolic bodily cleansing by which those who had already given themselves to virtue, justice, and piety might echo and symbolize in the flesh the life to which their spirits were already committed. Nothing could be farther from the dramatic summons of John's gospel as reported by the other surviving evidences.

The contrast is stark, but I think the explanation is simple and fairly obvious. Josephus wrote some sixty years after John's mission. If, as I have argued earlier, he wrote from information provided by a faithful remnant of John's followers, his account is not surprising. The crucial intervening fact is that things had not happened as John had predicted. The great threshing of judgment had not taken place. Undoubtedly, this failure of happening had led to the disaffection of some of John's earlier converts. Others clearly joined the Christian movement, some of them substituting the Christian gospel for the one they had learned from John, the rest trying to find among the Christians the fulfillment of what John had preached. (The Fourth Gospel's treatment of John is, to my mind, the best example of the latter case, for its insistence on John's witness to Jesus, often explained as a polemic against the disciples of John, is more probably an attempt to account for both their fidelity to John and their new commitment to Jesus. I will return to this in the final chapter.) The remainder, those who had been awakened to new life under John's ministry, those who had experienced "knowledge of salvation in the forgiveness of their sins" (Lk 1:77) and had tried to live accordingly, had now lived through a generation or two of postponement. Part of what had been known as John's gospel had not come to pass: neither the wrath nor the rescue had come about. Yet their own experience of repentance and forgiveness seemed to validate John's work. If they were to remain loyal to John, they had to adjust to what had not happened, and find another way of understanding the gospel of John the Baptist.

The Baptist source which Luke used for the Benedictus (Lk 1:68-79) seems to come from an intermediate time: the urgency is already dulled, and the view of John projected from the time of his birth is no longer the fiery gospel of the Synoptic memories but shows instead the taste of forgiveness and indefinite salvation that must have lingered among the faithful even while the apocalyptic expectation slowly waned by its delay. It was not as if nothing had happened. It was only that the dramatic expectation had not been fulfilled, even though John was now many years dead. The faithful followers had essentially two choices: either suppose a mysterious postponement of the cataclysm, temporarily or indefinitely, or give up its expectation altogether, on the grounds that John had misunderstood that part of his commission or on the grounds that they had evidently misunderstood that part of John's gospel. Behind the Benedictus seems to lie a hesitation. John still executes the office of Elijah, which may lead to the judgment that was popularly thought to be next on the agenda. But the emphasis is put on what we have gained in the meantime, whether or not a definitive judgment ensues. Things have changed, and for the better. No further questions asked.

Josephus was apparently in touch with those who had come to assume that the previously expected apocalyptic end was not in fact going to come. They had learned to live without the Baptist himself, and had preserved a more modest version of his baptism for themselves and for their children. They had reconstructed the Baptist way accordingly, reaffirming the values it had in fact secured for them or for their forebears, and abandoning those that had come to seem untrue. Josephus knew nothing of the original gospel of John—not the one-time baptism of repentance, nor the baptizer to come, nor the wrath, nor the definitive salvation—because the Baptist remnant from whom he got his information had learned to live with what had not happened and had worked out a preservable version of what was left. Josephus accordingly bears witness not to what John's gospel was, but to what remained of it in the minds and lives of at least one group of subsequent followers long after, when the original message had given way to one that could be lived with indefinitely. If scrutinized and considered closely, Josephus does not challenge the reconstruction of John's gospel that comes from the other evidences—he rather tends to confirm it.

CONCLUDING CONSIDERATIONS

My attempt so far has been to reconstruct from the surviving evidences the essentials of the gospel of John the Baptist. While I lament the paucity of the evidence, regret the absence of alternative testimony (if only Josephus had written two generations earlier!), and acknowledge the precariousness of any attempt to retrieve John's gospel from the Christian texts that preserve glimpses of it, I admit that I suppose the preceding account to be not only plausible but probable. I think this is what John preached. But because habits of tendentious Christian reading are still constantly applied to the texts dealing with John's gospel, I would like, before moving on, to reiterate more pointedly some of my observations about what John did *not* preach.

WHAT JOHN DID NOT PROCLAIM

First, John did not preach Jesus. This is true in two senses. On the one hand, there is no compelling reason to suppose that he knew Jesus (even if Jesus had been among the many who received his baptism), and less reason to suppose that he wished to point to Jesus as the fulfillment of his gospel, despite the Fourth Gospel's attempt to portray it that way. The historical John simply did not say, and probably did not know, who would accomplish the deeds that would end the world as we know it—and his gospel pointed to just such a dramatic end, not to a Christian interim. On the other hand, the gospel of John the Baptist does not point willy-nilly to Jesus, as if John's inspiration operated in spite of himself or in a way that would indicate Jesus once we had fuller information. Various early and modern Christians would like to have it that way, but they may not. There is no room. John's successor, in the terms of his gospel, would end it all abruptly, and soon, in judgment. That did not happen. John was wrong about that part of his gospel: the followers whom Josephus leans upon were right to decide that this was not a doctrine they should continue to cling to. Early Christians who maintained that Jesus would shortly enact the winnowing judgment proclaimed by John expressed a hope, not a knowledge—and the hope was effectually extinguished by the continuity of the world. Nobody in fact did what John said somebody would soon do. John was wrong. No attempt to rescue him by saying that he was really, consciously or unconsciously, speaking about Jesus will hold water. His gospel of the Coming One had nothing to do with what Jesus subsequently was and did.

Secondly, John's gospel was not Messianic in any reasonable sense of the word. It is commonly supposed that all Jews of John's time expected that a descendent of David would ascend some sort of preordained throne and rescue Israel to a pious sovereignty. That is simply not true. Some Jews did in fact believe something of the sort, but many had given up on any rescue in this world, and many others had transferred their hopes to direct divine interventions or a divinely arranged scenario of some indeterminate kind in which a Messiah had no part.[15] As far as we can tell, John had no place for a Messiah. He proclaimed another rescuer of greater proportions than had ever been attributed to a Davidic King. The omission of the Messianic title from John's gospel is no accident: the Coming One whom he announced was quite different from, and thoroughly independent of, the Messianic expectations held by some of his contemporaries. Tradition does not record whether or not he argued explicitly against Messianic expectations, but it clearly records a gospel that was non-Messianic.

Thirdly, John was not leading into the Christian gospel. The earliest Christian gospel took its point of departure from his, but that is a very different matter. John's gospel was influential enough, especially among the earliest Christians, to result in a variety of accommodations by which the Christian gospel might seem the continuous fulfillment of the gospel of John the Baptist. The accommodations are nearly all artificial and false. John had no idea of Christianity; he had no knowledge of, interest in, or room for Jesus the Messiah as Christian gospelling came eventually to understand him. John pointed to no gospel beyond his own. He evidently presumed that his was the final word before the deluge of holy spirit and fire. The followers of Jesus, who at first were also largely followers of John, wanted to see them in continuity, and wanted to see Jesus as the fulfillment of what John preached, or at least as a coda to his gospel. John would never have recognized Jesus as a fulfillment of his gospel, and would not likely have acknowledged that there was anything important that had not already been said or done by himself, until the Coming One should bring his definitive baptism of judgment.

Nor is it likely that those of John's followers who had really understood his gospel expected anything further. The indications for this are twofold. First, there is no reference, in the preserved earliest evidences of John's mission, to Jesus or to a Davidic Messiah or to a restoration of Israel's political sovereignty. These were not a part of John's expectation, nor of the expectation of those who had heard him well. Second, these early memories associate John with other terms and ideas which, properly appreciated, confirm that he was understood to be the usher of the impending judgment, the last warning before the end; the key associations are with Isaiah's voice crying in the wilderness, Malachi's preparing messenger, and Elijah.

HOW JOHN WAS SEEN

THE VOICE IN THE WILDERNESS

All four Gospels identify John the Baptist—through his own direct testimony, in the case of the Fourth Gospel—with a slightly distorted version of Isaiah 40:3: "A voice of one crying in the wilderness: prepare the way of the Lord, make straight his paths." A glance at the Isaian texts shows that this was originally more good news than a challenging command: Isaiah is announcing that the time of punishment is over, the Lord has forgiven, and the glory of the Lord is about to be revealed to all. Isaiah's gospel corresponds well to the good news preached by John, and its association with him is, if not inevitable, at least appropriate.

Part of the appropriateness has to do with John's association with the wilderness. Isaiah had said that the voice proclaims "in the wilderness, prepare the way of the Lord"—i.e., the voice itself was not necessarily situated in the wilderness, though the preparation was. The Greek version of Isaiah's Hebrew text places the voice in the wilderness, but that is not necessarily the only explanation for how the same change occurs in the version applied to John. John was in fact in the wilderness. Luke places him there for an indefinite period preceding his ministry: "...and he was in the wilderness until the days of his manifestation to Israel" (Lk 1:80), and makes it the place in which he was inspired and called to his work: "...a word of God came upon John the son of Zechariah in the wilderness" (Lk 3:2). Matthew begins his account of John by saying that "in those days comes John the Baptist proclaiming in the wilderness of Judea" (Mt 3:1). Mark reports that John was "baptizing in the wilderness, proclaiming..." (Mk 1:4). Matthew and Luke have Jesus ask concerning John, "What did you go out into the wilderness to see?" (Mt 11:7, Lk 7:24). Josephus alone offers no association of John with the wilderness—again, not out of any personal reluctance, for he himself had been the disciple of the ascetic Bannos and had spent three years with him in the wilderness;[16] he was well aware of the traditional associations of the wilderness with spiritual trial and renewal. His silence probably echoes a silence in his apologetic source, which emphasizes consistently the permanent and universal validity of John's spiritual way, minimizing the historical and geographical details of its origin. These silences do not count against the otherwise consistent association of John with a wilderness setting.

Christian interpreters occasionally suggest that the "Lord" whose way John was preparing was Jesus. It is clear that this is not Isaiah's meaning. His voice prepares for the God of Israel. That is exactly the intention also of the Qumran text which uses a more accurate quotation of the same Isaian verse to apply to the community that prepared the way for the definitive intervention they expected.[17] So it is too with the Gospels' application of this quotation to John the Baptist: the quotation differs slightly from the Isaian original, but no adjustment has been made to make it suggest Jesus. As it stands in the Gospels, it probably faithfully records what was said and thought about John before Jesus appeared on the public scene. What it means is clearly what Isaiah and Qumran meant. The gospel it characterizes is a gospel of the coming intervention of God himself, to save those who have been accorded his forgiveness, and to destroy the unrepentant.

MALACHI'S MESSENGER

In addition to the Isaian quotation, Mark prefixes a slightly confused quotation that is ultimately a mixture of Exodus 23:20 and Malachi 3:1—although Mark seems to be attributing it to Isaiah rather than to its real sources. The Exodus text quotes God speaking to Israel about the angelic guard whom he will send to lead Israel safely into the promised land: "I will send an angel before you to guard you as you go and to bring you to the place that I have prepared." Malachi's text has a radically different setting and meaning. A much later Israel has begun to murmur that the sinful are not being punished, that the God of Justice seems to be absent. God replies with an assurance and a warning of imminent action: "Look, I am going to send my messenger to prepare a way before me"—and after that, the Angel of the Covenant will visit the land with the purifying and destructive fires of judgment. Mark's text blends the two: "Behold, I am sending my messenger before your face, who will prepare your way" (Mk 1:2).

It is not obvious just where to translate "angel" and where "messenger," since the same word has both functions in both Hebrew and Greek, but it seems plain that the Exodus text means to be understood as a reference to an angel, and that the Marcan text, through its application to John the Baptist, means "messenger." Malachi is more ambiguous, and there are grounds for either reading, depending upon whether the text is to be aligned more with the Angel of the Covenant mentioned shortly thereafter or with the prophet mentioned some twenty verses later (Malachi 4:5), who is to be sent in warning and preparation before "that great and terrible day." Rabbinic commentators eventually identified the two with each other.[18] But whatever Malachi originally meant, it is clear that his text eventually came to be read as referring to a prophet who would precede the end: that is how it came to be associated with John the Baptist, not only in Mark's introductory remarks but also in Matthew and Luke, who represent Jesus as applying precisely the same conflated Exodus/Malachi quotation to John (Mt 11:10, Lk 7:27).

What does the Gospels' form of the quotation mean? John is obviously to be understood as the messenger in question. But whose way is being prepared, and before whose face? On the surface, it may appear that the original texts have been subjected to Christian manipulation, and that the way and the face of Jesus are intended. But the overall weight of evidence bears against this reading. First, nothing is made of it: neither Jesus nor Mark makes any such application. Both repeat the conflated text as if it were the original reading of Scripture, and neither takes advantage of a possible application to Jesus. Second, and more important, there is reason to believe that the conflation had already established itself in Jewish tradition without any reference to agencies other than the prophet/angel and God himself. The rabbinic commentaries signalled in the previous footnote explicitly join the Exodus text with the Malachi text and use them to interpret each other to mean that God will, before the end, send his prophetic-angelic messenger before the face of Israel to prepare their way to salvation. The meaning of the conflated text is exhausted without going beyond the reference to John's own gospel: its association with John is probably an authentic memory of the way he was perceived by his followers, and it confirms that John was aptly understood as preaching the final reprieve and preparation before the end.

If John was associated with the Malachi text in or shortly after his own time, there are two further ways in which an exploration of Malachi may lead to clues about John's gospel. One is the general nature of Malachi's vision of what was coming; the other is the identity of Malachi's prophet.

After the appearance of the messenger, according to Malachi, God's apparent inactivity will be swiftly remedied:

> And the Lord you are seeking will suddenly enter his Temple; and the angel of the covenant which you are longing for,[19] yes, he is coming, says Yahweh Sabaoth. Who will be able to resist the day of his coming? Who will remain standing when he appears? For his is like the refiner's fire and the fullers' alkali. He will take his seat as refiner and purifier.... For the day is coming now, burning like a furnace; and all the arrogant and the evildoers will be like stubble. The day that is coming is going to burn them up, says Yahweh Sabaoth, leaving them neither

> root nor stalk. But for you who fear my name, the sun of righteousness will shine out with healing in its rays.... (3:1-3,19-20)

Beyond the obvious resemblance between the main features of this promise and those of the gospel of John the Baptist, I wish to underline two points of interest. One is that Malachi's fiery judge is identified with the Angel of the Covenant—the superhuman agent of God who presides over righteousness as God defines it and who will in the end visit the earth with a fire that both saves and destroys. The resemblance to the thresher of judgment preached by John is clear: he does the work of the Lord's own just judgment, and it does not require a large stretch of the imagination to grasp how it might be said that his judgment will result in the gathering of his righteous (i.e., those who keep the Covenant which it is his office to supervise) into his own storehouse (i.e., the final Covenant, which faithful Israelites long for him to institute definitively). The language of John's gospel is consistent with Malachi's promise. And it is consistent in still one other way, for my second point of interest is Malachi's emphatic "yes, he is coming," or "yes, he is the coming one," *hinne ba*. This is one who is coming in the name of the Lord. The special meaning of Psalm 118:26, as a coded promise of a rescuing intervention to come, easily aligns itself with this more specific promise. The gospel of Malachi corresponds in intriguing details to the gospel of John the Baptist and is likely one of its major sources. If John was associated with Malachi's messenger, it may have been on grounds deeper and more compelling than the mere coincidence that both prepare the way for God's final judgment. John's gospel was evidently read in terms of Malachi. John may well have been responsible for this.

ELIJAH

It remains only to return to one last supporting evidence for my reconstruction of John's gospel, one which is also another link between John and Malachi. It is the association of John with Elijah—for Malachi concludes not with a reference to an unnamed prophet to come, but with the specific promise that "I am going to send you Elijah the prophet before my day comes, that great and terrible day. He shall turn the hearts of fathers towards their children and the hearts of children towards their fathers, lest I come and strike the land with a curse" (Mal 4:5-6). These were the very last words not only of the Book of Malachi but of prophecy itself as the books were apparently arranged in the days of John the Baptist.[20] Authentic prophecy was supposed to have ceased,[21] and this was therefore its last testament.

That John was associated, and sometimes identified, with Elijah is indisputably clear. The angel's prophecy to Zechariah, undoubtedly preserving a pre-Christian source concerning John (for it is faithful to the other earliest representations of John, and contains no Christian coloring whatsoever), says that John "will go before him [viz., God] in spirit and power of Elijah, to turn hearts of fathers to children, and disobedient ones in wisdom of just ones, to make ready for the Lord a prepared people" (Lk 1:17). This is clearly Malachi's Elijah. Other speculation on Elijah occurred in other texts (notably 1 Maccabees 2:58 and Sirach 48:10) but with different words or different thoughts. They gave rise both to a cautious general speculation that Elijah would return before the end, and to some specific speculations about just what he would do. The general presumption is echoed in the question of Jesus' disciples: "What is it then that the scribes say, that Elijah must come first?" (Mt 17:10; cf. Mk 9:11). Jesus replies with a specific reference to Malachi: "True, Elijah comes first, and will restore [*apokatastēsei,* precisely the word used in the LXX translation of Malachi for the Hebrew *heshib,* "turn"] all things"—but then adds "but I tell you that Elijah has now come, and they did not recognize him, but did with him as they wished" (Mt 17:12; cf. Mk 9:13). Matthew observes that "then the disciples understood that he spoke to them about

John the Baptist" (Mt 17:13). They should not have needed to draw the inference slowly: Matthew had already reported that Jesus, speaking in praise of John the Baptist, concluded by telling the disciples that "if you are ready to receive it, he is the Elijah who was to come" (Mt 11:14). Both Christian and non-Christian sources bear witness to the conception of John as Elijah.

When John the Baptist was identified with Elijah, just what was the value and import of the identification? For additional speculations about Elijah may have been in circulation. The scribes referred to by the disciples probably said more about the matter than the mere fact that he was to come, and if such other thoughts about Elijah are witnessed to only by much later documents, this does not preclude their having been known to popular rumor in earlier times. Opinions were not systematically collected for publication from the scholars of John's day, let alone from the tax-gatherers and prostitutes and other religiously marginal people who seem to be remembered as an important portion of John's penitents: notions that first appear in rabbinic lore some centuries later might well have been bruited about among the scribes and even the populace long before. Nevertheless, what it meant to align John with Elijah must be sought out first from the indications surviving in the earliest sayings about John. Convenient Christian hypotheses can be appealed to later-attested possibilities of evidence only after the earlier ones have been carefully weighed and measured.

Once this discrimination is made, the case is readily closed. The oldest texts offer striking positive and negative evidence that John's early reputation confirms the outlines of his gospel as I have proposed them. On the negative side, it is notable that although it would have been obviously advantageous to the Christian cause to conceive Elijah as the ordainer—even as the forerunner, but especially as the ordainer—of the Messiah, there is no early text that so interprets either John or Elijah. This was not part of an Elijan office. The idea of Elijah as commissioner of the Messiah may not have arisen for another century, when it is first attested,[22] and this for good reason: it depends upon a conflation of Malachi's version of the end (which offers Elijah but has no place for a Messiah) and a specifically Messianic version (none of which, in early texts, involves Elijah) which John does not appear to have encouraged or even to have left room for. On the positive side, the Gospels' references to Elijah stay close to the implications and even to the language of the Malachi prophecy: Elijah must come first (i.e., before the end) to restore all things (Mt 17:11, Mk 9:12), and John the Baptist either is Elijah in having done so (Mt 11:14, 17:12-13) or is working in the spirit and power of Elijah in his mission of turning hearts (Lk 1:17). What the Gospels attest concerning popular ideas about Elijah in the time of John and Jesus seems to fall short of subsequent Jewish imaginations about him. The early texts suggest that John was seen as Malachi's Elijah and no other. The most plausible conclusion is that in the earliest days of the gospel of John the Baptist, the role of Elijah was supposed, both in popular and in more sophisticated circles, to be essentially confined to the capacities given in Malachi's announcement of Elijah's return in the last of times, to turn Israelites' hearts to reconciliation and to prepare the Lord's way in the face of an imminent and definitive judgment.

This is not a diminishment of John, but a considerable enhancement. Elijah was the ultimate prophet, the effective herald of the end. In the view of John's believing contemporaries, no greater prophet had ever been given to Israel. Jesus is quoted as saying that John was more than a prophet: from those born of women, there has not arisen one greater than John the Baptist (Mt 11:11, Lk 7:28). For the Law and the Prophets governed the religious life of Israel until the appearance of John; but since then, John's gospel redefines what is promised and demanded (Mt 11:13, Lk 16:16). He is the Elijah who has long been awaited, the proclaimer of the definitive good news and both the sign and the agent of the final mobilization of the world under God's destructively and salvifically merciful judgment.

John's importance inevitably resulted in speculations about him. The Fourth Gospel reports the most predictable of these: he was thought to be "the prophet" (i.e., the one like Moses, who seemed to be promised before the end, according to a special late interpretation of Deuteronomy 18:15,18), or the Messiah, or Elijah (Jn 1:20-21; cf. Lk 3:15). Luke and the Fourth Gospel are undoubtedly right in representing that John resisted being called Messiah: to invoke that category was to misunderstand his gospel, however it may have showed an appropriate hope for the dawning of some kind of new era under his leadership. The suspicion that he might be "the prophet" showed a clearer appreciation of what he said and did. But above all, the guess that he might be Elijah proved that he had made himself understood, at least to some of his hearers. John demanded just such a change of heart and achievement of righteous life as was expected by Elijah. He preached the imminence of the judgment which Elijah was to be sent to precede. He proclaimed a gospel that closely resembled the gospel of Malachi that promised Elijah. He had begun to "restore all things," as the LXX version of Malachi's Elijah would have it, through the final conversion of Israel.

In short, the association of John with Elijah, apparently an early and firm development, is in itself a persuasive testimony that the gospel of John as it is preserved in the oldest evidences and susceptible of critical reconstruction is in fact the gospel that John proclaimed. The judgment was at hand. God was about to intervene definitively through a judging and angelically powerful Coming One, and had sent through John one last invitation and warning—good news or bad, depending on how one responded to it. Those who made themselves ready by repentance and righteous amendment of life would be saved and gathered into the divine storehouse; those who declined to do so and remained in their sins—no matter how they belonged to Israel or to Pharisaic piety or to any other imagined privilege of protection—would be swept away into the fire. This was the last chance, for unimaginable good or unspeakable ill. This was the gospel of John the Baptist.

2

The Gospel of Jesus

The public ministry of Jesus began without any privilege. He started from scratch. The idea that anything good could come out of Nazareth was apparently difficult or amusing to Nathaniel (Jn 1:46), and when Jesus preached in his own home town, the reaction recorded by Mark (6:3) obviously amounts to a skeptical "We know this fellow and all his family. How can we take him seriously?" The spectacular events and circumstances surrounding his conception and birth prefixed to the Gospels of Matthew and Luke have no parallel in the Gospels of Mark and John, and no echo whatsoever in the reception of the adult Jesus in any of the Gospels. It is not registered in any account of Jesus' ministry that anyone who heard him remembered that he had been marked as something special from the beginning. There is no recollection of guided Magi or summoned shepherds—not even of a birth in Bethlehem.[1] His ministry had no prior advantages in public relations. From the time he began to preach his gospel until the end, he was apparently on his own.

The gospel of Jesus was initially perceived as beginning where John the Baptist had left off. This is true in two ways. In the first place, there is an early tradition which holds that the public preaching of Jesus commenced only when, and possibly because, John was taken off the scene into prison by Herod. Mark dates the beginning of the gospel of Jesus thus: "And after the imprisonment of John, Jesus went into Galilee, proclaiming the gospel of God" (1:14). Matthew is still bolder about the connection between these two events: "And hearing that John was imprisoned, he departed to Galilee. . . . From then Jesus began to proclaim and to say, 'Repent: for the kingdom of the heavens has drawn near'" (Mt 4:12,17). In the second place, there is an early tradition which sees the basic gospel of Jesus as essentially identical to the basic gospel of John. The Matthean quotation just given, summarizing the first proclamation of Jesus, is word for word the same as Matthew's summary of the preaching of John (Mt 3:2). The similarity was close enough to inspire the rumor that the gospelling Jesus was none other than John the Baptist risen from the dead. (Mt 14:2, and Mk 6:14,16 make this Herod's opinion—but cf. Mt 16:14, Mk 8:28, Lk 9:19—and Lk 9:7.)

The chances are that these are basically accurate memories. Disciples of Jesus would have small reason to invent them, since they seem to subordinate Jesus to John, making Jesus appear to be a follower or at best a self-appointed junior partner who carries on the work of the master when the master can no longer continue. This apparent subordination was awkward enough to inspire corrective adjustments in the story. Luke, for instance, reports the imprisonment of John before he deals with the baptism of Jesus, and mentions no meeting between Jesus and John during their adult lives (Lk 3:20—4:14), thus leaving little room for discipleship. The Fourth Gospel offers an alternative correction, reporting that John was still active after Jesus had begun his public ministry and then adding "For John was not yet cast into prison" (Jn 3:24). This added remark is self-evident from the previous verse, and was therefore probably motivated by a desire to counteract the idea, recorded by Matthew and Mark, that Jesus' public life began only after, and perhaps only because, John had been jailed. Luke and the Fourth Gospel, in short, go out of their way to establish Jesus' independent importance and to avoid the impression that he was simply carrying on the work of John. Matthew and Mark, innocent of this corrective intent, are probably nearer the truth. The first stage of the gospel of Jesus probably struck many people as virtually indistinguishable from the gospel of John the Baptist, and Jesus himself was undoubtedly seen, by those who were in a position to compare, as carrying into Galilee the same gospel that John had proclaimed in the wilderness of Judea and in the region of the Jordan: "Repent! for the kingdom of God is at hand."[2]

If Jesus' gospel was, in its beginnings, seen as nothing more or less than the continuation of John's, there was nevertheless probably good reason to make a distinction between them. For there seem to have been some differences between the gospel of John and the early gospel of Jesus, even if they did not seem significant to the earliest tradition.

John preached a baptism of repentance. There is no reason to suppose that Jesus did so. The body of evidence clearly suggests that Jesus neither baptized nor spoke of baptism during the main part of his ministry. One text that weighs to the contrary, Jn 4:1, is immediately corrected by the following verse: "But actually Jesus himself did not baptize—it was his disciples." Baptism was resumed by the followers of Jesus after he was no longer with them, but Jesus himself, at least during the main part of his public ministry, did not baptize and did not preach baptism.[3] Whether this was because he thought baptism unique to John as the only true baptizer or because he thought it simply dispensable, we can never know. What we can know is that he differed from John in this: the baptism of repentance was not part of his own gospel.

Moreover, John's gospel of the baptism of repentance was intimately linked with his gospel of the greater baptizer to come. He characterized the imminent future cataclysm by reference to his own mission and to what he did in the waters of the Jordan. Jesus did not follow John in using the metaphor of baptism in speaking of what was finally to come. He appears to have shared with John the expectation of a grand judge who would come soon, but there is little reason for supposing that he used the titles employed by John—the Coming One, the One More Powerful than I. The characteristic title by which Jesus is represented as referring to the coming Judge is The Son of Man: there is no evidence that John had used this title before him.

In short, the gospel of Jesus began in clear continuity with the gospel of John the Baptist, so much so that some observers casually identified the two gospels. They were similar enough to permit Jesus to commend John as the initiator of the great good news. They were similar enough to justify the early tradition that thought Jesus to be carrying on John's work. But they were different enough, both in specific detail and in general emphasis, to validate the final stance of the followers of Jesus: Jesus did not simply repeat the gospel of John, but proclaimed a news that was in some respects genuinely new. It was not the Christian good news as we know it—that was not to come until a later stage of gospelling—but it was a good news as dramatic and hopeful as any before or since. The rest of this chapter will be concerned with its nature and content.[4]

THE DOMINION OF GOD

The core of the gospel of Jesus is neatly summarized in Matthew's account of the very outset of his public ministry: "Repent! for the Dominion of the Heavens is at hand" (Mt 4:17). Elaborations of this basic theme appear everywhere in the surviving accounts of Jesus' preaching and teaching. It was the beginning of his gospel, and continued to the end.

THE MEANING OF "THE DOMINION OF GOD"

The meaning of this term is far from obvious. It was not obvious even to Jesus' contemporaries, despite his various attempts to clarify it and correct misunderstandings. But one cannot understand the gospel of Jesus without some grasp of what he meant by the Dominion of God.[5]

Having quoted Matthew's formula for the essential gospel of Jesus, I must at once clear up a possible confusion. Matthew refers to the Dominion "of the Heavens" (*tōn ouranōn*). This means exactly the same thing as the Dominion of God. Matthew wrote in a tradition of Jewish piety that avoided using the name of God so as to be scrupulously careful about the Third Commandment. The first principle of this custom was to avoid always the actual pronunciation of the ancient Hebrew name of God that appeared in the Hebrew scriptures as JHVH.[6] By Matthew's day, it was customary in the reading of the Scriptures to disregard the fact that JHVH had been written in bolder times: the reader was obliged to substitute the word *Lord* (*Adonai* in Hebrew) in its place. Various circumlocutions and euphemisms developed in order to protect this principle further. One of them was the substitution of "Heavens" where one meant "God." Matthew's reference to the Dominion of the Heavens is simply his use (in which his received text is not entirely consistent)[7] of a standard delicate way of avoiding a direct reference to God. There is good reason for supposing that in doing so he was correcting Jesus rather than following him. Jesus was apparently not fastidious about such matters. He scandalized his contemporaries by addressing and referring to God directly and intimately; that was one of the things that got him in trouble with the conservative authorities. In any case, Matthew's delicacy is not the delicacy of Jesus: what Jesus preached was the Dominion of God.

The gospel of Jesus is essentially a gospel of the Dominion of God. I choose the word *Dominion* in place of the more traditional *Kingdom* because it seems to me to be a nearer English equivalent to the word, and the idea, that Jesus actually used. The underlying Hebrew word is *malkuth* (the Aramaic equivalents being derived from the same verbal root), and the basic thrust of the word designates the act of reigning, rather than the corresponding realm. *Kingdom* misses that emphasis and is accordingly misleading. But just as the present participle *gathering* slides easily into a designation of the group that is gathered, and the noun *government* has shifted to indicate not the act of governing but the personnel and policies that govern, so *malkuth* and its Aramaic equivalents eventually took on suggestions of the territory or populace subject to the king's rule. From the various statements attributed to Jesus, it appears that he was prepared to use the word with emphasis in either direction, reign or realm, rather indifferently; each implied the other anyway. *Dominion* preserves an original ambiguity that ought to be retained.

"The Dominion of God" was not a scriptural phrase. It does not occur at all in the Hebrew Bible, although God is often represented as a reigning king in various other phrases. Jesus clearly uses it as a sort of technical term—and so it evidently had become in popular usage, to judge from its occurrence in some pre-Christian Jewish writings and in the post-biblical literature stemming from the synagogues and from the rabbis.[8] Neither Jesus nor John the Baptist invented it; it had already been in general circulation. What it formulated does not seem to have been very precise: it could be used to mean roughly "the controlling power of God" or "God's right to be obeyed," or even to describe that hypothetical or future state of affairs in which God is fully and universally submitted to. It was not precise, but it was readily intelligible. When Jesus began to proclaim the coming of the Dominion of God, he could count on his audience's knowing in some general way what he was talking about: God is going to take over. He could also count on there being people who were eagerly hopeful for such an event. Luke characterizes Joseph of Arimathea as one who was awaiting the Dominion of God (Lk 23:51)—i.e., one who expected and believed that something would happen to bring the reign of God more completely upon Israel. Apparently there were many who cherished at least a general hope for something better to come. Simeon was "waiting expectantly for the consolation of Israel" (Lk 2:25), and Anna gave her good news to "all those waiting expectantly for deliverance in Jerusalem" (Lk 2:38). John the Baptist preached to people "waiting in expectation" (Lk 3:15). It was to such audiences that Jesus offered his gospel of the imminent coming of the Dominion of God.

REPENTANCE AND LOVE

That imminent coming was good news—but it was not meant to be unequivocally so, any more than the analogous news of John the Baptist was unqualifiedly reassuring. It is good news for those who are properly prepared; for others, it is first a warning. Hence Jesus shares with John a general call to repentance: since God is about to take over, you must change your life. The gospel of Jesus, like that of John before him, was an announcement of the imminent great happening, an invitation to belong to it, a caution about the kind of change of life that is a prerequisite for belonging, and a warning about the cost of being left out.

The single imperative "Repent!" was an injunction familiar enough to all Jews, but just what it entails was never self-evident. John had insisted that it is more than a regret or an apology for one's past waywardness: true repentance, the kind that brings full forgiveness and eligibility to be gathered into the divine storehouse rather than to be consigned to the flames, requires that one bring forth fruit worthy of repentance. One must become righteous. In John's case, Luke records some specific instructions by which John is supposed to have indicated what that means: share with those who do not have enough, be fair and honest, do not misuse your power (Lk 3:10-14). Jesus seems to have taken a somewhat different approach, at least somewhat different from what has survived in the scanty descriptions of John's teaching on the subject. Jesus summarized the heart of true repentance in the two great commandments of Deut 6:5 and Lev 19:18: first, you shall love the Lord your God with all your heart and with all your soul and with all your mind and with all your might (Mk 12:30; cf. the slightly different versions in Mt 22:37 and Lk 10:27);

and second, you shall love your neighbor as yourself (Mt 22:39, Mk 12:31, Lk 10:27).

Jesus seems to have seen these commandments at the center rather than just at the summit: "On these two commandments the whole of the Law and the Prophets depends" (Mt 22:40).[9] Accordingly, he attempted in various ways to explain the implications of repentance and of the great commandments, and thus of his gospel. The explanation was both surprising and sobering—surprising, because of the radically literal way in which he maintained the great commandments should be understood; and sobering, because of the extraordinary demands that result from taking them seriously.

The literal requirement of the first of the commandments is that one must give oneself over to God totally. Totally meant *totally,* not greatly, or considerably, or often; and "to God" meant *to God*—not to religion, or to pious observances, or to what the scholarly elders have taught. The particular instructions of Jesus follow accordingly. On the one hand, one ought to see God as inviting and deserving unqualified love—as a loving, caring, provident Father who can be completely trusted, a knowing and fostering Father who should be thoroughly obeyed, a generously forgiving and accepting Father to whom anyone can turn with unfearing confidence. Thus Jesus emphasizes that the seeker will find, the asker will receive, the knock on the door will be answered (Mt 7:7-8, Lk 11:9-10). God is good; he is in fact the only one of whom this word can be properly used (Mt 19:17, Mk 10:18, Lk 18:19); and if we, who are not good, still give good things to our children, how much more so will our good heavenly Father give us what is good (Mt 7:11, Lk 11:13)! He knows what we need before we ask it (Mt 6:8), and nothing is impossible for him (Mt 19:26, Mk 10:27, Lk 18:27); he keeps track of everything, from the hairs on our heads to the fall of the solitary sparrow (Mt 10:29-31, Lk 12:6-7), and will provide for our needs at least as readily as he provides for the needs of the birds and the lilies, which thrive under his providence (Mt 6:25-34, Lk 12:22-31). Because God is a compassionate, benevolent, and wise Father, we should above all strive to do his will, which encompasses all that is best. Hence the simplest prayer praises God and asks that his will be obeyed and accomplished on earth, as it is in heaven (Mt 6:10, Lk 11:2). Frail humanity may well also pray that God's will not permit trials that are hard for us to endure, but rather that we be delivered from evil and protected from testings (Mt 6:13, Lk 11:4). But in the long run, even that plea must have as its last word: "yet not what I want, but what you want" (Mt 26:39, Mk 14:36, Lk 22:42). Therefore his commandments must be obeyed in those instances where he has made his will known (Mt 19:18-19, Mk 10:19, Lk 18:20), and his governance must be trusted in those situations when his will is less obvious. And what we know especially about his will is that it calls us to love him with all our heart and soul and mind and might, and to love our neighbor as we love ourself.

The love of neighbor followed from the love of God because God had commanded it. It also followed from the love of God because it is one of the implications of love, properly understood. Matthew's Jesus gives the succinct injunction, "Then be you perfect, as your heavenly Father is perfect" (Mt 5:48; Luke's parallel, 6:36, says *merciful* in place of *perfect*). This is a maxim distilled from centuries of Jewish discussion and reflection on the implications of God's love for Israel and the requirements of Israel's love for God. The Book of Leviticus had already insisted on such reciprocity: "You have been sanctified and have become holy because I am holy. . . . You therefore must be holy because I am holy" (Lev 11:44-45). The sages of Israel knew that they should be grateful for what they were, and that they were what they were because God had loved them first. The only appropriate response would be to love God in return and to realize as fully as possible what his love was trying to make of them—the image and likeness of God. The Jesus of Matthew and Luke enforces the rigor of the conclusion: be Godlike.

And what is it to be Godlike? Matthew's conclusion follows from a simple argument of analogy:

> You have heard how it was said: "Love your neighbor"—and hate your enemies. But I'm telling you, love your enemies and pray for those who persecute you. Thus you shall become sons of your Father in heaven—for his sun rises on bad ones and good ones, and his rain falls on the righteous and the unrighteous. If you love those who love you, what deserving is there in that? Don't the tax-collectors do as much? And if you have a good word only for your brothers, what's the big accomplishment in that? (Mt 5:43-47; cf. Lk 6:27-35)

The essential point is that we have settled for too little. We have our own version of righteousness, one that makes excuses and cuts things to our ordinary size. We think ourselves entitled to hate our enemies: so we feel, and so we have been taught. But the impartial behavior of God shows that he does not hate his enemies. He loves them and "is kind to the ungrateful and the wicked" (Lk 6:35). We are called to be like him. Therefore, whatever the traditions of the sensible elders may say—whatever may be said even in some of the compromising statements of the Law—we must love our enemies and be benevolent even to our persecutors (Mt 5:43-45, Lk 6:27-28). We must turn the other cheek, give the extra garment, walk the additional mile (Mt 5:39-42; cf. Lk 6:29-30). Above all, we must forgive—thoroughly, generously, with all our hearts, even repeatedly forgive the same offender, if we are to be like God, who does all this and more (Mt 18:22). We must, in short, conform ourselves to the alternative summary of the second great commandment: "Whatever you want men to do for you, do thus for them: for this is the Law and the Prophets" (Mt 7:12; cf. Lk 6:31: "And just as you want men to treat you, treat them the same way").

There are, of course, ways of reading compromises into both the Golden Rule and the second great commandment. The latter is the easier to fulfill the more one suffers from, or affects, a self-hatred that disguises itself as humility: "as you love yourself" can become an escape clause. It is not difficult to persuade oneself that one does not really want others to compromise their comfort, their private property, or their outraged feelings on one's behalf—and that view establishes convenient limits for one's obligations to them. This is not the way Jesus intended himself to be understood. The norm is not our skill at taming these commands by skillful interpretation. The norm is God's love, and we are called upon to imitate that love, the only way of fulfilling all true righteousness.

The great commandments, as Jesus understood them, may perhaps be stated in a slightly different way as well. They summarize the Law and the Prophets—but the Law and the Prophets do not necessarily have the last word. The Law expresses God's will; but God is now on the move, is about to take over, and times are accordingly somewhat different. A new age is at hand. The Law and the Prophets defined the age that covered the time until John the Baptist proclaimed the good news of the imminent Dominion of God (Mt 11:13, Lk 16:16), but now that John's new proclamation has arrived, we turn to the new age, not the old one. God is pleased to give the Dominion (Lk 12:32), and it must now be our first preoccupation. First seek the Dominion of God—and God will take care of everything else needful (Lk 12:31; cf. Mt 6:33). God is shortly to make available a new and total way of becoming a true child of his, through the coming Dominion and the new era it will inaugurate. Belonging to the Dominion is all that is really important to us now. Hence we should be ready to sacrifice anything and everything to make it possible, like the merchant who sells all he has in order to be able to afford a once-in-a-lifetime purchase (Mt 13:45-46), or like the crafty man who stumbles upon a treasure and sells everything in order to possess it (Mt 13:44). The only true treasure, of course, is the heavenly sort—the incorruptible and inalienable treasure offered by God (Mt 6:19-20, Lk 12:33). It is now being offered in the impending Dominion of God, and no other treasure may be allowed to stand in the way. We should be ready to give up everything to follow God's will fully, like the widow with her mite (Mk 12:41-44, Lk 21:1-4). Worldly treasure, home, family, even an eye that leads us astray—anything that holds us back or stands in our way should be abandoned for the one great chance (Mt 10:37-39, Lk 14:26, Mt 5:29).

The choice is not even as hard as it looks, since thereby we not only acquire a greater treasure in the age to come, in the form of eternal life with God, but also in the meantime we will have all we need that treasures can buy and will acquire a better home and a larger and closer family among those who join in seeking the Dominion of God (Mt 19:29, Mk 10:30, Lk 18:28-30). An offer you can't refuse: the eventual rewards are incomparable, the temporary rewards are impressive, and to say no to the invitation is to refuse to do the will of God, which is not at all a good idea.

Anyone who repents fully and effectively—that is, anyone who brings forth the good fruit of righteousness and sins no more, who forgives and compassionates and cares for the needy, anyone who follows with simple literalness God's call to love God completely and to love one's neighbor as oneself—is not far from the Dominion of God (Mk 12:34) and will inherit eternal life (Mt 19:16-18, Mk 10:17-19, Lk 10:25-26, 18:18-20). And that is the only thing worth doing.

WHEN WILL IT COME?

When will the Dominion of God make its appearance? For the last two generations of scholarship on the Gospels, there has been a struggle to establish that the Dominion of God, as represented in Jesus' gospel, was not entirely future—that in some sense it had already taken root.[10] When Jesus proclaims that the Dominion of God "has drawn near" or "is at hand" (*ēggiken,* Mt 3:2, 4:17, 10:7; Mk 1:15; Lk 10:9,11), can he mean that it has already begun? Not readily with that verb; even though it can be stretched to that end, that is not its normal meaning. Nor when Luke's Jesus says that the Dominion of God is "in your midst" (*entos humōn,* Lk 17:21) does he mean that it is fully present: Luke's Jesus subsequently describes signs that will occur later to indicate that the Dominion of God is "near" (*eggus,* Lk 21:31). Later in the history of Christian gospelling there was an effort to claim that the Dominion of God was far more accomplished than unaccomplished, much more present than future. I will take up those questions later, especially in dealing with the Fourth Gospel. At the moment, when the issue is to reconstruct the gospel of Jesus, it appears to me clear that what must be said is that the Dominion of God was essentially something that would come in the future, with power, in glory and judgment. What had already begun was important, but small. But something had indeed begun.

To what extent did Jesus consider the Dominion of God a present event? To begin with, its proclamation had gone forth. The Law and the Prophets were the way that God had ruled until recently, up to the time of John the Baptist. But from the time of John, the Dominion of God is proclaimed, ready for people to shove their way in, up for grabs and people are crowding into it (Mt 11:12-13, Lk 16:16). The general announcement and invitation has now gone forth; the excited guests are making themselves ready, and are clearly planning to join the party. It's official; it's already on its way. But that is not merely an abstract statement concerning estimated time of arrival. The act of accepting the invitation is in fact an aspect of the feast itself. People are repenting, reforming, bringing forth good fruit: they have already begun to taste what it is to be embraced by the Dominion of God, to submit fully to God's rule, to live under a divine takeover. There is a new joy abroad in the land; people are already grasping a knowledge of salvation through the forgiveness of their sins and through lives lived in full love of God and neighbor. They will be saved in the end if they persist, but in another sense, as Luke rightly puts it, we can say that they are already in the process of being saved (Lk 13:23; cf. Mt 10:22, 24:13).

There are occasional teachings of Jesus that imply that the Dominion of God has already established a beachhead, a genuine beginning in the world. The most celebrated of these comes upon the occasion of the controversy about the exorcisms performed by Jesus. Against the accusation that he bests the demons by virtue of demonic powers, he argues that the devils would not war against themselves, that the children of the Jews cast out demons too, that no one would be able to contend with the demons without first mastering the strongest demon of them all (Mt 12:22-29, Mk 3:22-27, Lk 11:14-22)—and that if it be by the spirit (or as Luke puts it, by the finger) of God that Jesus exorcises after all, then the Dominion of God "is come upon you" (*ephthasen eph' humas*—Mt 12:28; see Lk 11:20). There is no need to get particularly excited about this latter text: all things weighed, it says no more, and no less, than the balance of other evidence, namely, that God is on the move, bringing his Dominion. If it is not present yet in full power, its effectiveness is already beginning to show: the world is thawing; repentance is spreading; unlikely plants are producing good fruit; and even the grip of the demons is loosened. The same implication seems to me to be present in those parables that speak of the slow, small start of the Dominion of God, steadily building to something grand and complete—like leaven in the loaf, like the tiny mustard seed that in time produces substantial and sheltering branches, and like the tiny band of followers that has already started to grow to substantial crowds (Mt 13:33, Lk 13:20-21; Mt 13:31-32, Mk 4:30-32, Lk 13:18-19; cf. Mk 4:26-29).

Something important had already started happening, then; but the full Dominion of God, completely realized in power, had not yet arrived. The small beginnings were only a foretaste of the great triumph to come. What was the nature of that triumph, and how would it take place?

NOT OF THIS WORLD

Those who heard Jesus' gospel of the Dominion differed widely in the beliefs and expectations with which they came to it. Some were clearly of a nationalistic political stamp. Some remained so even after Jesus' ministry was over. When Luke represents Cleopas on the road to Emmaus, expressing his now-disappointed hope that Jesus would be the one to redeem Israel (Lk 24:21), he is evidently supposing that Cleopas's expectations were that God would redeem Israel from the power of the Romans. The presumption represented on the lips of the disciples just before the ascension of Jesus is essentially the same: "Lord, will you at this time restore the dominion to Israel?" (Acts 1:6)—that is, return sovereignty into the hands of the people of Israel, as they once enjoyed ruling their own lives and those of nearby subject peoples. Luke apparently thought that many of Jesus' hearers, even his closest disciples, cherished this hope. Luke has the disciples usher Jesus into Jerusalem with a greeting that significantly alters an established formula. Adding one crucial word to the often-quoted verse 26 from Psalm 118, they cry out "Blessed is the *king* who comes in the name of the Lord" (Lk 19:38). Luke is not alone in this view of the disciples' expectation. Matthew and Mark, in their version of Jesus' entry into Jerusalem, quote the original psalm without emendation, "Blessed is the one who comes in the name of the Lord," but they join Luke in bearing witness to a more conventionally political sense of dominion present in the expectations of the disciples: Matthew adds "Hosanna to the son of David" (21:9), while Mark has them say still more pointedly, "Blessed is the coming dominion of our father David" (11:10).

This style of expectation is known from sources other than the New Testament, and is most perfectly preserved in the seventeenth of the Psalms of Solomon, which was written near the beginning of the period of Roman domination over Israel and captures an early version of the pious hopes that greeted the entry of Jesus into Jerusalem.[11] God is our ultimate King, says the psalmist, and the Dominion of God hangs in judgment over the nations; but God chose David to be king over Israel and will now send a son of David to drive out sinners and Gentiles and establish a holy rule over the land. The psalm closes by saying once again, as it looks hopefully into the future, that "The Lord himself is our king for ever and ever"—i.e., the Dominion of God is realized in the dominion of a righteous Davidic king, ruling with the protection and inspiration of God. It was possible to understand the Dominion of God as a political redemption brought about through the restoration of the Davidic monarchy in power and in justice. The Psalms of Solomon seem to understand it in this way; so do the disciples of Jesus who bring him triumphantly into Jerusalem.

But apparently not Jesus himself. Nor John the Baptist before him. John the Baptist's use of the title "the Coming One" differs markedly from the way it is used by the crowds in Jesus' Jerusalem entry, since John's gospel obviously refers to a mighty judge who comes in power to bring fiery wrath upon the earth—nothing so modest as a throne-restoring king, Davidic or not. Matthew and Luke report a story in which John hears of Jesus' activities and sends two disciples to him to ask whether Jesus is the Coming One or whether we should wait for another (Mt 11:2-6, Lk 7:18-23). The story is, to my mind, a clear fabrication. John's gospel was a gospel of a Coming One about whom there could hardly be any ambiguity about politics and Davidic sovereignty, as he threshed the earth with holy spirit and fire, gathering the righteous into his barn. What Jesus was now doing in no way resembled this. Of *course* John's Coming One was another, still to be waited for. The story is a way of suggesting, daintily and gingerly, that Jesus might be considered eligible, even from John's viewpoint, to be identified as the Coming One of John's gospel. That suggestion could arise only when the mere echoes of John's preaching remained, not the vivid memory of what it contained. The identification is out of the question—the story of the inquiry is as contrived as having Pope Paul VI send to ask Martin Luther King if perhaps he is the Jesus of the Second Coming.

Jesus himself seems to have had a radically different understanding of the Dominion of God from that expressed in the Psalms of Solomon and in the snapshots of Jesus' followers offered by the Gospels during the latter part of his career. He is represented as being largely indifferent about the presence of the Roman power, neither afraid of it nor belligerently opposed to it, but simply unconcerned about it. He does not seem interested in military strategy, or political organization, or ideas of revolution; Caesars and kings and hefty treasuries and the power to dominate others all appear to be beside the point as far as he is concerned, even if some of his followers take them more seriously. What Jesus looks for in the Dominion of God will come soon, but not as some sort of coup. It is much bigger news than that. God is going to take over, and in a way that makes any concern about the Jewish national aspirations seem petty and backward.

For the Dominion of God is not part of this present age or era: it belongs to the age to come (Mk 10:30), the new birth (*paliggenesia,* Mt 19:28), when those who endure to the end and are saved (Mt 10:22, 24:13) will be given eternal life (Mt 19:29, Lk 10:25, 18:18,30) and will be able to recline in the company of Abraham and Isaac and Jacob and the prophets (Lk 13:28-29). It will come in full power before the present generation is ended (Mk 9:1, Lk 9:27; cf. Mk 13:30, Mt 24:34, Lk 21:32), and until that time there is a chance for everyone to repent and reform so as to become a child of the Dominion, ready to enter it when it comes. But it will not come with a restoration of the Davidic throne or with the expulsion of the Romans. It will come with a total transformation—and with judgment.

THE JUDGMENT

The Dominion foreseen by John the Baptist was to begin with a cataclysmic judgment ushered in by the Coming One. The Dominion preached by Jesus was similar: it offered not merely the good news of salvation to those who prepared themselves by repentance and good fruits, but the bad news of judgment for the others, and a stern and terrible judge.

The idea of a large-scale day of judgment is ancient in Jewish tradition. In earlier days, the image was plausibly rooted in the visitation—for that was an alternative word used for the same idea of judgment—of the circuit-riding judge. His case expectantly prepared, the offended party waited for the day of visitation when he would be vindicated, shown publicly as the one in the right, and saved by just judgment from the oppression and threat from which he suffered. By the time of Amos in the eighth century B.C., a larger notion of rescue had arisen in an idea of the Day of the Lord; and Amos was already prepared to turn the idea against many of those who thought it comforting. He warned them that when the Lord made his visitation to give just judgment, some of those who supposed that they would be vindicated would be condemned and punished (Amos 5:18-20).

The coming Day of Judgment appears frequently as part of the gospel of Jesus. Chorazin and Bethsaida stand under judgment, and when the Day of Judgment comes, the Gentile cities of Tyre and Sidon will have an easier time than they, for Chorazin and Bethsaida were given a clearer invitation to repentance and declined it. Had Sodom been given the chance given to Capernaum, it would have repented and still remained: on the Day of Judgment, Capernaum will fare worse (Mt 11:21-24; cf. Lk 10:13-15). Sodom and Gomorrah will both survive the Day of Judgment more readily than the modern towns that disdain the gospel of the Dominion of God preached to them by the followers of Jesus (Mt 10:14-15, Mk 6:11, Lk 9:5, 10:10-12). Nineveh responded to Jonah's summons to repentance, and the Queen of the South responded to Solomon's wisdom; both will witness against this generation in the Judgment, for this generation did not respond to still greater testimony than theirs (Mt 12:41-42, Lk 11:30-32). In addition to various direct references to the Day of Judgment, the idea is shadowed in several parables that deal with a definitive punishment to be visited upon the wicked: in the Parable of the Tares (Mt 13:24-30,36-43), of the Dragnet (Mt 13:47-50), of the Careless Servant (Lk 12:45-48), of the Adversary (Lk 12:58-59), of Lazarus and the Rich Man (Lk 16:19-31), of the Wicked Husbandmen (Mt 21:33-46, Mk 12:1-12, Lk 20:9-18), of the Wedding Feast (Mt 22:1-14), of the Talents (Mt 25:14-30), and also in such a direct representation as Matthew's dramatic final judgment in which the judge assumes his throne, separates the sheep from the goats, and divides the world, according to its fruits, into everlasting punishment in the fire prepared for the devil and his angels, or everlasting life in the Dominion prepared for the blessed from the foundation of the world (Mt 25:31-46).[13]

Among the parabolic representations of judgment is the Parable of the Tares, in which the weeds sown among the wheat by the enemy are ordered to be left undisturbed until the harvest, then taken out from the wheat for burning, while the wheat is gathered into the barn (Mt 13:24-30). This is one of the rare cases of substantive parables which are given a full explanation within the Synoptic Gospels (the principal other example being the Parable of the Sower, Mt 13:1-9,18-23; Mk 4:1-9,13-20; Lk 8:4-8,11-15—but see also Lk 12:35-48). Whether or not the explanation in this case originated with Jesus, it certainly treats the parable in a way representative of how its original hearers would probably have understood it. The good seed is the sons of the Dominion, and the tares are the sons of the evil one. The harvest is the end of the world, and the reapers are the angels, who at the end will gather up out of the Dominion the scandalous and the ones doing lawless things and will cast them into the fire, while the righteous shine like the sun in the Dominion of their Father (Mt 13:36-43). Those who had heard John the Baptist preach of the coming harvest of judgment, through which the good grain would be gathered into the barn of the Dominion and all else would be hurled into the fire, would be likely to hear with such ears as these. The reaping angels are usual agents of the final judgment, and they play here a conventional part, echoed elsewhere in the preaching of Jesus and in earlier Jewish literature. The major curiosity of this interpretation is that whereas the basic organization of the parable suggests that the sowing husbandman is essentially analogous to God himself, as the founder of things and the director of the harvest's destruction and salvation, the explanation reproduced by Matthew identifies the sower and the harvester as the Son of Man. Occupying roughly the same position as John the Baptist's Coming One, the Son of Man in this vision of the final judgment by which the Dominion of God is established may well come, if not from Jesus' own explanation of the parable, then at least from an apt memory of Jesus' gospel, for it is consonant with the gospel of Jesus as we find it elsewhere in the Gospels. The Son of Man is a frequently recurring figure in Jesus' preaching and teaching, and the gospel of Jesus cannot be adequately understood without coming to terms with this enigmatic and fascinating problem: Who or what is the "Son of Man," and how does he figure in the gospel of Jesus?

THE SON OF MAN

The task of reconstructing early forms of gospel is land-mined with difficulties. The body of extant evidence is smaller than one would wish; the editorial interference in the received texts is difficult to detect and still more difficult to see through; the disagreements and inconsistencies within the texts are hard to adjudicate. But one of the most complicated of all the problems is the ambiguity of much of the central terminology. "The Dominion of God" meant one thing to the rabbis, another thing to the author of the Psalms of Solomon, still another in the preaching of Jesus; the one who comes in the name of the Lord could be, for various expectant interpreters, Elijah, the Messianic Son of David, or an avenging angel. Meanings shift from context to context, and the honest but naive expectation that one usage can be reliably used to interpret another has caused endless confusion. Of all the key terms made elusive by such shifts of meaning, none is more vexingly complicated than *son of man.*[13]

THE MEANING OF "SON OF MAN"

The first difficulty, the puzzling oddity of the term, is not hard to overcome. "Son of X" is a common Semitic construction, used to indicate that the thing or person spoken of is a member of X or can be characterized by the quality X, or is derived from X. Thus "the sons of the Kingdom" and "the sons of the Evil One" (Mt 13:38) are those who belong respectively to salvation and damnation; and "the son of peace" (Lk 10:6) means someone who is peaceable or who deserves peace. "Son of Aaron" denotes a priest, all of whom are theoretically descended from Aaron; and when Mark (or his source) clarifies the still-obscure nickname "Boanerges," he considers it sufficient to translate it into Hebraized Greek as "sons of Thunder" (Mk 3:17).

But although the construction is commonplace and its basic thrust easy enough to grasp, it is used in shifting ways that make its meaning hard to pin down. It can mean that the thing or person in question is a preeminent exemplar of X, or even *the* preeminent exemplar: "the son of perdition" means Judas in Jn 17:12, but the same title when used in 2 Thess 2:3 means essentially the same as "the Antichrist." "Son of David," while basically meaning merely "Davidic descendent," came to mean the special descendent, the Messiah. (It may even have been used, by some people, without any thought of literal ancestry, as a mere code-phrase amounting to nothing more or less than Messiah, whether or not descended from David.) Contrariwise, the notion of being a son of Abraham was extended to include those who follow Abraham's example, whatever their genealogical ancestry, and could exclude lineal descendents who had lost their eligibility to share in God's promise to Abraham. The construction "son of X" is, in short, basically intelligible, but slippery. Sometimes we simply do not know what it means. When Jesus refers to Zaccheus as "a son of Abraham" (Lk 19:9), it is hopelessly unclear whether he refers to his Jewish ancestry or his righteousness or his share in the Promise.

Fundamentally, "son of man" means "human being." It is not basically a title of respect but a fairly neutral designation—and more often than not, it is used in explicit or implicit contrast with something greater, and means essentially "mere mortal." When the Psalmist asks in wonderment, "What is man that you should spare a thought for him, the son of man that you should care for him?" (Ps 8:4), it is clear that "man" and "son of man" mean the same, and that it is not intended to be understood as a particularly dignified status. When God repeatedly addresses Ezekiel as "son of man," he is giving orders to a servant with a reminder that puts him firmly in his lowly place. The phrase can even become contemptuous, as when Balaam, under irresistible inspiration, declaims that "God is no man that he should lie, no son of man to draw back" (Num 23:19). For the basic meaning to be complimentary or dignifying, it requires a context that contrasts it with something plainly inferior, such as foxes or birds or monstrous beasts.

The basic meaning, however, is only where the word starts; it does not restrain it from taking on a variety of other shadings or technical values. This is, of course, not a phenomenon peculiar to Hebrew and Aramaic. Consider the variety available in English. "Man" can be entirely neutral, but often isn't. "Isn't that just like a man!" is not complimentary; Antony's summary statement about the dead Brutus, "This was a man," is a high eulogy. "Hey, man . . ." offers a title that may be contemptuous, casually familiar, or affectionate, depending on the context rather than the tone of voice. "Man," in a definition of anthropology or in a biology textbook, is a universal collective term. "The Man" is in some circles a recognizable reference to the police, in others a reference to God.

And thus it was also, alas, with "son of man" in the days of Jesus' ministry. The term was highly variable in weight, flavor, and meaning. It could be used to mean nothing more than "human being," which is clearly the sense of the term lying behind Mk 3:28, "all sins will be forgiven the sons of men" (Matthew's parallel text has simply "men," 12:31). It can be a general plural even when gramatically singular, and even with the definite article, as is demonstrated by Ps 8:4, where "the son of man" obviously means humankind. That this usage endured into New Testament times is suggested by Matthew's version of the healing of the paralytic (9:2-8, cf. Mk 2:10, Lk 5:24), for after Jesus has scandalized some of the company by pronouncing the paralytic's sins forgiven and then healed him as a sign that "the son of man has authority on earth to forgive sins," the witnesses praise God as the giver "of so great authority to men." Whether or not Matthew had understood Jesus properly is at the moment beside the point: the essential matter is that Matthew here understands "the son of man" to be a legitimate way of meaning "men." I suggest that this is the best way, though obviously not the only way, to understand the conclusion of the incident in which the disciples pluck grain on the Sabbath (Mt 12:1-8, Mk 2:23-28, Lk 6:1-5). It is they whose behavior is challenged; it is not reported either that Jesus plucked grain or that he gave his disciples permission to do so. His justifying conclusion, that "the son of man is lord of the Sabbath" is probably intended to mean just what Mark's preceding verse supposes it means: "The Sabbath came about for the sake of man, and not man for the Sabbath"—i.e., the Sabbath is a gift which human beings are empowered to make use of, not something they are subjected to. Similarly, the contrast of the son of man with foxes and birds in Mt 8:20 and Lk 9:58 suggests the generic sense of humankind rather than something that would single out the ironic disadvantages of Jesus himself.

All the same, the homely uses of "son of man" as simply equivalent to "man" or "men" are relatively few in the nearly seventy instances in which the Synoptic Gospels use the phrase. There are many examples in which it is plainly used as Jesus' reference to himself, a mere circumlocution for the first person singular pronoun: the son of man is about to be betrayed to the priests, the son of man is going to suffer, the son of man will be betrayed as it is written, delivered to crucifixion to give his life for the ransom of many, the son of man will be in the earth three days, the son of man will be raised from the dead. Nothing could be clearer. In these cases "son of man" means "I, Jesus." What, if anything, else is conferred by the use of the phrase in these instances is a matter of considerable dispute. "Son of man" functioning as "I" is hardly impossible ("What's a man supposed to do?" often functions effectually as "What am I supposed to do?"), but it is not clearly attested in the surviving evidences of Hebrew and Aramaic usage as meaning "I."[14] It seems distinctly odd. I will return to this issue later, but note in passing that this personal-reference use of the phrase is, in all its clear instances, confined to Jesus' predictions of his passion, death, and resurrection.

There is one other typical use of the phrase, and it is this one that makes all the difference between a minor problem and a major one. "Son of Man" is a title by which Jesus refers to the one who will preside over the definitive end—his at least rough equivalent of John the Baptist's Coming One. In various remarks put in the mouth of Jesus by the Gospels, the Son of Man is the one who sows the good seed in the Parable of the Tares (Mt 13:37) and the one who, when the time of harvest comes, will send forth his angels to gather the iniquitous to be burned (Mt 13:41). Before the present generation is over, the Son of Man will be seen seated at the right hand of divine power (Mt 26:64, Mk 14:62, Lk 22:69) and will come like lightning (Mt 24:27) in the clouds of heaven (Mt 24:30, Mk 13:26, Lk 21:27) with his angels (Mt 16:27, Mk 8:38, Lk 9:26) to sit on the throne of judgment (Mt 19:28, 25:31) and will separate the two classes of humankind like sheep from goats (Mt 25:31-33). Again, nothing could be clearer. This "Son of Man" is neither a mere mortal nor an ordinary human being nor humankind in general. He corresponds rather to Malachi's Angel of the Covenant and to John's Coming One. He is the Lord of the Great Judgment.

THE BACKGROUND OF "THE SON OF MAN": THE BOOK OF DANIEL

The curious use of an otherwise lowly title for such a figure would probably have been impossible to explain had we lost the last-written of the books that finally made it into the Hebrew Bible, the Book of Daniel. Its lateness (the parts crucial for our purposes were evidently composed between 167 and 164 B.C.), and the fact that parts of it (including the crucial parts) were written in Aramaic rather than Hebrew, undoubtedly weighed against its chances for admission to the canon. Its canonization in spite of these disadvantages suggests that it was extraordinarily valued.[15] Various other evidences support that supposition. It was, during the period in which Christianity had its beginnings, an especially revered part of Scripture—and it holds the main key to the meaning of "Son of Man" in the gospel of Jesus.

The book of Daniel is really a collection of various quite different parts, including the story of Daniel in the lion's den, the story of Suzanna and the Elders, and the story of the three young men in the fiery furnace. None of these parts seems to have had much effect on the formation of earliest Christian gospelling. The one that did is quite different from them all: the vision of Daniel in Chapter 7.

Daniel's vision is essentially a reassurance to the beleaguered rebels of the Maccabean revolt that God is about to intervene and restore the Dominion to the people of Israel. It looks back over the history of Israel during the previous few centuries, recounting through the symbolic beasts of Daniel's dream the various powers that had conquered Israel—the Babylonians, the Persians, and finally the worst of all, the Greeks. It recounts in a knowledgeably detailed way, though in symbolic representations, the history of Israel up to the time of the Greek ruler Antiochus IV; and then, partway through the story of his reign, the historical detail stops abruptly, and the vision begins much more vaguely to tell what was to happen next (Dan 7:8,21). That change in informedness obviously marks the time of its composition.

Whoever wrote Daniel's vision apparently did so in the critical years of the crisis that arose over the attempt of Antiochus IV to suppress the religion of the Jews and replace it with a more Hellenistically sophisticated equivalent. The actions of Antiochus were supported by a substantial part of the most influential Jews.[16] Many had already adopted Greek ways and were ready to cooperate with Antiochus' program of reform. But the heavy-handedness of Antiochus was the last straw for the Jewish conservatives: they rebelled, despite their outnumbered and inadequately equipped condition. They retreated into the hinterlands and prepared for a final showdown with the enemy. It is in this context that the vision of Daniel arose, with its detailed understanding of what had gone on before in the history of Israel, and its more generalized hopes for what would follow. The hopes were projected into the same schema in which the history had been symbolized, and were represented accordingly.

In the first part of Daniel's vision, oppressive conquerors had been represented as beasts—a lion with eagle's wings for

Babylon, a leopard for Persia, and an indescribable monster for the Hellenistic Greek regime that had conquered and taken over the Persian empire. Israel had been subject to all these in turn. The symbolism of the beasts is an elemental representation of the author's horror and contempt for the oppressors of the Jews: these are powerful beasts; but, as beasts, they are subhuman. A partial concession is made to Babylon. Jews had been deported to Babylonian territories at the time of the Babylonian conquest, early in the sixth century B.C. The Persian conquest of Babylon took place some two generations later, and when it became possible for Jews to return to the land of Israel, many of them decided to stay where they were: for many of them, the land of Babylon was the only home they knew. The Babylonian territories remained an important center of Jewish life for centuries thereafter, and produced not only one of the greatest Jewish teachers of all time, Hillel, but even the principal Talmud. At the time of the Maccabean revolt, Babylon had already ceased to be the enemy: it was at the very least a place of flourishing Jewish life. Hence the symbolism of Daniel pays a delayed compliment to Babylon by making its symbolic beast more human: "Its wings were torn off, and it was lifted from the ground and set standing on its feet like a man; and it was given a human heart" (Dan 7:4).

Within the symbolic scheme of Daniel's vision, even a moderate degree of humanization is an improvement for beasts. Therefore, when the vision gets to what is supposed to be the ultimate end, the rescue from the Hellenistic beast of the author's own time, the expected and hoped-for divinely ordered triumph of the people of Israel is represented by another symbolic figure altogether—not a beast this time, but "one like a son of man":

> I gazed into the visions of the night,
> and I saw, coming on the clouds of heaven,
> one like a son of man. (Dan 7:13)

The beasts had arisen from earth: theirs was the power of earthly conquest. But the restoration of Israel that was hoped for in the desperate times of the Maccabean revolt could come only from heaven, only from the power of God intervening on behalf of his people in what they supposed to be their last-ditch stand against the pagan forces (see 1 Macc 18-19). Hence the symbolism of the vision of Daniel. Finally, God establishes the right and righteous rule, imaged as a human being in order to establish the ratio: the Dominion of Israel in the power and service of God is to the great empires of history as a human being is to a beast.

Israelite sovereignty would be restored. This new man-like figure approaches the divine throne and

> On him was conferred sovereignty,
> glory and dominion,
> and men of all peoples, nations, and languages
> became his servants.
> His sovereignty is an eternal sovereignty
> which shall never pass away,
> nor will his empire ever be destroyed. (Dan 7:14)

Such was the hope of the Maccabean revolt.

The meaning of the symbolism is clear enough to anyone familiar with the symbolizing techniques of the time. For those who are not, the Book of Daniel gives an explanation, probably a later addition, that makes things still clearer. "Those who are granted sovereignty are the saints of the Most High, and the dominion will be theirs for ever, for ever and ever" (7:18). Those who are truly faithful to God, resisting the impositions of Greek-inspired reforms, will take over the world.

The immediate relevance of Daniel's vision to our discussion is that it provides the missing link for explaining how Jesus came to use the title "Son of Man" for the exalted and glorious judge who concludes his gospel. The resemblances are obvious. Daniel's vision represents the new and final Dominion of Israel as "one like a son of man," who has glory conferred upon him, who is given kingship, who comes on the clouds of heaven "when the time came for the saints to take over the Dominion" (7:22), and who rules all nations as his servants (7:14). In the gospel of Jesus, at a secret and unspecifiable time appointed by God (Mt 24:44, 25:13; Lk 12:40), the Son of Man will come in glory (Mt 16:27, 24:30, 25:31; Mk 8:38, 13:26, 14:62; Lk 9:26, 21:27) and with power (Mt 24:30, Mk 13:26, Lk 21:27), in the clouds of heaven (Mt 24:30, 26:64, Mk 13:26, Lk 21:27), in his Dominion (Mt 16:28), as a king (Mt 25:34), and all the nations will be assembled before him to be subject to his judgment (Mt 25:32).

There are differences between Daniel's symbolic "one like a son of man" and Jesus' Son of Man. In Daniel's scheme, God himself sits on the throne of judgment and deals with the nations before glorified Israel is ushered in to take over (Dan 7:9-12); Jesus' Son of Man sits on the throne of judgment (Mt 19:28, 25:31) and settles affairs with the nations (Mt 25:31). Jesus' Son of Man will come with angels (Mt 16:27, Mk 8:38, Lk 9:26); angels are not expressly mentioned in the corresponding part of Daniel's vision, though they may be present among the "saints" (i.e., the holy ones, a term sometimes used for angels) of the Most High; but in any event, the angels of the gospel's Son of Man execute the judgment under his direction (Mt 13:41, 24:31; Mk 13:27), and Daniel says no such thing. Jesus' Son of Man is not simply derived from Daniel: in many respects, he more closely resembles the Coming One of John's gospel. But Daniel's vision has clearly made its mark on the gospel of Jesus.

This was probably inevitable. Daniel's vision was undoubtedly well known and much revered among the people who responded to John and Jesus. On the one hand, it was conveniently accessible: it is one of the very few parts of Scripture written not in Hebrew but in Aramaic, the general language of the people. But that is a minor consideration. The major one is that Daniel vies with Malachi as one of the two clearest promises of rescue and salvation in all the books that eventually stood as Holy Scripture.

Now: there were two major dispositions in Jewish piety, corresponding to two major tendencies in the books which came to be considered Scripture. One is founded on the conviction that there is nothing new under the sun—everything important has already been given and provided for, and the world will never change; the task of pious people is to accept what God has given and commanded, and to live faithfully within those limits: thus the main drift of wisdom literature. The other strain is founded upon the conviction that God will respond to the hunger of his people for something better—that he will intervene when the ripe moment comes, to punish the wicked, reestablish Israel's sovereignty, change people's hearts, restore to humanity the glory that he bestowed upon the newly-created Adam, kill or convert the Gentiles, raise the dead—whatever belonged to the unsatisfied dreams of those who worshipped him: thus one of the recurrent thematic strains of the prophetic literature.

These two modes are not mutually exclusive: they have a tendency to seep into each other. The prophetic borrows heavily from wisdom, and wisdom sometimes permits itself to dream about prophetic promises. Both have deep religious dignity, both have been carefully thought out, both have their cheap parodies and weaknesses and invitations to laziness. I do not presume now to adjudicate between them. The main point is this: John and Jesus preached gospels, good news. The essence of gospel is a promise of change, a promise that answers a hope for change and characteristically asks for belief that it will take place. Quite naturally, the people who responded eagerly to the gospels of John and of Jesus were especially the people who were of the prophetic tendency, though a call to personal change could readily be heard by those whose understanding had been formed in the image of wisdom. Quite naturally, the people who were of the wisdom tendency were likely to have been skeptical about these gospels, to the extent that they seemed to promise dramatic external change. Quite naturally, those who found their hopes authorized and confirmed and specified by a gospel were inclined to believe it. Quite naturally, they reacted impatiently to those who were skeptical. Quite naturally, the movements in which they became involved looked back with fond respect on those who, even though they had not received a gospel, were waiting for one: hence Luke's reverent attitude toward Simeon, whom he characterizes as "a righteous and pious man, waiting for the consolation of Israel" (Lk 2:25). Quite naturally, those who were waiting took special refuge in those Scriptures that assured them that they were right to be expectant, the Scriptures that offered them a gospel, however vague. Daniel's vision was inevitably among the most important parts of Scripture for the people who responded positively to what Jesus gospelled. And since Jesus was gospelling, and evidently revered the Scriptures, Daniel was appropriately one of the books that guided his expectation and his message.

There are two important corollaries to this description of the situation. One is that the expectant had their own expectations, and longed for them to be confirmed with authority. Luke's Simeon seems carefully discreet: he has confined his expectation to an ambiguous "Consolation of Israel" and is apparently ready to take whatever God means to offer along that line, hopeful that he will recognize it when it comes—if indeed he should be so fortunate as to have it come before he dies. That was probably an uncommon condition. Most of the expectant had formed a specific idea of what they had a right to expect. Many of them presumed that God must have in mind to vindicate Israel by making the Jews the masters of the world, and that was what they looked for in a gospel.

The dream of a restoration of Israelite sovereignty, whether or not raised to so high a power as Daniel's, was not only the hope of the Maccabean revolutionaries: it remained, even after the collapse of the regime they managed to establish and sustain, the persistent hope of the people of the land. The intermediate relevance of all this to the gospel of Jesus is that

Daniel's vision was written when a vigorous hope of Israelite sovereignty was reawakened, after centuries of discouragement. That hope was not forgotten when the successful Maccabean dynasty declined and fell. When the Romans took over, the old sentiments were once more reawakened, and many of those who hoped in Israel looked for a definitive restoration of power such as Daniel's vision encouraged. That inevitably meant that any powerful new presence in Israel would evoke hopes of Jewish sovereignty, either on the large scale envisioned by Daniel or in a more modest way. That, I think, is how we may best explain the term "Herodians" as it occurs in the Gospels: these are the people who were ready to settle for the fact that under Herod and his successors, the Jews had secured at least a modest version of sovereignty—at least they now had a king again.[17] Others remained more ambitious, more faithful to what Daniel seemed to promise. Their expectations were part of the problem that John and Jesus had to face, since many of the people of the land were impatient for a grand political salvation, and supposed that the one they were waiting for, whom they thought of as Messiah or as the One Who Comes in the Name of the Lord, would cast off foreign rule and reestablish sovereignty in Israel.

Given the already-eager expectations, both John and Jesus were inevitably conformed, in the minds of the hopeful, to what popular expectations required. Given enough desire, one can find what one is looking for. John first, and then Jesus, became rumored as the king who would bring Israel back into prominence, if not into world domination. Some who were of this mind undoubtedly came to realize that this was not the gospel of John or of Jesus. Probably many of them defected at that point, to wait for a gospel that told them the good news they wanted to hear. Others presumably were more normally careless, and simply heard from these gospels what they wanted to hear, then eagerly spread the word that the Messiah had come. Given enough interpretive room, they could claim that the Messiah was speaking in an elusive code that disguised the real message from all but the True Believers, who knew how to make interpretive allowances that would shape their understanding of either Jesus or John to their own previous expectations. Others heard what John and Jesus preached, heard it more or less accurately, and then decided to accept it, surrendering their earlier suppositions with some discomfort in order to conform themselves to this new and unexpected gospel, even without a Messiah or a political deliverance. Of such, says the gospeller, is the Dominion of God.

I will return to this point in the next chapter. At the moment, I must deal with the second corollary, which is that the imposition of a previous mold is not the only way in which gospels were deformed by their hearers. One could also reinterpret the gospeller in terms of the gospel. Some of the hearers of John's gospel may have guessed that he himself would be the Coming One; some of the hearers of the gospel of Jesus who realized that he was not proclaiming a Messiah evidently came to believe that he himself was or would be the Son of Man whom he preached.

JESUS AS SON OF MAN?

There is no warrant in the evidences preserved by the Synoptic gospels for identifying Jesus with his Danielic Son of Man. Whenever Jesus speaks of the glorious judge, he does so in the third person. Attempts of modern or ancient interpreters to get around this fact, and to make it appear that Jesus was speaking of himself, are simply carrying on the tradition of deformation. This is not what the texts say. To the everlasting credit of the early Christian communities, Jesus' sayings about the Son of Man who would come in glory are apparently preserved in something close to their original form in the Synoptic Gospels, which nobly resisted the temptation to make them self-references—a temptation to which the Fourth Gospel succumbed. What Jesus said was allowed to stand without much interference in the Synoptics, however mystifying it must have seemed to those who had come to believe that Jesus and the Son of Man were identical.

The temptation was not totally resisted even by the Synoptic tradition. As I remarked earlier, there is one striking pattern within the Synoptic uses of the title "Son of Man" in which Jesus is clearly referring to himself. With one or two trivial exceptions, all of the clearly self-referential uses of the term fall into an outline of the gospel of the Apostles—i.e., the preaching of the early Church, which I will treat in the next chapter. The Son of Man will be betrayed (Mt 17:22, Mk 9:31, Lk 9:44) by a wretched man and according to the Scriptures (Mt 26:24, Mk 14:21, Lk 22:22), with a kiss (Lk 22:48), delivered into the hands of the chief priests (or of men, or of Gentiles, or of sinners—Mt 16:21, 17:22, 20:18, 26:45; Mk 8:31, 9:31, 10:33, 14:41; Lk 9:22, 9:44, 18:32), must suffer (Mk 9:13, etc.), as it is written (Mk 9:12, 14:21, Lk 18:31, 22:22), at their hands (Mt 17:12, etc.), and be delivered to death (Mt 17:23, etc.) by crucifixion (Mt 20:18, 26:2), will be three days in the earth (Mt 12:40, Mk 8:31: cf. Lk 9:22, 18:33), and will be raised from the dead (Mt 17:22, Mk 8:31, 9:31, 10:34, Lk 9:22, 22:22). It is very neat: too neat. It is simply unthinkable that Jesus ever made such precise predictions, since it would then be impossible to account for the firmly attested total demoralization of his closest followers as he went through his arrest, passion, and death, and the equally well attested incredulity with which they received the first news of his resurrection. Besides, the gospels candidly admit that when he made these clear predictions, his disciples simply did not understand what he was saying. This pattern arises from a natural impulse to say, retrospectively, that everything was in fact in order, even during the darkest and most confusing days, that nothing had really got out of hand; it was all part of the plan, and Jesus had done his best, however unsuccessfully, to make this clear in advance, just as one would expect him to do. The fault lay only with the disciples, for not understanding until later what he had tried to tell them.

I have in a previous book[18] offered an explanation of how these fancied predictions came to be projected into the teaching of Jesus (not his gospel, for they are represented as private communications to the disciples, not part of his public proclamation). Eager to satisfy the natural impulse to find such reassuring forewarnings in what Jesus had told them, the post-resurrection disciples found ways of interpreting earlier sayings of Jesus so as to see in them coded messages of this sort, and then represented them as being offered without the code. The most obvious and blatant example of the process occurs in Mt 12:38-42, where Jesus refuses to work any sign to convince the people except the sign of Jonah, i.e., an authoritative call to repentance. Luke's version of the same story (Lk 11:29-32) realizes that this is all there is to it—and so does Matthew's other version in 16:1-4. But in Matthew's account in Chapter 12, he inserts a clever interpretation that totally reverses the thrust of the passage and makes the denial of a sign a prediction of Jesus' death and temporary entombment: "as Jonah was in the belly of the fish three days and three nights, so the Son of Man will be three days and three nights in the heart of the earth" (12.40). Here we get a lucky glimpse of the process of perceiving an originally intelligible saying as if it were a mysterious code, breaking the code on the basis of later happenings, and then reporting the results overtly. I think it very likely that the Gospels contain the residue of other instances, in which the original statement itself has dropped away, leaving only the decoding interpreter's results, put plainly into the mouth of Jesus.

What is especially curious and interesting about all this is that this pattern of predictions somehow emerged with a consistent attachment to Jesus' use of the title "Son of Man" as a self-reference—even the emerging instance of the Jonah interpretation shows this odd mannerism. The use of "Son of Man" as clear self-reference appears consistently in this pattern of references to Jesus' passion and death, and only in this pattern. How are we to account for this?

SON OF MAN AS DOMINION OF GOD

I would like to offer a tentative hypothesis, which I think makes more overall sense than any alternative I know. It begins with the proposition that Jesus read Daniel more accurately than most of his contemporaries and nearly all of his successors did. I propose that Jesus' Son of Man is, in the last analysis, the collective body of the righteous. That is what Daniel's symbolic figure stands for, and that, I propose, is what Jesus meant. True, he spoke of the Son of Man in the third person singular, as if he were an individual. So did Daniel, shifting indifferently between his symbol and the group it symbolized:

> And sovereignty and dominion,
> and the splendors of all the kingdoms under heaven
> will be given to the people of the saints of the Most High.
> His sovereignty is an eternal sovereignty
> and every empire will serve and obey him. (Dan 7:27)

The switch from "the people" to "his" and "him" is neither a grammatical blunder nor a textual error. It is the flexibility of the mode of presentation: when we are within the symbolic structure, the singular is appropriate, and when we are on the more literal level, the plural is required. The two are, properly understood, exactly equivalent. The author of Daniel, expecting us to understand that, is free to shift as he pleases.

I suggest that when Jesus referred to the Son of Man as a singular, this was neither more nor less than what Daniel had done with the figure whom Jesus borrowed from his vision. On the level of the symbol, already canonized as such by Daniel, the singular is appropriate. It stands for a collective.[19]

Gospel exegetes have occasionally remarked that Jesus never speaks of the Son of Man and the Dominion of God in the same breath.[20] The general conclusion has been that these must come from two different traditions. The simpler solution is that they come from two different levels of the discourse of Jesus. They are absolutely identical. The Son of Man is the symbolic way of referring to what on a more literal level must be called the Dominion of God—i.e., the collective body of the righteous who, in the power of God, will enjoy the ultimate glory.

The references to the glorious Son of Man in the gospel of Jesus do not obviously impose this idea of a collective. They seem to be pointing to an individual. They were probably, in fact, understood by many of his hearers as a reference to an individual. Many of them, after all, knew and cherished the gospel of Malachi and the gospel of John, and might readily misunderstand Jesus' faithful use of Daniel's symbolism as if it were a variant on Malachi/John. Many of them probably already misread Daniel himself in that way, as the majority continue to do in our own time. The writers of the Gospels probably thought that the Son of Man was a single glorified person, and probably thought that it was Jesus himself. It is to their credit that they apparently did not impose the latter belief on their representations of Jesus' preaching. It is also to their credit that they report the sayings about the glorious Son of Man in such a way as to leave them all as clearly susceptible of a symbolic-collective meaning as is the Danielic original.

If the Son of Man and the Dominion of God are in fact identical, alternative ways of referring to the same reality, then it should be illuminating to watch what happens when we apply the gospel of the Dominion of God as a way of interpreting the gospel of the Son of Man. "The Dominion of God is at hand" translates "the Son of Man is going to come soon." The Synoptic description of the tribulation to come ends "and then they will see the Son of Man in a cloud, with power and great glory" (Mt 24:30, Mk 13:26, Lk 21:27). Luke adds "When these things, then, are beginning to occur, raise yourselves up and lift up your heads, because your deliverance is drawing near" (Lk 21:28). Two verses later, he says the same thing in the other mode: "When you see these things occurring, know that the Dominion of God is near" (Lk 21:31—Mt 24:33 and Mk 13:29 say ambiguously either "he is near" or "it is near"). All three Synoptic Gospels report a remark by Jesus about the Son of Man coming in glory with angels, and all three follow it with Jesus' assurance that there are some standing there who will not taste death until the great moment arrives (Mt 16:27-28, Mk 8:38-9:1, Lk 9:26-27). But there are differences among the three gospels in their characterization of the great moment. Luke says that they won't taste death until they see the Dominion of God; Mark says that it won't be until they see the Dominion of God come in power; and Matthew says that it won't be until they see the Son of Man coming in his Dominion. There is no disagreement here, and no invasion of substantially alternative traditions. All three are saying the same thing, and all three are recording the gospel of Jesus: Matthew has remained in the symbolic discourse of the Son of Man, while Mark and Luke have shifted to its equivalent alternative, the language of the Dominion of God. It is not improbable that Jesus too had so shifted from time to time, as Daniel had done before him: it was not important which language was used at a given moment, since the meaning was the same. The glorified Son of Man is the Son of Man in his Dominion is the Dominion of God is the Dominion of God in power.

And so it runs throughout the Synoptic tradition's use of these terms. If the wicked and unrepentant must tremble at the advent of the Dominion of God, so must they at the coming of the Son of Man. If the Son of Man sits upon the throne of Judgment (Mt 19:28), Jesus' followers will do so too (Mt 19:28, Lk 22:30): there is no inconsistency in Jesus' saying both that judgment belongs to the Son of Man and that they will be judges. And if the Dominion of God, while coming in full power and glory only in the future, has already in some ways begun, so too the glorious and powerful future advent of the Son of Man—or, in Luke's more telling expression, the time when "the day of the Son of Man is *revealed*" (Lk 17:30—the emphasis is of course my own)—has already started to arrive, to be revealed. And therein, I suggest, is the solution to the problem of Jesus' references to himself as the suffering Son of Man.

THE SON OF MAN'S SUFFERING

The Dominion of God had already started in a modest way—a mustard seed that would eventually grow into a glorious tree. There were already sons of the Dominion. They had not yet entered it, in the full sense, but they already belonged to it. They did not have an easy time with their compatriots: they were condemned, disdained, mocked, resisted with unbelief, and probably from time to time, physically abused. Jesus had been rejected in his home territory of Galilee, criticized by hostile skeptics, denounced by outraged conservatives, and threatened with violence. We are not told that he was scourged in the synagogues, but his reported warning that his followers would be thus treated (Mt 10:17, 24:9; Mk 13:9; Lk 21:12), may have been rooted in direct personal experience. Even though the movement touched off by the gospel was the true way of the Lord, it did not thrive in this world. There is a difficult saying in Matthew, repeated in a modified form by Luke, in which Jesus bears witness to John the Baptist as the initiator of the dawning day of the Dominion of God: "From the days of John the Baptist until now, the Dominion of the heavens is being broken into, and men of violence have maltreated it" (Mt 11:12). This is immediately followed by the verse that reads "For all the prophets and the law prophesied until John—and, if you can receive it, he is the Elijah who is to come." The latter verse is important for context: Matthew's Jesus seems to be suggesting not only that John has initiated a new era, but that he fulfills what the Law and the Prophets were talking about. The previous verse clearly implies that the Dominion of God has somehow been accessible since the time of John's gospel. Luke's Jesus confirms this reading, saying that revelation was "the Law and the Prophets, up to John: from then the Dominion of God is preached, and everyone is breaking into it" (Lk 16:16).

I have translated these controversial verses in a slightly unconventional way, though one which the Greek originals will allow, in order to release what I believe to be their basic meaning. They clearly agree that a great change came about with John, that somehow the Dominion of God started to become available. In the context of the verse that follows it, Mt 11:12 can fairly be supposed to say something about taking advantage of the availability. Luke is more ambiguous, but the flow of his verse invites the same assumption. The main interpretive question is what is meant by the verb *biazetai,* which I have deliberately (and with grammatical warrant) rendered in two slightly different ways in the two texts, "is being broken into" in Mt and "is breaking [into]" in Lk. Its root is the same as the word *biastai,* which I have translated, uncontroversially, as "men of violence," though perhaps "ruffians" might be more exact. I believe that Matthew's verse makes most sense if understood as I have translated it—that is, once John opened the door, all sorts of people have been shoving their way in (i.e., taking advantage of the invitation by an abrupt and surprising repentance and reformation)—and then, punning on the rough verb he has just used in a positive sense, Matthew gives the verse a new and more sobering turn: ruffians have harassed and abused it. The movement is successfully under way, and people are aggressively getting on the bandwagon; but other aggressors are doing violence to it. The other aggressors, the men of violence, the ruffians, are the opponents of the movement—those who abuse the Dominion itself by speaking against it, and abuse its first members with punishments and beatings.

How extensive the problem was, we cannot know. But one stark instance was, and remains, especially clear: John the initiator was himself imprisoned and executed. It is hardly likely that his zealous followers escaped punishment altogether. Jesus saw what was happening, and drew the appropriate conclusion. One might suppose that God would arrange that the great good news would be given an easy path, but that was apparently not the way he had organized things. On the contrary, the true gospel had met with great resistance and with startling violence. That is, then, presumably the way it must be, the way God wills—and undoubtedly the way revelation is written; for if the Law and the Prophets were leading up to John, then a careful search of the Scriptures should disclose that it was ordained and prophesied to be like this, and that therefore everything is still in order, in some mysterious way known only to the divine purposes. Hence the death of John is in conformity with the Scriptures: "Elijah has come, and they did to him whatever they wished, just as the Scriptures say about him" (Mk 9:13; cf. Mt 17:12). The Dominion of God, through those who preach it and begin to populate it, must undergo abuse. Or if we translate the same statement into Jesus' other idiom, we get precisely the formula with which Matthew concludes the reference to the scandalous treatment of John: "Thus the Son of Man must suffer at their hands" (Mt 17:12; cf. Lk 6:22: "Blessed are you when men hate you, and when they excommunicate you, and revile and cast out your name as evil for the sake of the Son of Man"). The movement must receive abuse and punishment. People will do violence to the Dominion of God. The Son of Man must suffer. All these statements mean exactly the same thing. Jesus saw what was happening, and trusted implicitly in God. If things are so, then it is because they must be so. The Son of Man must now suffer. It is only after the time of suffering that he can enter into his glory and become ready to be the one who comes in the name of the Lord to execute the great harvest of judgment.

From this point on, the gospel of Jesus again merges with the gospel of John the Baptist, echoing most of the main motifs and drawing to approximately the same conclusion. But it is perhaps worth noting in passing that it is at least possible that, from Jesus' point of view, there had never been a significant divergence between these two gospels. I think that John had taken his cue from Malachi, and that his gospel accordingly proclaimed an individual quasi-angelic judge to come. I think that Jesus took his cue from Daniel, and accordingly gospelled a righteous collective that would be revealed and glorified and set up in judgment. But the resulting symbolic figure in the Daniel/Jesus gospel looks very much like the more literal figure in the Malachi/John gospel, and it is not unthinkable that what Jesus understood John to mean by his elusive and unnamed Coming One was precisely what had been presented in Daniel's vision—a collective of the glorified righteous, presented in the guise of a glorious and powerful quasi-angelic individual. In short, Jesus may have thought that his gospel's Son of Man was identical to John's Coming One. If so, he would have thought his message to be in virtually complete accord with the gospel of John the Baptist.

But in some respects, Jesus went farther than John. There is, for instance, no reason to think that John preached the necessity of suffering. That was apparently not something that Jesus had learned from John's gospel, except in the larger sense: it was John's gospel that brought about John's suffering and death. This was obviously an enormously important factor in Jesus' grasp of the scheme of things. It seems to have been what launched his own gospelling mission, and what introduced into it the note of greatest divergence from John. If it was from the main outlines of John's gospel that Jesus acquired the main outlines of his own, it was apparently from John's fate that Jesus became most thoroughly convinced that those who belong to the Son of Man, whatever their future glory, are ordained to suffer.

It is not credible that Jesus made clear and specific predictions of his own betrayal, passion, crucifixion, and resurrection. It is fully credible that he warned his disciples that the Son of Man must suffer. He turned out to be far more right than they had ever dreamed, and when the shock of his ignominious death had worn off, giving way to the wonderment of his resurrection, the disciples could remember and understand in a new way what he had meant by his warning. Jesus had to suffer. They too would probably have to suffer. He had predicted this. Suffering is one of the essential features of the Son of Man during the first phase, before he comes in glory. Gradually, as they combed their memories of his parables and other teachings, they found ways to suppose that Jesus had foretold his career of suffering in precise detail—hidden in the parabolic saying about Jonah, and undoubtedly in other parables, teachings, and casual remarks that would yield the other predictions if squeezed by the "right" interpretive method. The predictions now seemed quite clear. Why had the disciples not understood at the time? Because they were too dim, too dull-witted to grasp them. Gradually, as the remembrance of the specific interpretive maneuvers fell away from the tradition, only the results were left: clear and open statements placed on Jesus' lips. Each of them bears a fossil relic of its ultimate origin. Jesus is represented as calling himself "the Son of Man"—a distorted and faint but nevertheless appropriate recollection that virtually all, and perhaps absolutely all, the predictions were ultimately derived from the one main remembered truth: Jesus had told them that violence will be done to the Dominion of God—that the Son of Man must suffer.

The passion predictions are represented as private communications to the closest disciples. The reason for this could be that his teaching about the suffering of the Son of Man had in fact been given in private, as a hard truth that only the closest and most faithful followers were ready to hear—if indeed even they were ready. I do not think this is a likely explanation. The parable of Jonah is said to have been uttered openly; the prediction it was subsequently thought to contain was theoretically public property, and the direct statement that eventually made its way into Matthew 12:40 is portrayed as a public pronouncement. It seems to me much more likely that the Gospels' representations of Jesus' exclusiveness in the passion predictions derived rather from the exclusiveness of their retrospective discovery: only the faithful inner circle found out what they took to be the hidden meanings in Jesus' preaching, and this historical fact made its way into the story in the form of clear but private disclosures to the few, which even the few did not understand at the time.

But the real, historically true, predictions of the passion were apparently not secretly given. Jesus is represented as saying to the people in general, not to the inner circle alone, that the Dominion of God suffers violence. The parallel statement about the Son of Man was probably given just as openly. It was not a secret. It was plainly uttered, and plainly audible. It was not withheld for the few but revealed as a helpful, if grim, forewarning to all who cared to belong to the Dominion of God and had ears to hear. But it seems not to have been merely a warning, much less a lament. The suffering of the Son of Man was a part of Jesus' gospel as the ordained prelude to the Son of Man's promised glory.

THE FADING OF "SON OF MAN" FROM THE GOSPEL

"The Son of Man" is a title tightly associated with Jesus in the New Testament insofar as he is, with one exception (Acts 7:56), the only one ever to use it. It appears nearly seventy times in the Synoptic Gospels and a dozen times in the Fourth Gospel—but outside the Gospels it is used only in the one exceptional instance in Acts. The alternative term, the Dominion of God, is used frequently by various voices in other New Testament books, from John the Baptist to the Book of

Revelation. But "the Son of Man" is left as Jesus' term almost exclusively.

I suggest two possible explanations for this curious phenomenon—both of which may be true, for they are mutually supportive rather than alternatives. The first is that the title "Son of Man" became more difficult to understand once the gospel of the Son of Man (alias the gospel of the Dominion of God) reached beyond Palestine—and most of the books of the New Testament arise from the Christianization of other territories. The term "Dominion of God" shows up in other Jewish literature, from the Psalms of Solomon to later rabbinic writings. It is given varied meanings, but the variations are all on a basic theme; there is good reason to believe that it was an intelligible and at least modestly useful way of communicating even to the Jews of the Greek-speaking Diaspora what this new gospel was about. But the same is not true of the term "the Son of Man." It is not attested in rabbinic literature, and there is no known example that clearly antedates Jesus himself. Daniel's near-equivalent, "one like a son of man," would of course pave the way for understanding it where Daniel was well known. But the strong market for Daniel's vision was in Palestine, where an urgent movement for liberation from the Romans was afoot, and where some hope for deliverance was extensively cultivated, and where the influence of John the Baptist had raised a new fervor of expectation. The apocalyptic interests of the compilers of the library found at Qumran, indicated by the various apocalyptic writings found in the excavations there, was primarily a Palestinian phenomenon. Outside the Palestinian territories there are few evidences of great interest in apocalyptic literature or in apocalyptic ideas. A title that was allusive to Daniel's vision may not have been readily intelligible to Diaspora Jews, let alone Gentiles, who would probably find the basic Semitic construction of the phrase rather odd, and all further steps to its understanding still more difficult.

The second explanation of why "Son of Man" is Jesus' term almost exclusively is suggested by the pattern of sayings in which Jesus is represented as using the phrase to mean "I"—always in conjunction with his passion. I suggest that those who heard the gospel of the suffering of the Son of Man tended to understand the term to mean "the Dominion of God under the aspect of its preliminary suffering" and eventually, once it was so particularly aligned with the suffering of Jesus himself, took it to mean "Jesus as sufferer," a role that evidently ended when the resurrection ushered him out of that dark phase, across the threshold of glory. If this special usage had in fact developed—and the evidences suggest it had—then once the resurrection had taken place, Jesus had in effect ceased to be the Son of Man. The title was no longer applicable. To the extent that it was useful at all, it was merely to celebrate by contrast the triumph of his glorification over his earlier career as suffering Son of Man. The formulation to which this naturally gave rise is echoed at the beginning of Paul's Epistle to the Romans, where he emphatically affirms the two stages of Jesus' operation. Jesus had "become the seed of David according to the flesh" (i.e., was a Davidic descendent insofar as he was a "son of man" in the elementary sense of "mere human being"), and then, through the resurrection from the dead, his fleshly phase had given way to the phase of glory. Almost inevitably, the title applied to this latter stage is "Son of God" (Rom 1:3-4).

OTHER ELEMENTS IN JESUS' GOSPEL

SON OF GOD

"Son of God" is a title that was applied to Jesus in the next stage of gospelling after Jesus. But at the moment, the issue is what Jesus himself preached. Was the title "Son of God" a part of his gospel?

Before answering, it is necessary to make some cautionary distinctions. This phrase, like its parallel, "Son of Man," carries a variety of values. The basic meaning is "someone who has a special relation to God."[21] This basic sense took several specific forms in the Hebrew Scriptures. One early and persistent use of the phrase was a designation of angels, who have the privilege of God's more immediate presence or Lordship, and are called sons of God in something of the same spirit in which high officials in ancient Near Eastern courts were called sons of the king (e.g., Gen 6:1-4, which contrasts the "sons of God" with the "daughters of men"—cf. Ps 89:5-6, where the "sons of God" are members of the heavenly court of God, or Job 1:6 and 2:1, where they are God's attendants).

Another recurrent use is to designate Israel. As the specially chosen of God, under his protection and love, Israel itself is the Son of God. In Exodus (4:22-23), God orders Moses to tell Pharaoh, "This is what Yahweh says: Israel is my first born son. I ordered you to let my son go to offer me worship." Hosea has God say, "When Israel was a child, I loved him, and I called my son out of Egypt" (Hos 11:1).

If Israel is collectively the Son of God, the leader of Israel may be so styled in a preeminent sense. God tells Nathan that Solomon is the one chosen by God to inherit the throne: "I will be a father to him, and he as son to me" (2 Sam 7:14; cf. 1 Chron 28:6). Psalm 2 uses two statements in apposition: God says "This is my king, installed by me on Zion, my holy mountain. . . . You are my son, today I have become your Father" (Ps 2:6-7).

While the monarchy remained, the king could be called Son of God. After it had disappeared, there was a natural inclination to use the title in conjunction with the hoped-for restorer of the throne, the Davidic Messiah to come. But the inclination seems to have been largely resisted. While some Gospel texts (e.g., the high priest's question in Mt 26:63—cf.

Mk 14:61, Lk 22:67,70—and Peter's confession in Mt 16:16) treat the title "Son of God" as if it were readily understood as equivalent to "Messiah" ("Christ"), surviving Jewish literature rarely makes the equation. If indeed it was current at the time of Jesus, it seems to have fallen into disuse subsequently, perhaps in reaction to the Christian usage.[22]

When applied to an individual, the term "Son of God" was sometimes used to designate a righteous man (Sirach 4:10, Wisdom 2:18). But the root notion remains: it is one who is especially dear to God.

New Testament texts sometimes apply the title to Jesus with a much more ambitious meaning than this. But the gospel of Jesus does not use it for himself, and Jesus is cagy about its application to him by others. The title "Son of God" is offered by others as a question or an affirmation, but it is not a title claimed by Jesus in the Synoptic Gospels. The main tradition has him answer ambiguously the high priest's proposal of this title in the Sanhedrin trial (Mt 26:63-64, Lk 22:70, and some, though not most, ancient manuscripts of Mk 14:61-62). The same is true of the temptation by Satan in the wilderness (Mt 4:3,6; Lk 4:3,9), in which Jesus evades the title with equal success. Demons who are about to be exorcised occasionally use the title (Mt 8:29; Mk 3:11, 5:7; Lk 4:41, 8:28), but Jesus no more shows his hand with them than with Satan or the high priest. The accounts of Jesus' baptism (Mt 3:17, Mk 1:11, Lk 3:22) admit a voice from heaven identifying Jesus as the speaker's beloved son, and so do the accounts of the Transfiguration (Mt 17:5, Mk 9:7, Lk 9:35), but the testimony of a voice from heaven no more belongs to the gospel actually proclaimed by Jesus than does the angelic testimony at Luke's annunciation that he will be called Son of God by others (Lk 1:32) or that he is technically entitled to it (Lk 1:35). Similarly, the testimony of the centurion (Mk 15:39—he and others in Mt 27:54) that Jesus must be the Son of God is not Jesus' proclamation but another's confession. Mark's introductory verse uses the title, and in conjunction with the title Christ (i.e., Messiah), but does not claim that Jesus proclaimed or accepted either of them (Mk 1:1). Matthew reports that after the stilling of the storm, the passengers of the threatened ship paid homage to Jesus as the Son of God (Mt 14:33), but there is no reply from Jesus.

Mt 16:16, where Peter declares that he believes Jesus to be "the Messiah, the Son of the Living God," seems at first to be more promising. Jesus does not quite say that Peter is right, but he does commend him for having had this revealed to him not by any ordinary human judgment ("flesh and blood did not reveal to you," 16:17) but by "my Father in heaven" (16:17). Nevertheless, this is not good historical evidence. Strategically, this verse is exactly parallel with the two verses—also unique to Matthew—in which John the Baptist demurs at Jesus' approach and is reassured (Mt 3:14-15). Both are statements designed to protect an early Christian sense of what was hiddenly so in the earliest days, both are slightly elusive in that they do not make Jesus say a clear yes, while giving the impression that *yes* is what it all amounts to, and both offer incidents of sufficient importance that it is flatly incredible that the other Gospels would not have found and used them if they had historically taken place. The parallel accounts in Mk 8:29 and Lk 9:20 acknowledge that Peter took Jesus to be the Messiah, but they do not record that Jesus commended him for doing so, nor do they use "Son of God" as an alternative title. Jesus' approval of Peter's insight in Mt 16:17, like the brief dialogue between Jesus and John the Baptist, must be discounted in any attempt to reconstruct what really happened. A similar verdict must fall on Jesus' reply at his trial before the Sanhedrin, even though most texts of Mark have Jesus affirm the high priest's use of "Son of God." The main tradition has him answer ambiguously, "This is what you are saying." The question, in the Greek text, has the same form as a positive statement, except for the inflection in the original voice and the question mark in the written text: "You are the Son of God?" Jesus' reply is therefore hopelessly evasive. It does not affirm, it does not deny; it allows the possibility of either acceptance or rejection of the title, and it winds up saying nothing that could either be adequate legal grounds for his indictment as a pretender to a throne or a clear denial that he thought himself entitled to such a claim.

That in turn leaves two classes of sayings in which the term "Son of God" is used in conjunction with, or by, Jesus. One is the mockery of Jesus at the time of his crucifixion, in which Matthew's account has anonymous passersby jeer "If you are the Son of God, then come down from the cross" (Mt 27:40). Plausibly, this is simply a reference to the placard which Matthew has just said was written over his head as an accusation, "THIS IS JESUS, THE KING OF THE JEWS" (Mt 27:37). That is, here "Son of God" seems to be precisely equal to "the King of the Jews" and is therefore evidently Messianic in meaning. The same is apparently true of the taunt which Matthew says came from the scribes and chief priests and elders (Mt 27:41-43), for so Mark and Luke understand and report the scoffings of passersby, scribes, rulers, soldiers, and fellow-victims, all of whom tease the crucified Jesus as "Messiah," "King of Israel" or "King of the Jews" (Mk 15:29-32, Lk 23:35-39). There must, however, be one qualifying remark: Matthew's scribes and chief priests and elders are not simply relying on the sign above his head or the general gossip: they claim that "he said, 'I am son of God'" (Mt 27:43).

Technically, they were undoubtedly right. He had claimed to be son of God. It is interesting that they do not accuse him of having claimed to be *the* Son of God, and it is tragic that they thought the claim to be *a* son of God foolish or outrageous or unintelligible or whatever else lay at the heart of their objection. But if the claim to be son of God was offensive to them, then they picked the right victim: for the indications are that the gospel of Jesus not only enlisted himself under that title but tried zealously to enlist others.

"Blessed are the peacemakers," says the Jesus of Matthew's Sermon on the Mount, "for they shall be called sons of God"

(Mt 5:9). And then he passes to the next beatitude, as if it is no less dramatic. And indeed, it is not any less dramatic. It reads "Blessed are those who are persecuted for the sake of righteousness, for theirs is the Dominion of the Heavens" (Mt 5:10). The two conclusions are essentially identical. To belong to the Dominion of God—to be a part of the glorified Son of Man—is the same as being a son of God. This is abundantly clear in the text shared (more or less) by Mt 5:45 and Lk 6:35: love your enemies (and do other analogous things, on which Mt and Lk differ unimportantly) in order that you may (thus Mt: Lk has simply "and you will") become sons of God.

We are all invited to become sons of God. That is what it means to belong to the Dominion of God, to become a part of the Son of Man, to become genuinely righteous. Of course, in the full sense one is a son of God only when all is fulfilled, just as the Dominion of God does not come about *in power* until then, and just as the Son of Man is not revealed in his glory until then. But in the meantime it is underway. We are already practising. We are urged to think of God as our Father, and to pray to him as our Father. Jesus even instructs his followers to use a more tender and familiar term, *Abba* (which had approximately the intimacy of *papa* in French, not—as has sometimes been suggested—the cozy casualness of "daddy," which had not been culturally invented yet).[23] Those who so address God are quite obviously at least in the process of training to be children of God in the sense promised by the Sermon on the Mount—and most likely Jesus encouraged them to start now to think of themselves as sons (and daughters, though a sexually unbiased term is, for readily comprehensible cultural reasons, only occasionally represented in the Gospels) of God, just as his gospel seems to have proclaimed that the Dominion of God has already started to emerge and that the Son of Man has already begun to be subjected to oppressors and scoffers and men of violence. The title "Son of God" was indeed a part of the gospel of Jesus: it applied to everyone who would faithfully accept it and live accordingly.

Its primary meaning lies in the future: as Luke's Jesus says, those who are sons of the resurrection are therefore sons of God (Lk 20:36). But one may start any time one is ready to start. Jesus had started.

THE RESURRECTION

The sons of the resurrection are fully sons of God. I have said almost nothing in this chapter about Jesus' proclamation either of his own resurrection or of others'. This is for good reasons. The main good reason is that Jesus is not reported to have said much about either subject, and what he is reported to have said about the former is, as I have previously argued, unreliable testimony. Not "unfortunately unreliable," since the question of the occurrence of his own resurrection depends in no way whatsoever on whether he predicted it or even whether he knew secretly that it would take place in a unique and dramatic fashion. I have no difficulty in supposing that he might have, in a more general way, spoken to his disciples about his own eventual resurrection, because it seems clear that he shared the widespread—not universal, but certainly widespread—Jewish belief that the righteous who have died will eventually be raised to the life of a new age.

Resurrection is not a traditional Jewish belief, if one takes the usual perspective of modern scholarship and thinks of "traditional" as meaning "as far back as one can trace." But if one places oneself in the setting to which the gospel of Jesus was addressed, a belief in resurrection was traditional: a little less traditional than the holiday feast of Thanksgiving is in the United States of America at this moment, but much more traditional than Santa Claus, or the notion of a United States of America—let alone one that stretches from sea to shining sea. That is, it was traditional enough to have been taken for granted as a firmly established reality by many of those to whom Jesus preached. The Pharisees, who were the identifiable "denomination" most admired by the people, believed with some passion in the resurrection, against the scoffing opinions of the Sadducees (who seem to have had little impact on Christian origins, and disappeared from even Jewish religious history within a couple of generations). A resurrection of the righteous was clearly presumed by the author of 2 Maccabees, writing some two centuries before Jesus proclaimed his own gospel (2 Macc 6:9-23), and it is also clearly present in the later visions of Daniel (Chapters 10-12), which are still earlier. By the time Jesus preached his gospel, he was preaching to a people who on the whole presumed that the righteous would be raised when the end came. It was not necessary for him to convince them.

The extant Gospels are undoubtedly right in giving the impression that Jesus did not much attend to this question, because it was not really a question unless raised by wily Sadducees, who want to trap Jesus into a puzzle that will force him to confess that a belief in the resurrection entails embarrassing problems (Mt 22:23-33, Mk 12:18-27, Lk 20:27-40). His response to the attempted trap shows at least a determination not to be caught in it. He apparently believed in the resurrection of the righteous.

As one who was pursuing righteousness with heroic determination, he undoubtedly was confident that he would be raised in the last days, to be a part of the Dominion of God, a member of the Son of Man. When he faced the prospect of his death on its very eve, he is reported to have announced that this was the last time he would share in such a meal until everything is fulfilled in the Dominion of God (Lk 22:16,18, Mt 26:29, Mk 14:25). At this point, the indications were obviously ominous, and there is good reason to suppose that he expected eventually to be resurrected if the killing did in fact take place. He did not presume to say when his resurrection would come about; that was not part of his gospel. Even the general resurrection of which it would be a part was only incidentally mentioned by him here and there: presently unrepayable virtuous deeds will be rewarded in the resurrection of the righteous (Lk 14:14), and the Queen of the South will be raised up in the Judgment (Mt 12:42, Lk 11:31) to condemn the unrepentant Jews of Jesus' own day. The resurrection of the righteous was evidently not much proclaimed in the gospel of Jesus—it was taken for granted.

THE NEW TEMPLE

The reports of Jesus' trial, in the accounts of Matthew and Mark, contain an interesting piece of byplay (Mt 26:59-61, Mk 14:55-59). Both of them report that false witnesses came forward with the claim that Jesus had said that he could (thus Mt) or would (thus Mk) "destroy the Temple of God and in three days build it" (thus Mt—Mk says "destroy this temple made with hands, and in three days will build another made without hands"). But they are not persuasive, and the trial turns to another issue.

Since the false witnesses were unsuccessful, it is curious that these accounts bother to mention only this one enigmatic charge without trying to explain what it meant, or why anyone would think it a grave misconduct for Jesus to have said anything so odd anyway. It grows more curious when we glance at the Fourth Gospel, where the Jews who ask for a sign during Jesus' first public doings in Jerusalem are offended to hear Jesus' answer: "Destroy this temple, and in three days I will raise it" (Jn 2:19). Thus Matthew, Mark, and John agree that Jesus had in fact been reported as having said something offensive about the Temple. Was the report true, or false? And what was at stake?

On the balance of evidence, I should think that the answer has to be: the report was true. Let me give two kinds of indication. One is what he notoriously did in the Temple upon his arrival, remembered as one of his very first acts in Jerusalem and reported in all four Gospels. The other is a set of sayings that when added together seem to indicate that the charge against him was substantially true. What was at stake will become clearer in my next chapter; in Jesus' time, it had to do with his radical gospel of true worship.

First, the incident generally known as "the cleansing of the Temple" (Mt 21:12-13, Mk 11:15-17, Lk 19:45-46, Jn 2:14-16). That is a rather euphemistic expression, given the way the incident has been usually understood, but it takes on, ironically, a greater appropriateness if we read more exactingly. Cleansing from what? All four accounts are agreed that he disrupted all the commercial interests being pursued in the outer precincts of the Temple, turning over tables and tossing out the buyers and sellers (though Luke, whose reverence for the Temple may account for his omission of the saying about destruction and rebuilding, typically soft-pedals the more violent details, and just speaks of the expulsion of the vendors). The three Synoptics then quote Isaiah 56:7, suggesting that the essential meaning of the episode has to do with the contrast between a house of prayer and a den of thieves (the Fourth Gospel supplies in its place the rather more limp and unspecific—but equally pro-Temple—citation from Psalm 69:9: "My zeal for your house consumes me"). Apparent conclusion: the incident was directed at purging the holy house of vulgar commerce.

Of course, when most readers remember the cleansing of the Temple, they also remember how extreme Jesus' reaction was, and it is not so much the overturning of dove-sellers' chairs that comes to mind as a whip of cords. This occurs in the Fourth Gospel only, not in the Synoptics. And what did Jesus want a whip of cords for? The answer seems obvious: to drive the merchants out of the Temple. El Greco tells us so—but not the Bible. Admittedly, Jn 2:15 is often translated that way, but that is because of a false picture that lingers in our minds. It is not what the text says. The verse before mentions his finding the money-changers and the sellers of various beasts, and then verse 15 runs like this: "And having made a whip out of rushes, he drove them all out of the Temple—both the sheep and the oxen—and he poured out the coins of the money-changers, and overturned the tables." What he drove out of the Temple with a whip of cords was not people but animals—the people are referred to after this action, not as an integral part of it. And then, in verse 16, he says to the dove-sellers, "Take these things away: don't turn my Father's house into a house of merchandise." Take what things away? Most likely, the doves: the other sacrificial creatures had already been driven out with the whip; now the doves should follow, and those engaged in trafficking over sacrificial animals should clear out. The cleansing of the Temple was only in a secondary way a cleansing from commerce. It was a cleansing of a house of prayer from the practice of the sacrificial cultus.

Second, there is a small set of sayings that supports this general presumption and provides a coherent pattern from which the various evidences can be explained and reconstructed. There are basically two branches. One is found in a brief incident reported with minor differences in all three Synoptic gospels. In Matthew's version, Jesus' disciples, much impressed with the Temple buildings (some of them quite plausibly were making their first trip from Galilee to Jerusalem and were seeing them for the first time: they were quite splendid, from all we know), come to show them to Jesus. Instead of marvelling with them, he replies: "Do you see all this? I tell you seriously, there should not be left a stone on a stone here that will not be thrown down" (Mt 24:1-2; cf. Mk 13:2, Lk 21:6). Luke has Jesus also make a similar statement in Lk 19:44, but the context is slightly changed: it is just after the entry into Jerusalem, and the statement is applied to the coming devastation of Jerusalem in general by enemies, with no particular singling out of the Temple. Both versions are thus found in Luke, and both make sense. But the one all three Gospels share, dealing specifically with the Temple, chimes more interestingly with the Synoptic trial accusation, and with the parallel Johannine saying, about the Temple. And it is perhaps worth noting that the first thing Luke reports of Jesus after having him announce that not a stone will be left upon a stone in Jerusalem, is that he then enters the Temple—for the cleansing. A case can be made for the good sense and plausibility of either the Temple or the Jerusalem versions of the stone-upon-a-stone saying, and they may both be authentic. But if one of them is not, it is bound to be the latter, probably invented by Luke, or more likely by his source, as a way of reducing the scandal of the Temple version. Jesus said that the Temple should be destroyed, or, in Luke's version, will be destroyed. Either would in itself be a source of scandal to many members of his Jerusalem audience—both those for whom the Temple was a source of civic pride and those who had journeyed a considerable distance to sacrifice there, the one place where God had chosen to be worshipped. Some of them undoubtedly believed that God would make the Temple as permanent as heaven and earth themselves, and that to say it could or should be destroyed might well be considered a blasphemy either against God's glory that dwelt invisibly within the Temple, or against his power to preserve it even from invading armies, or against his faithfulness to his own Law. But Jesus did not think it blasphemous, because he apparently thought that the Law itself was due for alteration.

What was his complaint against the Temple? He does not call it an offensive and impious construction, as a Samaritan might. It was evidently a place for teaching, and presumably a place for prayer, as far as he was concerned. But he does not seem to think it a place for authentic worship through the sacrifice of animals. That was not because he would prefer to sacrifice animals elsewhere, but because his gospel included the news that animal sacrifice was really not to the point. Matthew twice has him quote Hosea 6:6, to assert true obedience to God over the mistaken emphasis on obedience among the more Law-abiding: "I want mercifulness, and not sacrifice." The first instance is when Jesus is criticized for eating with sinners and tax-collectors (Mt 9:10-13). From one common point of view, such an action is dangerous, disrespectful of the Law, and very likely productive of the kind of impurity that might require offering a sacrifice. From Jesus' point of view, it was proper to imitate the righteousness of God by imitating his loving mercy, and therefore, far from being an impediment, it was an aspect of precisely the most authentic worship possible. Mercifulness, not sacrifice: Law of purity and Temple cult have been taken far too seriously, at the expense of more important things. They could pass away—but the mercy of God cannot.

The second instance of the Hosea quotation is even more decisive. It occurs in Mt 12, just after Jesus has been criticized for the liberties taken by his disciples with the rules governing the Sabbath. Jesus counters by pointing out that their beloved David violated the Law when he ate the bread of the Presence, which is reserved only for the priests, and that the priests themselves can be argued to be technically violating the Sabbath by continuing to work in the Temple. The obvious answer to the latter argument, and one that was likely used in catechetical instruction to clear up this very problem in consistency, is that the Temple is so important that the usual Sabbath laws are not binding on those who are dedicated to its service. That is the context of Mt 12:6-8, where Jesus gives his ultimate answer: "I'm telling you that here we have something greater than the Temple. If only you had known what this is—'I want mercifulness, and not sacrifice'—you would not have condemned the blameless. For the Son of Man is Lord of the Sabbath."

Here are exactly the same central themes that dominate the gospel of Jesus. What is taking place here, manifest in the very liberty from Sabbath Law being shown by these disciples of the true gospel, is greater than the Temple. They are free from blame, and anyone who really understands the true righteousness—not the Law, not the Temple, but the greater righteousness that is the Dominion of God imitating God's mercy—would know enough not to blame. The Sabbath does not dominate, but is used and dominated by, those who belong to the new order, the Dominion of God, the collective Son of Man.

And that is the ultimate reason for Jesus' detachment from the Temple and for his willingness to speak of it as overrated, taken much too seriously, an occasion of distraction from the true righteousness. He was undoubtedly guilty of saying that it might be destroyed, possibly even of saying that this might be a good idea. He apparently did speak against sacrifice in the course of speaking for mercifulness, just as he spoke against the Sabbath laws. He evidently did believe that these things would be changed, and that when true worship of God finally came to pass, it would definitely not consist of the offering of sheep and oxen and doves—and that now was the time to begin thinking that way. True worship would take place within the obedient righteousness of those who belonged to the Son of Man, to the Dominion of God: that is what will replace the Temple and is already something greater even in its modest beginnings, just as it is more important than the Sabbath. If the old Temple should vanish—and he very likely both thought and taught that it was doomed to extinction—it would soon be replaced anyway by the new Temple: the Dominion of God, the Son of Man. The witnesses against Jesus at the trial were not entirely false. They may not have got his wording right, but he had doubtless said something of the sort. Part of his good news was that the old Temple, for all its splendor, was already obsolete and was in the process of being replaced by the new and true Temple, where the worship of God would finally be what it was always supposed to be.

JESUS' QUARREL WITH THE PHARISEES

Jesus does not seem to have been much impressed with the religious history of Israel. Most of the time, God's people had not been very faithful to his commands, or obedient to his will.

It is not so much that human beings are intrinsically wretched and unworthy, for Jesus seems to admit that there are righteous people in the land now, and have been in times past. When the young man replies modestly that he has kept all the commandments from his youth, Jesus does not challenge his discernment but simply loves him (Mk 10:21). Jesus came especially to call sinners, and he acknowledges that not all those who seem to be righteous really are—but it is not his style to assume that they aren't. Still, on balance it appears that righteousness is rare in the land. God has consistently, through the Law and the Prophets, summoned his people to justice, mercy, generosity, love; his people have characteristically responded by neglecting these great duties and commandments. They have been rapacious and oppressive to one another; they have defrauded and abused, withheld and neglected, and generally acted as if they had no idea what love of neighbor might be. As for the service of God himself, they have been careless of what God really requires of them, and they substitute in its stead sacrifices in the Temple or public shows of devout piety or scrupulosity about trivial rules.

Jesus seems to have disliked especially the self-deception that kept some of his contemporaries from seeing that they were successfully observant about many small matters while failing enormously in the most important ones. This he seems to have supposed was rather typical of the history of Israel, where the prophets kept reminding the people of their infidelity and were rejected for doing so and sometimes killed.

Hence the quarrel of Jesus with the Pharisees was a special modern instance of a perennial problem, not a peculiar disdain for them as such. What made them a recurrent preoccupation in Jesus' criticism was in part the fact that their message was popularly esteemed and was deceptively close to his own.[24] The Pharisaic party had given intense attention to their own version of the proposition that, above all, one must seek the Dominion of God and his righteousness—what was eventually called, among the rabbis, "taking on the yoke of the Dominion of God." What they understood by this was that they must accept gladly, and follow as scrupulously as possible, exactly what God wanted of them, taking as few risks of disobedience as they could. They too were motivated by love and gratitude, and knew that they stood in awe before the grace and goodness of God. They wanted to be uncompromisingly faithful. Over the years, they had developed traditions and customs of observance that were meant to honor God's expressed will as thoroughly as possible. They too wanted to be righteous as God is righteous; and righteousness at this level meant, among other things, that they must be careful to observe all that is commanded and to avoid anything that might compromise their observance. The strictest observers therefore took pains to avoid mingling with Gentiles and unobservant Jews: to do so might mean that they would inadvertently participate in a meal that was not prepared according to the commandments of God, which they were vowed to respect in every detail.

There seems to have been a special clash between Jesus and the Pharisees, and it appears to have worked both ways. The Pharisees had mainly two reasons for opposing Jesus and his gospel. The first was that, in their view, he took too lightly the detailed requirements of the Law. His detached attitude toward the Sabbath (the observance of which the Pharisees treated with particular rigor, giving thanks to God for the chance of serving him in doing so) was an affront and a scandal. This was precisely the sort of thing they were attempting to correct in the religious laxity of the people. His disdain for the traditions of observance which they had carefully developed and cultivated was scarcely tolerable, but his readiness to take issue with aspects of the Law of Moses was outrageous.

A second ground lay in the Pharisaic skepticism about the authenticity of the gospel of the Dominion of God. They had not believed John the Baptist and had not received his baptism (Mt 21:25-32, Mk 11:30-31, Lk 20:4-5; see also Lk 7:30). They apparently discouraged others from doing so, and it is probably to such opposition that Jesus refers in Mt 23:13: "Woe to you, scribes and Pharisees—you hypocrites! You close up the Dominion of the Heavens in the presence of men: for you do not enter, nor do you allow the ones entering to enter." The question about the source of Jesus' authority for doing what he does (Mt 21:23, Mk 11:28, Lk 20:2), while not labelled a question of the Pharisees, is undoubtedly one they shared and thought they could answer.

The quarrel was mutual. Jesus had three principal points of contention with them that served as the basis of important disagreements. First, and most important, was a difference of opinion on how to understand God's self-revelation. Jesus apparently believed that God had revealed himself as a merciful and generous Father, and that any theologizing that was to be done had to conform to that. The Pharisees also believed that God had revealed himself as a merciful and generous Father, but trusted much more than Jesus did in the supposition that this merciful and generous Father was also dead serious about the details of the observance prescribed by his Law. Hence the quarrel about divorce. The Pharisees took God at what seemed to be his word. His word, as registered in Deuteronomy 24:1, clearly said that a man may put away his wife if she displeases him. They therefore accepted God's permissiveness on the matter. The Pharisaic school of Hillel, however reluctant they may have been to come to such a conclusion, concluded that God's Law ruled that any form of displeasure was sufficient. The rival school of Shammai hedged a bit and claimed that more material grounds ought to be required. Both schools were trying to come up with a righteous and reasonable understanding of what was in fact written. Their differences were within those bounds. But Jesus offered a scandalously bold counteropinion: a covenantal love was forever, with no escape clause. That is the way in which God dealt, and deals, and will forever deal with those to whom he has given his love and promise. If the Law says otherwise, that must be just a concession made by Moses to an unruly people who were unable to understand and imitate God's ways.

The original and basic ways of God are expressed not in the permissive text but in his original definition of what it means to marry: two become of one flesh (Gen 2:24). It is absurd to think of dividing what is one flesh. The argument which Jesus proposes in Mt 19:1-12 and Mk 10:1-12 is turned on a quotation from Scripture, but it was probably rooted in his radical understanding of what it means to love, and therefore imitate, God—and therefore to love as God loves, with unshakable fidelity. If Scripture offers a compromise, then the less Scripture it! It must be a compromise of a lesser authenticity, the word not of God but of Moses. God has said who he is: this cannot be he.

The second ground of disagreement of Jesus with the Pharisees concerned what the Pharisees did in their own teachings about how to keep the Law. If Jesus thought they took Scripture too seriously and God's deepest self-revelation not seriously enough, his impatience was almost inevitably far greater with the Pharisees' reverent attitude toward the special rules which they themselves had admittedly ordained to make sure that God's will, as expressed in the Scriptures, would be uncompromisingly observed. There were also other ordinances, equally observed within the group, which were faithfully followed because they seemed appropriate or because they were authoritatively imposed—obligations which the Pharisees realistically called "burdens" and which, once imposed, must be faithfully borne. Jesus evidently spoke about both with scorn: both those that were rooted in Scripture and those that were pure pious invention did not deserve the sort of care and attention paid them by mindful Pharisees. Needless washings, restrictions on companionship, special modes of dress, dietary niceties, fussy observances—what had all this to do with the generous Father who called us to be like him? Thus the snide remarks by Jesus on all these issues: Pharisees clean the outsides of cups and dishes (Mt 23:25); they are scandalized to see Jesus eating with tax-gatherers and sinners (Mt 9:10-13); they wear exaggerated versions of the garments prescribed in the Law (Mt 23:5); they are overcareful about ritual defilement from what they eat (Mt 15:10-20); they pay tithes even on their garden herbs (Mt 23:23). Jesus' principal irritation came from the failure of some practicing Pharisees to perceive the absurdity of their scrupulosity about small matters when they were careless of what was really important. But it is clear that he also held the practices themselves in some contempt: they were simply not to the point, and anyone who thought they mattered much was just not in tune with the truth.

The third ground of difference of Jesus with the Pharisees is relatively trivial, though it has unfortunately often been treated as the main point. Many of the Pharisees were, inevitably, men of ordinary moral sensibility. They professed, and pursued, a zealous devotion to the commandments of God and to the traditions of the Elders, but they still permitted themselves to make money from clever maneuvers, to grow well-to-do on rents from poor tenants, to be contemptuous of tax-gatherers and whores, to take pleasure in being admired and deferred to. The Pharisaic teachings discouraged such abuses, but hypocrisies—both the cynical and the merely inconsiderate—we have with us always. Such inconsistency is a standard feature of all time. Jesus seems occasionally to have attempted to jar the Pharisees out of this inconsistency with angry critical rebukes. Such hypocrisy was, given his gospel's standards, the ultimate parody of the truth: to suppose oneself safely within God's rule, while in fact missing exactly the attitudes and behaviors that characterize God himself. Hence the railing of Jesus at the hypocrisy of some members of the Pharisaic party: while strictly keeping the tiny laws of their own, motivated by vanity rather than piety, they are heedless of the impurities of their own hearts, and they neglect the far deeper duties of faith and mercy (see previous references). These failings were not universal among the Pharisees; but in the judgment of Jesus, they were at least common enough to prove that, as an organized movement, the Pharisees had not managed to get their values and priorities in order. Hence the requirement that our righteousness must exceed that of the Pharisees if we are to be fit for the Dominion of God (Mt 5:20). To outdo even the most rigorous and strictest of the ways of piety undoubtedly seemed initially impossible to many of Jesus' hearers, until such an arresting and scary challenge caught their attention long enough to make them realize that true righteousness lies not in the multiplication of observances but in doing what really counts.

The only thing that really counts, Jesus argued to the Pharisees and to all others, is an imitation of God that really shows understanding—and real understanding cannot be oppressive, cannot be proud, cannot enrich itself at the expense of others, cannot satisfy itself with the keeping of routine observances while the central demand is left unattended. Real understanding is patient and kind, never jealous, or boastful, or ready to take offense, or resentful—but is always ready to excuse, to trust, and to endure whatever come. Paul's celebrated praise of love (1 Cor 13) is one of the points at which Paul is most exactly in tune with the gospel of Jesus, which proclaimed that the commandment to love God is the main calling in life, that it is not burdensome but life-giving, that the life it gives overflows automatically to the giving of life to the neighbor, and that the neighbor is anyone at all—tax-gatherer, Samaritan, sinner, enemy, persecutor, crucifier. That is the yoke and burden of the Dominion of God, and if one truly understands, then the yoke is easy and the burden light.

THE ULTIMACY OF GOD'S MERCY

Before concluding my treatment of Jesus' gospel, I wish to address myself to a matter which will have occurred to attentive readers as a possible inaccuracy in my reconstruction—or, to more trusting readers, a possible inconsistency in the gospel of Jesus. I have alleged that the gospel of Jesus represented the Father as inexhaustibly merciful. Yet there are various passages in which Jesus seems to be warning his listeners against God, as if the Father restrained his wrath only with difficulty and would soon let himself go in furious vengeance. If it were so, it was a grievous fault—but I think it was not so, and I wish to conclude by taking up a bit of slack that Jesus, for good reason, did not take up in his preaching of his gospel. According to his gospel, is the way of God finally more a matter of justice than of mercy? Or to put the question more rudely: did the gospel of Jesus demand more mercy of human beings than it attributed to God?

Occasionally, Jesus seems to be saying that God's forgiveness is conditional upon our forgiving those who have done us wrong: the parable of the Unmerciful Servant (Mt 18:23-35) concludes with the king, wrathful at his servant's failure to apply the lesson of mercy that he should have learned, turning the servant over to the torturers until he pays the huge debt that of course he can never pay. Matthew's Jesus then gives the moral of the story: "And thus my Father in heaven will do to you unless you each forgive your brother from your heart" (Mt 18:35). "And when you stand in prayer," says Mark's Jesus (Mt 11:25), "forgive, if you have anything against anyone, so that your Father in heaven may forgive you your misdeeds."

This is undoubtedly more a scare tactic than an inconsistency. The king of the parable has already not merely given his servant more time, as he requested, but has in fact totally cancelled a debt of staggering size. He did not wait to check out the servant's own mercy before forgiving him. The Lord's Prayer does not mean "Forgive us our trespasses *to the extent* that we forgive those who trespass against us," but *precisely as* we do so.

Now, a prayer that pleads "please imitate us," especially when it comes from the gospel of Jesus, is neither being silly nor presumptuous: it is merely a kind of calisthenics prescribed for the spiritual muscle-tone of one who is praying. It agrees to pretend that it is up to us to initiate the quality of forgiveness, and that the measure we measure out will determine how it will be measured to us; it agrees to forget for the moment that God far outdistances us in mercy. It helps us avoid the risk of counting so heavily on his generosity that we neglect the call to become like him. It keeps us from settling back into our own spontaneous inclinations and falling into the trap of treating our neighbor as *we* will, rather than in the way God wills. The Lord's Prayer that would be more exactly consonant with the gospel of Jesus would say something like "Please keep on forgiving us our trespasses (as we realize you intend to do), and we will try to imitate your example." But in addition to its being too clumsy for such an elegantly compact prayer, such a clause would not exert enough discipline on the speaker. Better to pretend that God has to be persuaded by our initiative. That way, we will be more inclined to keep striving for the righteousness that really imitates God.

It is in the same spirit of discipline that Jesus probably offered his other bracing admonitions. One set emphasizes the difficulty of becoming fit for the Dominion of God: the way is narrow and terribly rough, and only a few will make it; many are called but few are chosen; most of the seed is defeated by the rocks and birds and thorns—and just try getting a camel through a needle's eye! The tactic is familiar to anyone who has tried out for a tough team, taken a premedical course, or been to boot camp: let them know that it will be demanding, and scare them into giving their all by warning them that they will otherwise be cut from the team, failed out of the course, die in combat. Another tactic was to invoke the fires of Gehenna: if you don't shape up entirely, you will burn forever (Mt 5:22,30, 10:28, 18:8, 23:33; Mk 9:43-48; Lk 10:15, 12:5; and various other texts). Such had also apparently been the gospel of John the Baptist, certainly in the threat of punishment and probably in the warning that few will make it. Was this what Jesus really believed?

Despite his occasional characterizations of sinners as the devil's seed, or as irredeemable hardhearts, or as whatever might make his listeners eager not to be one of them when the showdown came, neither the gospel nor the behavior of Jesus suggests that this is what he actually thought of them, or of anyone. No one can be written off, because the Father's mercy is limitless. Through John's mission and his own, Jesus had seen many hardened sinners change their ways and their lives and turn to bearing the fruits of righteousness. Doubtless he had also seen many who had thus reformed slip again, back into their old lives, or lose heart under pressure, or even forget and come to disbelieve the good news by which they were invited to share in the Dominion of God. But even then, it was not all over for them. The Father remained ready to forgive even these, if they would only turn again: seven times, seventy times seven, or whatever it might require, until the end comes and the opportunity is definitively lost.

Lest that time come before they are found and gathered into the flock, Jesus sought out sinners and tried to persuade them. His main persuasion was the good news of the Dominion of God, not merely what it would eventually be but also what it already was. But he was not above using, along with it, the bad news of what it might cost to decline this invitation. The religious history of Israel in general and the contemporary case of the Pharisees in particular proved how easy it was to be smug, to fail to realize one's own unrighteousness. There was also clear proof of how easy it was to despair and to fail to realize that one can really change and be changed. Sinners of both kinds needed to be jostled, informed, teased, cajoled, encouraged, warned, and if necessary even scared to life. For the sinner, whether smug or hopeless, was not really wicked but sick and in need of the physician who could bring healing of the malady (Mt 9:12, Mk 2:17, Lk 5:31). Hence Jesus' impatience with the Pharisees' disapproval of his associations. If they had understood what God had meant in demanding mercy, they might realize that the enlightened merciful were called to this: to rescue the lost sheep and make them ready and willing to enter the Dominion of God. And hence also the parables and pronouncements that emphasized how long God has patiently but vainly waited for good fruit to be produced. Things have always been bad, bad enough to deserve a terrible judgment. But God has offered one more chance, one more undeserved and generous delay before the Dominion comes with power. During that brief reprieve, the door is open to anyone. The proud Pharisee can see the error of his ways and repent; the whore and the exploitative tax-collector can see the error of their ways and repent.

Jesus warns his followers against trying to second-guess God about the timing of the great event. It will be fairly soon, but no one knows exactly when—not even the angels in heaven (Mt 24:36, Mk 13:32). Just as he was reluctant to presume any knowledge of this detail, so it is likely that he was not certain how God would finally act when the ripe moment came. In the meantime, his own work was to help the ripening. He knew from the Scriptures that God had occasionally threatened severe punishments and had apparently carried out some of the threats. This was enough warrant for him to repeat such threats to his audiences—even to elaborate them. Any effective technique was worth a try.

But if Jesus was consistent about his understanding of his own gospel—and he appears to me to have been impressively consistent—then he quite plausibly had the same sense that all bright children have in similar circumstances. What Father threatens is an index of how important it is to obey, not a reliable prediction of what will happen to the disobedient. Here and there we get glimpses of a supposition that an eternal Gehenna is not quite the style of the Father to whom he demands obedience, and glimpses also of a supposition that the few who will be chosen will in fact be many.

One of these occasions occurs in the offhand remark that when the Dominion of God finally erupts into full power, it will be like the time of Noah's flood. The basis of the analogy is that many people think it is business as usual and do not heed the prophetic warning—and then, suddenly, the threat comes true. But Jesus does not follow the analogy to say that in this case, as in the case of Noah, only a handful will be saved. The estimate is closer to fifty percent: "I'm telling you, that night there will be two in one bed—the one will be taken and the other left. There will be two milling grain in the same place—one will be taken and her companion will be left" (Lk 17:34-35; Mt 24:40-41 differs only in trivial details, including a decorous substitution of 'two men in the field' for Luke's two people in bed). Luke's version offers also a comparison between the destruction of Sodom after Lot's departure and the Sodomites continuing to live it up as before. But the comparison is not pursued far enough to fool the really attentive listener. The punch line is the same: one taken, one left. For the breakthrough of the Dominion of God, there is nothing remotely resembling the statistics of the Noah and Sodom episodes.

Neither is there anything resembling the punishments visited upon Sodom and upon Noah's scoffers. Those who are to be saved are "taken"—like Lot and Noah's family, removed from those who are not members of salvation. But what happens to those who are ineligible is not discussed. There is no further word about flooding or brimstone or Gehenna or perpetual tortures, just as in Mk 13:27 the angels gather up those who are ready and nothing is remarked about what happens to the others. It is as if Jesus thinks that the tragic plight of the unprepared is sufficiently established by the mere fact that they are left behind, like the foolish virgins outside the closed door (Mt 25:10-12) or like the thoughtless and improvident servants who weep in the darkness and gnash their teeth with regret when they are denied admission because of their failure to respond appropriately (Mt 8:12, 24:51, 25:30, Lk 13:28)—or like those whose preoccupations led them to decline their invitations to the feast, who never even know what they are missing as others are summoned to take their place (Lk 14:16-24).

It seems to me likely that Jesus believed that God would not punish those who failed to accept the great invitation. He would give them a chance and then leave them to perish normally, either regretful or bewildered or unaware, while the children of the Dominion of God are separated out for a permanent and indescribable life of joy. Those who do not want to belong will not have to belong. Neither will they be tormented for making that choice. And the question of how many of those there will be is obliquely addressed by one other small pattern of evidence.

The blind Pharisees on the one hand, and the careless liberals on the other, were obviously a vexation to Jesus. But in one pattern of his sayings, the issue is not that either class will be excluded—he warns them that they will have only a humble place. Matthew's Jesus is adamantly insistent on the enduring importance of the commandments of the Law, and he enforces his point by declaring that not a jot or a tittle will pass away, and that anyone who breaks even the least of the commandments and teaches others to take such liberties will be—what? Abandoned by God? Destroyed? Burned forever, like a perpetual Temple sacrifice? No. This one will be least in the Dominion of God (Mt 5:18-19). And the unbelieving Pharisees, who failed to do God's will by their failure to believe that John the Baptist came in the way of righteousness—what is their punishment? They will suffer the humiliation of having whores and tax-collectors precede them into the Dominion of God (Mt 21:31-32), just as the vineyard laborers will be humiliated to behold the mercy of the generous owner who is ready to pay as much to the latecomer as to the one who has labored all day (Mt 20:1-15). The last will be first and the first last (Mt 19:30, 20:16, Mk 10:31, Lk 13:30); he who humbles himself shall be exalted, and he who exalts himself shall be humbled (Mt 23:12, Lk 14:11, 18:14). These have to do with relative positions of dignity within the Dominion of God, not with the question of whether one will be permitted to enter. The Pharisee and the breezy libertarians may be in for a shock—but if they have truly, however benightedly, striven for righteousness and the love of God and neighbor, then the worst that can happen is a humble place in the Dominion of God.

If salvation depended upon what we can do, it would be impossible. But with God, *everything* is possible (Mt 19:26, Mk 10:27, Lk 18:27). It is likely that no one will be damned. It is imaginable that all the sick will eventually be healed, that no sheep will stay lost. It just may be that in the deeper recesses of Jesus' understanding, not clearly announced in his open gospel but allowed to peep out from time to time, like a news leak, he either believed or hoped that his gospel's characterization of God was so right as to exclude the possibility of loss. At least it was clear from his gospel that loss will be minimized and that for many whom he occasionally threatened with the fires of Gehenna, what he thought really in store was a relatively lowly place in the Dominion of God. That, given his gospel, was not much of a threat. He did not say where the Dominion of God would be situated, or when it would arrive, but he did insist that for all the power and glory visible in John the Baptist when he preached—even though no one born of women has ever been greater than he—the least in the Dominion of God will be still greater (Mt 11:11, Lk 7:28) and will shine like the sun, like angels, in the Dominion of the Father (Mt 13:43, 22:30, Mk 12:25, Lk 20:36). And, as Matthew's Jesus then adds, let him hear who has ears to hear.

3

The Gospel of the Apostles

The gospel of Jesus was not a Christian gospel. Jesus was its proclaimer, but he was not its content. The Christian gospel, properly so called, did not arrive on the scene until after the crucifixion and resurrection of Jesus. It was a gospel *about* Jesus, and those who proclaimed it were Apostles.

I do not mean that those who proclaimed this gospel happened also to be Apostles, or that those who were commissioned as Apostles happened to preach this gospel. I am rather defining what Apostle means in this chapter and probably meant originally: an Apostle is a proclaimer of a gospel about Jesus, a Christian gospel. The gospel of the Apostles that is the subject of this chapter is the gospel preached by those who were in a privileged and authorized position to bear witness to what God had done and would do in and through the Jesus who had overcome death.

THE APOSTLES AND THEIR MESSAGE

Who were the Apostles? And what was their gospel? These two questions became enormously important in the Church of the second century as Christians, assailed by a variety of new proclamations and teachings, turned to reaffirm their roots in the original Christian gospel as propounded by the original proclaimers. It is largely concern over these two questions that first brought about the collecting of early Christian documents and the eventual formation of the New Testament as the authoritative sources for discerning the right answers.

As a result of this collecting, most of the surviving literature produced by the first two generations of Christians—and therefore most of the evidence by which we must discover who the Apostles were and what gospel they preached—is preserved in the pages of the New Testament. But not much of it was written by, or even in the time of, Apostles. Several of the New Testament books incorporate memories and oral traditions and even written sources from very early times—but none of these books achieved its present form until much later. The gospel of John the Baptist and the gospel of Jesus must be reconstructed from Gospels written some thirty to fifty years after the fact, and the reconstruction must deal with a variety of reinterpretations and editorializings that come between us and the original happenings. The gospel of the Apostles was subjected to just as much rethinking as these previous two gospels, and reconstructing it requires just as much labor and imagination. For the days of the Apostles were volatile days, a phase of gospelling history in which the ground was shifting rapidly, a time in which the eventually settled continents were still adrift and not yet clearly indicating where they would find their stable places. When the story was gathered together at a later time, it was told mainly from the perspective of that later time, and bent to its shape. To locate and correct the distortions that resulted requires a good deal of surmise, conjecture, and hypothesis; the complicated and tangled evidence hides as much as it discloses, and some of the hiding derives from a deliberate attempt to provide simpler and more comfortable answers than history had in fact offered.

Consider, for instance, one of the few early texts that managed to be preserved despite its not having been included in the New Testament, a small church manual evidently compiled in stages during the first few Christian generations. Utterly lost from view for centuries before its surprising rediscovery in 1875, it is usually known as the *Didache*; its full title translates as "Teaching of the Twelve Apostles: Teaching of the Lord through the Twelve Apostles to the Nations."[1]

The title promises a clean answer to the questions about the identity of the Apostles and the content of their gospel—but the title is utterly fanciful. The document itself never mentions Twelve Apostles or makes any further reference to its own authorship. Indeed, it implicitly denies that authentic Apostleship can be discerned as easily as the title suggests, for it treats Apostles as a type of itinerant prophet and offers instructions about how to tell genuine Apostles from charlatans. The pretense that the true Christian gospel is simply the gospel of the Twelve Apostles belongs to the title only, and is a late and wishful imposition on a document that knows no such thing.

The lore of the Twelve Apostles is deeply implanted in early Christian thought, and is especially prominent in the book on which we must principally rely for evidence of the gospel of the Apostles—Luke's account, written as a supplement to his Gospel for the purpose of recounting the earliest days of the Church, now known as the Acts of the Apostles.[2] Acts was written more than a generation, perhaps two generations, after the gospel of the Apostles began, and much of the material gathered by Luke had already been rethought and recast in a way much more subtle—but not less distorting—than the way in which the title of the *Didache* is misleading about its contents. This chapter will be especially concerned with what Luke collected into Acts, because that is a large proportion of the only evidence that survives.[3] To use it discriminatingly, we must understand how to identify and circumvent its biases, some of which are Luke's and some of which were already imposed on the material he received.[4] One of these biases is precisely the myth of the Twelve Apostles.

THE MYTH OF THE TWELVE APOSTLES

Christian history has repeatedly shown how convenient it can be to assume that the true Christian gospel was the uniform proclamation of those Twelve who exclusively held the office of Apostle by formal appointment. The idea took hold fairly early and has remained firmly in place ever after. But it is not sound, and discovering the gospel of the Apostles requires that we dismantle this myth.

There is early evidence for a special group known as the Twelve.[5] Paul tells the Corinthians that according to the tradition he himself had received, the second resurrection appearance of Jesus was to "the Twelve" (1 Cor 15:5). It is sometimes suggested that the Twelve originated precisely then, constituted by the fact of the resurrection witness; but all four Gospels set their origin earlier, during the public ministry of Jesus, reporting that he appointed twelve of his disciples in a special way (Mt 10:1,5; Mk 6:7; Lk 6:13; Jn 6:70) and referring to them thereafter as "the twelve disciples" (Mt 20:17) or "his twelve disciples" (Mt 10:1, 11:1)—or, more frequently and more significantly, simply "the Twelve" (Mt 26:14,20,47; Mk 4:10, 6:7, 9:35, 10:32, 11:11, 14:10,17,20,43; Lk 8:1, 9:1,12, 18:31; 22:3,47; Jn 6:67,70,71)—and representing them as Jesus' closest and most loyal companions during the days of his gospelling, and the recipients of privileged teachings.

The Synoptic Gospels claim that the Twelve were also Apostles,[6] recording that Jesus incorporated the Twelve into his own mission, gave them authority, and sent them forth to heal and preach (Mt 10:1,7-8; Mk 6:7,12-13; Lk 9:1-2,6). The verb used for their sending-forth is the usual and non-technical *apostellō,* and the Twelve are accordingly called *apostoloi,* apostles: those who are sent (Mt 10:2, Mk 6:30, Lk 9:10). But if the verb is non-technical, the same is not necessarily true of the noun. Luke tells of another mission in which Jesus sends forth a group of seventy disciples to preach the gospel of the Dominion of God (Lk 10:1-20), following the same pattern as in the sending-forth of the Twelve (Lk 9:1-10); but although the same verb is used, *apostellō,* the seventy are not referred to as *apostoloi*. The omission is not accidental. The title *apostle* is apparently reserved. Luke's first use of it comes at the point where Jesus selects twelve disciples, "whom he also named apostles" (Lk 6:13), and the verb for *named* is precisely the same as in the subsequent verse, where Jesus names Simon "Peter." "Apostle" is evidently a technical and restricted term.

Were the Twelve really appointed "apostles" during Jesus' ministry, or is Luke projecting into that period a technical title that emerged only later? For our purposes, it matters little. Even if the Synoptic tradition is right in representing that Jesus chose a special Twelve before his crucifixion and entrusted them with a gospelling mission as "apostles," they were not yet pertinent to this chapter. The "gospel of the Apostles" is the Christian proclamation about Jesus. But there was no such thing before Jesus' crucifixion. The gospel preached by his disciples during his public mission was, as one would expect, his own gospel, the gospel of Jesus. "They proclaimed that [people] should repent," says Mark (Mk 6:12), while Luke more explicitly has Jesus send them to "proclaim the Dominion of God" (Lk 9:2). Matthew is still more precise: "And going on your way, proclaim, saying that the Dominion of the Heavens has drawn near" (Mt 10:7), which is also what Luke's Jesus tells the seventy disciples recruited for the other major gospelling mission (Lk 10:9). The gospel of the Dominion of God and the preparation for that Dominion was the gospel of Jesus, and those who assisted Jesus in proclaiming it can at best be considered "apostles" with a small *a,* only an embryonic version of the capital-A Apostles who would later introduce the Christian gospel.

It is only in the post-resurrection setting that the Apostles emerge as the appointed proclaimers of a new gospel, and the Synoptic tradition emphasizes the privileged position of the Twelve and reports a new commission. It is they who are the main recipients of Jesus' post-resurrection appearances (Mt 28:16-17, Mk 16:14, Lk 24:33-43), and who are charged as "witnesses of these things" (Lk 24:48) to extend the gospel universally (Mt 28:19, Mk 16:15, Lk 24:47). Their witness to Jesus' resurrection, after their association with his mission, is the foundation of their authority as Apostles and the foundation of the gospel they are now to preach. It seems, in fact, to have been primarily with an eye to their eventual role as resurrection witnesses that Jesus had singled them out in the first place; for according to Acts, the risen Jesus became visible "not to all people, but to those witnesses previously appointed by God—to us, who ate and drank with him after his rising from the dead—and he commanded us to proclaim to the people and to testify that this is the one designated by God as judge of the living and the dead" (Acts 10:41-42; cf. 2:32, 3:15, 5:32).

As Acts advances the story beyond the Synoptic tradition, Luke shows how deep a partisan he is of the Twelve Apostles as the founders of Christianity. His sense of the exclusiveness of their leadership emerges especially in his report about the way in which the remaining eleven become twelve once more. There is no obvious reason why they cannot continue as the special Eleven, nor is it obvious that anyone else would be eligible to join their privileged ranks, but Peter announces as the first order of business after Jesus' ascension that they must replace Judas. The conditions of eligibility are strict: the new twelfth Apostle must be one of those "having associated with us all the time in which the Lord Jesus went in and out among us, beginning from the baptism of John up to the day when he was taken up from us—one of those become with us a witness of his resurrection" (Acts 1:21-22). Two candidates who qualify as such intimate fellow-travellers of the twelve apostles are put forward, but only one of them can be admitted to fellowship in what is clearly to be understood as a closed college of Twelve with a single vacant Apostleship. The lot falls to Matthias, "and he was counted with the Eleven Apostles" (Acts 1:26). Thereafter, Luke can use "the Apostles" and "the Twelve" interchangeably in his reports of life in the early Church (Acts 6:2,6), and the Twelve Apostles, now restored to their rightful number and fully confirmed in complete Apostolicity as longtime associates of Jesus and witnesses of his resurrection, are the authoritative leaders for preaching, teaching, decision-making, and all forms of governance (Acts 2:14,37,42-43; 4:33-37; 5:2,12,13,18,29,40-42).

And thus Luke confirms the hints given by his Synoptic colleagues about the special standing and authority of "the Twelve Apostles" (Mt 10:2, Mk 6:7,30), by carrying the story farther than they had done, into the early life of the Church, where their authority and standing come into full bloom and their distinctive gospel may finally emerge. This is the kind of understanding from which the title of the *Didache* was composed: there are Twelve and only Twelve Apostles, and the true gospel and the governance of the Church have been given into their hands.

This picture is familiar enough. It is still the usual lore of Christian churches. The problem is that it is not true.

It is probably true that there was a special group of Twelve who were resurrection witnesses. We have Paul's word that this was part of the early solemn tradition, and there is no strong reason for suspecting otherwise. It is certainly true that "Apostle" was a title of high rank in the early Church, designating an authentic agent of the gospel about Jesus. But it is not so clear that all the Twelve were Apostles, even if some of them were. Much more to the point, it is undeniable that there were Apostles who were not members of the Twelve.

PAUL AND OTHER APOSTLES

The evidence for Apostles who were not of the Twelve is hardly obscure. Even Luke himself provides some of it, for although his scheme of the closed Apostolic circle is notably strict and consistent, he strays from it twice, by referring to Paul and Barnabas as Apostles, despite their lack of membership in the Twelve (Acts 14:4,14). But more revealing and more forceful evidence is provided not by Luke but by Paul, one of those to whom he so extraordinarily accords the Apostolic title. It is by measuring Luke against Paul that we can best come to a balanced perspective on what constituted Apostleship, and on what gospel the Apostles preached, apart from what Luke thought about both questions.

When Paul credits the Twelve with the second resurrection-appearance of Jesus, he does not refer to them as Apostles at all, let alone as *the* Apostles (1 Cor 15:5), and two verses later, when he lists another appearance to "all the Apostles," he is clearly not speaking of the Twelve, since he has just listed them separately. In fact, he is not really referring even to all the Apostles, for he has one more appearance yet to mention—the one to himself, "the least of the Apostles" (1 Cor 15:8-9). If Paul's humility leads him to confess that he is not worthy to be called an Apostle (1 Cor 15:9), it also requires him to acknowledge that by the grace of God he is what he is (1 Cor 15:10). And what he is is an Apostle, as he boldly proclaims in the opening verse of nearly every one of his extant epistles.

These opening verses strike a somewhat polemical note, in fact, and this note is echoed elsewhere in Paul's writings. Paul was called to Apostleship (Rom 1:1, 1 Cor 1:1), neither self-appointed nor appointed by other men but so designated by God and by Jesus Christ (Gal 1:1), set apart for the gospel of God concerning his resurrected Son, Jesus Christ our Lord (Rom 1:1-4). Paul sets out his credentials. His authenticity as an Apostle is clear not only from his having been appointed directly by God and from his having seen the risen Christ (1 Cor 9:1, 15:8) but also from the "signs of the Apostle" he has displayed (2 Cor 12:12) and from the effectiveness of his evangelizing. "Are you not my work in the Lord?" he challenges the wavering Corinthians: "If to others I am not an Apostle, nevertheless I am to you, for you are the seal of my Apostleship in the Lord" (1 Cor 9:1-2).

Paul was aware that there can be ambiguity in a claim to Apostleship and that there are such things as "false Apostles, deceitful workers, transforming themselves into Apostles of Christ" (2 Cor 11:13). But he stoutly insisted that there was no ambiguity in his own case. He is an Apostle. His right to the title is grounded in his having seen the risen Christ and having received the special calling to what he recognizes as the highest office in the Church (1 Cor 12:28). That he is not a member of the Twelve is evidently of no significance whatever: his authority is on an equal footing with any of them (2 Cor 12:11), and his gospel's authenticity is not subject to question by anyone at all (Gal 1:7-9). He does not tell us who, or how many, are included among "all the Apostles" (1 Cor 15:7), nor is he specific about how to discriminate a genuine Apostle from an imposter, but his testimony about his own case forcefully and unequivocally demands the conclusion that Luke was quite right in twice referring to Paul as an Apostle (Acts 14:4,14) and quite wrong in his otherwise promoting the myth of the Twelve Apostles.

From what we have just seen, it is clear that the gospel of the Apostles was not simply the message of the Twelve, nor the preaching authorized by James, nor the proclamation of Peter. No description of the Apostolic gospel can possibly be complete unless we include in it the gospel preached by the Apostle Paul. When we do so, we are forced to conclude further that the gospel of the Apostles was not an invariant and uniform doctrine. Some of its forms, and some of its agents, were sometimes disputed. What it was at the beginning of Apostolic preaching is not the same as what it later became, and the progress of its development involved some duress and controversy. In short, the smooth and harmonious picture painted by Luke in Acts is not a true record of its early days. To get behind that picture and come closer to what more probably happened in the formation of the gospel of the Apostles, we must therefore take a closer look at Paul, who shows some of the seamy side of the story, and then a closer look at Luke, who reveals more than he had meant to reveal about the seamy side.

THE OPPOSITION TO PAUL'S PROCLAMATION

It is sometimes only by slight interruptions of the fabric's smoothness that we can become aware of the seam underneath. Consider this curiosity: Paul struggled indignantly against those who would deny him the title Apostle; yet Luke, despite an admiration for Paul that gives over half of Acts to recounting and celebrating his successes, not only generally withholds the title from Paul but defines the conditions of eligibility in such a way as to exclude Paul permanently from being considered an authentic Apostle. How can we account for this disjunction in Luke?

The first step, I believe, is to note that the issue is not really the name of Apostle, but the gospelling authority it stands for. Paul's battle was not for his status but for his gospel, and his detractors were pursuing not a personal dislike or a professional envy but a theological principle.

It is in Galatians that the issue bursts out most clearly. Paul's successful mission to Galatia had been succeeded by a competing mission, whose agents maintained that Gentile converts to Christianity must submit to certain constraints of the Jewish Law (Gal 3-5, *passim),* most particularly circumcision (Gal 5:1-6, 6:12-15). Moreover, this countermission insisted that these were the terms of the real gospel, and evidently alleged that although Paul ordinarily preached in these terms (Gal 5:11), he had illegitimately watered down the gospel to make it more palatable to the Galatians (Gal 1:10), behaving in a rather irresponsible way and deforming the gospel which the leaders of the Church had given him to preach (Gal 1:1,12,16, etc.). Paul denies the charges with fervor: there is one gospel and only one, and it is the gospel of freedom in Christ that he had preached to them; this is the gospel he himself learned not from men but from God, and any other gospel that contradicts it, be it preached by men, angels, or even (heaven forbid!) Paul himself, is not a gospel at all but is simply accurst (Gal 1:6-9).

Galatia was not the first battleground on which Paul had fought this issue. He reports that when he was in Antioch, some had come from James in Jerusalem and observed the customary Jewish refusal to share meals with uncircumcised Gentiles, even influencing Peter and Barnabas to separate themselves from the Gentile converts (Gal 2:11-13). Moreover, Paul's visit to Jerusalem had been complicated by Law-conservative "false brethren" who attempted to bring Paul's gospel of freedom into servitude by insisting that the Gentile convert Titus be circumcised (Gal 2:1-4). Paul's stand had been the same in those cases: these were *false* brethren, opposing a true Gentile Christian liberty as proclaimed in Paul's Apostolic gospel; and when Peter had wavered over the full legitimacy of such freedom, Paul had faced him down, berating him for being disloyal to the truth they knew they shared in the gospel of Christ (Gal 2:11-18). Whatever Peter might preach among the Jews, and whatever might be the customs in James' Jerusalem community, Paul's gospel of Gentile freedom in Christ is the authentic Apostolic gospel, and is not to be tampered with.[7] And this time it seems that Luke is firmly on Paul's side, for that is precisely the overall message of Acts 15. The chapter begins with Judean Christians coming to Antioch to insist on the circumcision of Gentiles, proceeds through Paul's appeal to Jerusalem, and concludes with the Apostles and Elders issuing a formal decree that Gentile converts are not subject to circumcision nor to the Mosaic Law (Acts 15:1-29). Paul's gospel of Gentile freedom is thus vindicated in an irrevocable and public way. A gospel preaching circumcision for the Gentiles cannot be authentic, at least from then on. The opponents of Paul's gospel must therefore have been either immoderate conservatives who refused to recognize the authority of the Church to confirm Gentile freedom from the Law (and therefore are of no moment in any attempt to discover the gospel of the Apostles), or they were the less reactionary opposition that had formed legitimately before the contentions about the matter had been officially sorted out.

Luke's account clearly favors the latter explanation. Once the issue has been formally disposed of in Acts 15, we hear no more of any Christian opposition to Paul; before that time, Luke reports that even Peter's fraternizing with uncircumcised Gentile converts had resulted in his being called to account in Jerusalem, where he managed to satisfy the objectors that all was in order (Acts 11:1-18). The incorporation of Gentiles into Christian salvation had, after all, been something of a surprise; it is entirely understandable that in its early stages, some would be uncertain about what the rules were and that some conservatives would insist that Gentile converts must be brought into proper Jewish observance before they could fully qualify. Hence a temporary distrust of Paul's gospel, and therefore of his Apostleship, could readily arise among the Jewish Christians of Jerusalem.

It is therefore not the problem of opposition to a gospel of Gentile freedom that needs explaining, but rather Luke's account of the solution to that problem. For while Luke vindicates Paul, he does not do so on Paul's terms. He works instead in a way that is consistent with the myth of the Twelve Apostles. His treatment deserves a closer examination, because it illustrates features of Luke's overall myth of Christian origins that pervade his story of the gospel of the Apostles—and since we are dependent on what Luke wrote in Acts for so much of the relevant evidence, it is important to know how to read him critically.

LUKE'S MYTH OF CHRISTIAN ORIGINS VS. PAUL'S EVIDENCE

When the issue of Gentile circumcision arises in Antioch, Paul and Barnabas go to Jerusalem to consult the Apostles and Elders (Acts 15:2). In Luke's account, it is on their authority, not Paul's, that the solution is promulgated (Acts 15:22-23). Moreover, the major intervention in the debate that gives rise to this solution is not Paul's but Peter's. Peter reminds the assembly that it was he who had been chosen by God to preach the gospel to the Gentiles (Acts 15:7) and that God had confirmed his converts by giving them the Holy Spirit, showing that their hearts had been purified by faith (Acts 15:8-9). He therefore concludes that Jewish customs should not be imposed on Gentiles, since all are saved not by Law but by grace through faith in Jesus: "Now, why then are you putting God to a test, to place a yoke on the neck of the disciples which neither our fathers nor we are able to bear? But through the grace of the Lord Jesus we trust to be saved—and they too in the same manner" (Acts 15:10-11). Paul and Barnabas offer their parallel testimony, which Luke does not bother to quote. James—whom Peter had already implicitly designated as his successor when Peter left Jerusalem (Acts 12:17)—then acknowledges that Peter's account of God's first acceptance of Gentiles into his own people squares with what Scripture had foretold, and concludes that they should do as Peter has argued.

Paul's role in this important event is, according to Luke, incidental and dispensable. Peter initiates the Gentile mission, tells the authorities how it should be understood, and leaves it to his acknowledged successor to summarize the result. Peter's argument has been persuasive. The Apostles and Elders agree. Paul apparently need not have been at the meeting at all.

The irony is that the argument which Luke places in Peter's mouth seems originally to have been used not by Peter but against him, and by the Apostle Paul himself. Paul tells the real story to the Galatians. It happened in Antioch, when Peter had knuckled under to certain persons who had come from James, and withdrew from his customary table fellowship with Gentile converts. Paul thought this an infidelity to the gospel, and opposed Peter to his face:

> I said to Peter in front of everyone, "If you, being a Jew, live like the Gentiles and not like the Jews, how can you

> force the Gentiles to do things the Jewish way? We, Jews by nature and not Gentile sinners, yet knowing that a man is not justified by works of Law, except through faith of Jesus Christ—even we believed in Christ Jesus so that we might be justified by faith of Christ and not by works of Law: for by works of Law no flesh will be justified." (Gal 2:14-16)

The resemblance between Paul's story and Luke's is not likely to be only coincidental. Apparently, Luke knew about a crucial controversy in Antioch between Paul and Judean conservatives, and knew about the argument that ultimately prevailed even with the Jerusalem leaders. But either Luke or his source has robbed Paul to pay Peter: the gospel of Gentile freedom, from its inception to its formal endorsement, has been given into the hands of the Twelve Apostles.

Luke's sources may have done much of the work of crediting this development to the Twelve Apostles, but Luke's reporting of the beginning of the Gentile mission shows that he contributed some editorial labor of his own in that direction. When Peter reminds everyone in Acts 15 that he had been the one appointed by God to take the gospel to the Gentiles (Acts 15:7), he obviously means to take us back to the story of his experience with Cornelius. This breakthrough is first reported by Luke in Acts 10:1-48 and is then recounted by Peter to the Jerusalem community in Acts 11:1-18 and is received with general rejoicing. That happy ending is then immediately followed by an abrupt change of subject as Luke narrates that those who were scattered in the persecution about Stephen travelled abroad, preaching at first only to Jews but eventually to Gentiles as well (Acts 11:19-20). This too points back to an earlier report, the persecution mentioned in Acts 8:1-3, which Luke had concluded by remarking that "then those who had been scattered went about gospelling the word" (Acts 8:4). The two passages are clearly linked. Luke seems to have worked from a source that told of the persecution, scattering, preaching, and first evangelizing of Gentiles. Why does he depart from this source at Acts 8:4 and not resume it until Acts 11:19? The obvious answer is that this delays the news about Gentile converts in Antioch until after the first Gentile mission has been given to Peter through visions, successfully executed to the accompaniment of signs and wonders, and granted the supervision and approval of the Jerusalem Apostolic community. Luke's editorial management insures that Providence introduces innovation through the careful authority of the Twelve.

In short, Luke, in managing the material bearing on the gospel of the Apostles, has taken some pains to assure his readers that the Twelve Apostles (and especially Peter as their leader) were in charge of the early Church and executed that charge mainly through Peter—with conservative caution, taking the dramatic step of extending the gospel to the Gentiles only with hesitation, with clear signs of God's invitation, and with the thoughtful, considered approval of the Apostolic community at Jerusalem. His overall scheme is designed to be reassuring to those who want to see the predominantly Gentile Christianity of Luke's own time in maximum continuity with conservative Judaism and with the duly delegated authority of Jesus himself.

Paul is accordingly subordinated and sometimes marginalized, his independent Apostolic authority basically unacknowledged, his gospel of Gentile salvation muted, his defense of it attributed to Peter. Luke was probably influenced in this by the views of Paul's opponents, for in his reports of Paul's early movements in Acts 9—his reception by Ananias, his sojourn among the disciples in Damascus, his visit to Jerusalem and consultation with the Apostles, his preaching in Judea—Luke seems to have drawn from a source that repeated essentially the same compromising rumors that Paul denies in Galatians 1. But even if some of Luke's treatment of Paul derives ultimately from Paul's detractors, Luke's intent is not to detract. It is rather to fit his admiration and approval of Paul into a system that will validate Paul as an authentic agent of the gospel of the Apostles, faithfully executing the mission that God had given to the world through the authority of the Twelve Apostles.

Luke's overall myth of Christian origins is extremely attractive. As a revelational scheme, it has almost everything—prediction and fulfillment, novelty with recognizability, clear authority, order, continuity, comprehensiveness, closure, mercy and justice: all the aesthetic and theological virtues. Its appeal is still powerful enough to overwhelm critical thought even among people who can see the seams, note the myth's inconsistencies with other evidence, and perceive that it is much too implausibly tidy. It is not hard to see why Luke adopted it. But it is important to note that he did adopt it, and that his handling of Gentile freedom is only one example of its influence on Acts: this general myth of Christian origins pervades Acts, coloring the material Luke selects, his interpretation of its meaning, his inventions and omissions and connections—nearly everything.

That is not to say that Luke simply wrote historical fantasy based on a convenient myth. Luke claims, at the beginning of his Gospel, that he has taken some trouble to investigate and report what really happened. I think he may be believed; the Gospel of Luke appears to be a true child of the Synoptic tradition as Luke received it. I think it reasonable to suppose that he wrote Acts in much the same way, working from information he had received and trying to present it in a way that makes coherent and satisfying sense.[8] But his taste for coherence and satisfaction was a special taste, and it was formed in the image of the myth he accepted. Furthermore, the information at his disposal was limited, requiring him to smooth out his story, supplying missing connections and explanations by surmising what was plausible; and his sense of what was plausible was influenced by the myth that guided his overall account.

He needed such guidance, especially since the information available to Luke about the earliest Jerusalem Church was surprisingly incomplete. Its incompleteness is disguised by Luke's presentation, which concentrates the early chapters of Acts almost entirely on Jerusalem, giving the appearance of a considerable body of recollections, with the individual events interspersed with various casual and vague generalizations that seem to be (and are undoubtedly meant to seem to be) summary digests of ample memories. But the impression thus created is an illusion. This may readily be seen if we consider the title that tradition bestowed at an early stage upon the book: The Acts of the Apostles. How close is this to being an appropriate title? It is in fact not very close at all. What was Thomas up to, or James, the brother of John? We are given no idea; for nothing is mentioned about Thomas, and despite the prominence of James in Luke's Gospel, in Acts all we learn about him is that he was killed in a persecution under Herod (Acts 12:2). As for Andrew, and Bartholomew, and Matthew, and all the rest who are routinely listed in Acts 1:13 as the Apostles—and we may even add the newly elected Apostle Matthias—nothing at all is reported of their Apostolic work. What did James the brother of Jesus do, apart from presiding over the meeting reported in Acts 15, and how did he rise to prominence? For that matter, what became of Peter after his quiet departure to Caesarea in Acts 12:19? Apart from his sudden reappearance to testify in Jerusalem in Acts 15, we hear nothing. *Why?*

Given the detailed and ample treatment Luke accords the adventures of Paul, the only sensible answer is that he simply did not have much, or perhaps *any,* information about the others. What would possibly have kept him from presenting it if it had fallen into his hands? He knew a good deal about Paul, and perhaps had access to a travel-diary written by someone who had occasionally accompanied him;[9] hence he is able to fill half of his second book with Paul's story, sometimes inaccurately but mostly in a manner consonant with everything else we know from other sources. But he must have known little or nothing about the other Apostles. He had a few stories about Peter, but even these give less information about the earliest Church than they may at first appear to do: the more detailed ones (in Acts 9-12) are situated outside Jerusalem, and arise from a time when Peter no longer resided there. In the second half of Acts, we learn virtually nothing about the Christians of Jerusalem. In the first half, despite Luke's fondness for the Twelve, and despite his having concluded his Gospel by having Jesus send them to preach to all nations, we hear nothing about their missions and never see them preaching, not even in Jerusalem, where they apparently remain—the one exception being Peter, the only member of the Twelve whom Luke represents as preaching the gospel of the Apostles. But notwithstanding Peter's prominence in the early chapters, where he does virtually all the work entrusted to the Twelve, even he becomes a shadowy figure. Luke leaves obscure the reasons for Peter's sojourn in Joppa (Acts 9:43), is evasive about his eventual departure from Jerusalem (Acts 12:17), and never mentions him again after his unexplained presence in the council of Acts 15. His replacement by James as leader of the Jerusalem community (acknowledged abruptly in Acts 12:17 and apparently presumed throughout Acts 15) is never accounted for—nor do we hear any significant news about James thereafter.

What all this indicates, it seems to me, is that Luke had much less information about the early Jerusalem community than he lets on, and that his myth of Christian origins probably inspired a fair amount of invention and guesswork in the course of his marshalling what he had. So it is not likely that we can recover the historical truth by accepting his account at face value. Luke's picture of the early days of the gospel of the Apostles needs to be handled with critical tact; our attempt to reconstruct that time and that gospel must counterbalance Luke's mythic imaginings with some critical imagination of our own. And that is precisely the task at hand.

THE FIRST GOSPEL OF THE APOSTLES

UNDERSTANDING THE RESURRECTION

Had Jesus' closest followers adequately understood the gospel of Jesus, his crucifixion might have spurred them to a more fervent proclamation of it, as Jesus seems to have been spurred by the death of John the Baptist. But all accounts agree that they were fearful and disheartened. Not a single member of the Twelve is said to have remained with him to the end. The Synoptic tradition is probably right in representing that they scattered back to Galilee, leaving the burial of Jesus' body to others. It appears that the gospel had died with Jesus.

And so it was resurrected with him also. The accounts are not agreed on just where or when or to whom the first resurrection appearances took place, but that does not matter very much. All accounts agree that the fundamental fact is that the Apostles came to know Jesus as risen from the dead, and the gospel was alive once more.

But what gospel? The answer is not as obvious as it might seem. It is easy to assume that the witnessing Apostles were immediately prepared to proclaim salvation through belief in the resurrection and Lordship of Jesus, and to initiate immediately the full Christian gospel of the Apostles. But what are the grounds for such an assumption? How did the Apostles *acquire* this new gospel?

It did not come automatically with Jesus' resurrection, for while that clearly vindicated his gospel, it did not establish a new one to take its place. What else did Jesus' resurrection prove? It reestablished his authenticity and gave a special position to the witnesses, but there are virtually no necessary implications beyond that. Believing in Jesus' resurrection was possible through trust in the witnesses; but understanding the meaning of Jesus' resurrection must have been a problem from the start, for the witnesses as well as for those to whom they preached.

One potential solution to this problem of understanding the resurrection is offered by the Gospels and Acts, which represent that Jesus conversed with his disciples (especially the Apostles) after his resurrection. Such an event clearly affords the possibility of having Jesus brief the Apostles on the significance of his resurrection, even on the content of the new gospel they were now to proclaim. This is attractive and convenient in a number of ways, especially in its most popular version, found at the beginning of Acts, where the risen Jesus appeared to the Apostles "by many convincing proofs, being seen by them through forty days and speaking the things concerning the Dominion of God" (Acts 1:3). Forty days of teaching could clarify a lot of things.

But Acts' forty days of tutorials can find no support in the other versions, not even in the ending of Luke's own Gospel. All three Synoptic Gospels have Jesus disappear shortly after his resurrection (the Gospel of Luke seems to allow less than a day between resurrection and ascension), and the instructions given by the risen Jesus are few and vague. Mark's Jesus tells the Apostles to preach an unspecified good news, adding that unbelievers will be condemned while believers will be saved and will work wonders (Mk 16:15-18), and then leaves them, without instructions on either resurrection or gospel. Matthew's Jesus announces that all power has been given to him and sends the Apostles to make disciples of all nations, teaching them to observe what Jesus has commanded (Mt 28:18-20), whatever that may be. Luke's Jesus teaches them to understand that the Scriptures ordain the Messiah's suffering and resurrection to glory (Lk 24:25-27,32,44-46), but otherwise adds only that repentance and forgiveness of sins are to be preached in his name to all nations (Lk 24:47). Those whom the risen Jesus sends forth in the Fourth Gospel (Jn 20:21) are sent without instruction, told only that they have the power to forgive and retain sins (Jn 20:23). And to the inconsistencies, the incompletenesses, and the oddities of these accounts may be added the earliest surviving record of what happened, Paul's testimony to the Corinthians in 1 Cor 15:1-11. Paul lists the various appearances of the risen Jesus, and attests that they are important to the preaching of the Apostles, but says nothing about any communications received on those occasions, though it would have been useful for him to do so in support of his point. He evidently knows only that the Apostles saw, not heard.

Even in Acts, for all its forty days of briefings, the Apostles do not seem to understand any better at the time of Jesus' ascension than at their first discovery of his resurrection. At the beginning of Acts, they are still far from grasping what was eventually to become their distinctive Apostolic gospel. Indeed, it seems that they had still not fully comprehended even the gospel of Jesus, for just before his ascension they are still dreaming about the restoration of political sovereignty to Israel as the culmination of what Jesus had started (Acts 1:6).

The inescapable conclusion, it seems to me, is that we cannot rely on stories of face-to-face instruction of the Apostles by the risen Jesus, whether for forty days or forty minutes. This is evidently not how the Apostles really came to understand what Jesus' resurrection meant or what their distinctive gospel was supposed to be. How then did this change come about?

The Apostles were alone with a private and very startling experience that needed interpretation, and they understood themselves to be called to proclaim a gospel. But no one except themselves alone was in a position to tell them what to think and what to preach. They had somehow been graced as Apostles and witnesses, and they had to learn what was to be learned by reconsidering, in the light of the unexpected crucifixion that had dashed their hopes and the resurrection that had even more unexpectedly restored them, their main sources of authoritative understanding: the Scriptures, the teaching and career of Jesus (and of John the Baptist before him), and their own habits of thought.

The first effect of the resurrection was presumably to restore to the Apostles the convictions that had been stolen away by the crucifixion: the gospel and the gospeller they had known were indeed fully authentic, vindicated by God, supported by divine power. The crucifixion may not have destroyed their faith in the truth of the gospel; it certainly need not have done so if they had understood Jesus well, for his message had provided for the possibility and even the likelihood of the suffering and death of those who belonged to the Dominion of God. John, after all, had not been discredited by his inglorious death at Herod's hands. But the Apostles had wavered, and saw from their own experience that the crucifixion must compromise the credibility of any gospel they could preach in Jesus' name. The resurrection gave tham a gospel again.

But it was still essentially the gospel they had known, the gospel of Jesus as it had developed and perfected the gospel of John the Baptist. They had no other new information and no other gospel, only their witness to Jesus' resurrection as a confirmation of the gospel he had commissioned them to proclaim.

The essence of the first post-resurrection gospel must therefore have been the impending Dominion of God and the universal necessity of repentance. That is what the Apostles were used to. That is the gospel they themselves had accepted and the only gospel they could have been trained to promulgate. They wanted to win others to it. They could scarcely have failed to play their trump card, the one that had definitively taken their own once-wavering confidence: Jesus, the gospeller extraordinary, had been raised from the dead.

Life is full of surprises, especially for the trusting and unwary. The Apostles undoubtedly thought that their witness to the news of Jesus' resurrection would make their gospel definitively persuasive. But it was bound to have, for the most part, exactly the opposite effect, stimulating most of their hearers simply to dismiss their testimony—and with it, their gospel—as being too flatly incredible.

The credibility of the gospel of John the Baptist had not faced this problem. Jesus evidently saw John's death within a divine providential plan, foretold by the Scriptures and resembling the usual fate of authentic prophets. John's death was regrettable, but no occasion for loss of confidence in what he had preached. The sign of his gospel's truth was the sign of Jonah: he preached the judgment and the need for deep and lasting repentance, and it worked—not universally but impressively, both before and after his death. But the incorporation of Jesus' resurrection into a new gospel shifted the center of gravity from something public to something very private, and thus, ironically, probably weakened rather than strengthened the public credibility of the gospel of the Dominion of God.

The earliest results of the Apostolic preaching must therefore have pointed up an acute need to understand further the meaning of Jesus' resurrection in order to make it more readily believable. The witnessed fact was not enough. It had to be shown to make good sense within God's providence, and that meant that it had to be shown to be part of the revealed divine plan blueprinted in Scripture.

UNDERSTANDING THE SCRIPTURES

Just how the Apostles went about reinterpreting the Scriptures, we unfortunately (and rather surprisingly) do not know. That it was done there can be no doubt. Paul's testimony is the earliest we have, and for Paul it was already a routine part of the Apostolic gospel that Jesus "was raised on the third day, in accordance with the Scriptures" (1 Cor 15:1,4). But we do not know much about how they read the Scriptures to support the claim that they predicted Jesus' resurrection. What has been passed down is obviously incomplete. We know they had a particular way of reading Psalm 16 (Acts 2:25-28,31; 13:34-37), Psalm 110 (Acts 2:34-35), Isaiah 55:3 (Acts 13:34),

Habakkuk 1:5 (Acts 13:40-41). But (as can easily be seen by anyone who ponders only these sample instances) the new readings sometimes involved intricate interrelationships of reinterpreted texts, and the surviving examples may be only the tip of the iceberg. Neither Paul nor anyone else tells us which texts were used to verify the claim that Scripture predicted a resurrection "on the third day." Luke, projecting this reinterpretive industry back into the fancied instructions of the risen Jesus, claims that "beginning from Moses and from all the prophets . . . in all the Scriptures" the key events about Jesus were foretold (Lk 24:27; cf. 24:44-46). This detailed correspondence may have been more an article of faith than an actual accomplishment, but it was an important principle. The scope was potentially huge, embracing reinterpretations of all the Scriptures, and the room for ingenuity is indicated by the regrettably few examples that were preserved. The conviction that the texts secretly pointed to Jesus and could be bent to fit him probably made much more impact than the particular reinterpretations.

Making Scripture predict Jesus' resurrection—especially making Scripture *in general* point in this direction—required considerable interpretive ingenuity. No less was required in the second project, making theological sense of the matter. It is one thing to say that God had predicted a surprising fact—say, the Babylonian Exile, or the establishment of an Israelite monarchy, or the building of the Temple—but quite another thing to make sense of it, to make it seem appropriate despite its surprise. Theology hungers after appropriateness. Whether that hunger is itself theologically appropriate is, from a historical perspective, entirely beside the point: the historical point is that the hunger was there, and made a difference. Jesus' resurrection was asked to make sense, and making sense meant making *religious* sense, and as much as possible.

The resulting interpretation of Jesus' resurrection invested it with meaning boldly and dramatically. It was not an offhand miraculous validation of the authentic gospel but a providentially central event, a major revelation: indeed, *the* major revelation. This is what revelation was really all about. Against the hesitations of their hearers, the Apostles claimed an urgent and ultimate significance; if you dismiss this (and especially if you dismiss the gospel on this account), you miss the *whole* point: this *is* the point on which everything turns; Jesus is the point on which everything turns. What have you thought the Scriptures promised? This, and he, must be understood as fulfillment. Do you read Deut 18:18-19 as a promise of an eschatological prophet (and evidently many did)? This is he (Acts 3:22-23). Do you think prophecy in general points to a special time of rescue (and evidently many did)? This is it, and this is how (Acts 3:24). Do you think the promise to Abraham holds more than what has already been realized (and evidently many did)? This completes it, through him (Acts 3:25-26). And, above all, moving well beyond Scripture to popular lore: do you think that God has promised a Messiah (and evidently many did, quite fervently)? Then know he has come, and this is he, the risen Jesus.

UNDERSTANDING THE MESSIAH

This latter point, about the Messiah, appears to have been the most salient among an overkill arsenal of claims, the one that most caught popular attention even if not the one most promoted at first. Probably it was *not* the one most promoted at first, since the career of Jesus did not conform conveniently—or, indeed, at all—to what the Messiah was supposed to be. But popular expectation *would* have a Messiah, despite the fact that Scripture made no such promise;[10] and the Apostles (who may well have continued to cling to this popular expectation, despite Jesus' lack of encouragement and his gospel's lack of room for such a notion) said yes, this is he. This claim was part of the logic of the general claim that, whatever you are looking for, this is he. It was against the grain of Scripture, against the grain of popular Messianic expectation, against the grain of the gospel as proclaimed by John and by Jesus, and quite unnecessary theologically. But, by popular demand, Jesus became Messiah.

Jesus' followers (or at least some of them) had been eager to fasten this title upon him during his pre-crucifixion gospelling. Indeed, their eagerness was probably an important contributing factor to his conviction and death. But there is no good reason to suppose he shared it. The role had no place in the gospel he preached, nor in the gospel of John the Baptist before him. Jesus did not look for a restoration of the Davidic throne. The one occasion on which Jesus is reported to have discussed the Messianic expectation of his contemporaries shows him arguing that the scribes and Pharisees must be wrong in supposing that the One Who Is to Come in the Name of the Lord can be a descendent of David. But the general popular hope in a Davidic rescuer, supported in some quarters by scholarly argument, proved too strong. Rather than setting the notion aside, as Jesus seems to have done in the interests of a grander gospel, the Apostles put forward the claim that Jesus was he—that in spite of the public appearance of failure and discredit, he had been constituted as Messiah by his resurrection and exaltation (Acts 2:36—cf. Acts 4:27), or that he had all along been Messiah but had not been recognized (or indeed, recognizable) as such because of a misreading of what Scripture had promised and required.

Eventually, the Apostles made Jesus the key figure in the gospel of John the Baptist. He was identified as the One Who Comes, following John to complete his work, even to the extent of baptizing with fire and the Holy Spirit. He was identified with his own gospel's Son of Man, the one who will preside over the coming Judgment, and with the King who organizes the Kingdom that is to come. He was identified with the eschatological prophet, the messenger of the New Covenant, and probably with Elijah. There were ways of making sense of all of this by bending Scriptural interpretation and the words of

John's and Jesus' gospels to the shape of Jesus' career. The major impediment to this enterprise was Jesus' apparent radical disqualification: he had been executed publically as a criminal. No agent of hope was expected to conclude his mission in such a way. No message that proclaimed the importance of such a one could fail to deal with the stumbling block of the cross.

UNDERSTANDING THE CRUCIFIXION

If the meaning of the resurrection was at first difficult to puzzle out, the meaning of the crucifixion must have been flatly baffling. Its impact seems to have been uniformly and universally negative. Even after the gospel of the Apostles had acquired considerable experience and sophistication, it remained a stumbling block to the Jews and folly to the Greeks, as Paul testifies (1 Cor 1:23). At the very first, the crucifixion seems to have been fairly devastating to the Apostles themselves, and it was undoubtedly a greater impediment to the reception of the earliest Apostolic gospel than was the awkwardness of their resurrection witness. How did the gospel of the Apostles deal with the cross?

There is reason to suppose that the cross was given no positive value in the beginnings of the Apostolic gospel. The first proclamation presented in Acts asserts that the crucifixion took place in accordance with God's will and foreknowledge, but claims no more than that (Acts 2:23). The second proclamation proposes it only as the fulfillment of the Messiah's promised requirement of suffering (Acts 3:18). The third proclamation presents it as a horrendous and ironic blunder on the part of the Jewish leadership, rejecting precisely the destined agent of their salvation (Acts 4:10-11), and this is also the main emphasis of Acts 5:28,30 and Acts 10:39, as well as a point of minor emphasis in Acts 2:23 and Acts 3:13-15. It is likely that this lack of positive claims is close to the historical truth. The crucifixion appeared to be a divine judgment against Jesus. The most obvious theological response is to remove that appearance through the claim that it is part of God's plan, that it was anticipated in the Scriptures, and that the judgment falls not upon the victim but upon those responsible for his death. Doubtless, this response already existed in a prefabricated form, for dealing with the scandal of John the Baptist's execution had provided a precedent. John's enemies had done to him what they pleased, as it had been written (Mk 9:13), and as it had been done to prophets before him. Jesus had followed the same pattern—and woe to those who have done this to him, unless they repent in the face of the new and more urgent summons proclaimed by the gospel of the Apostles.

The treatment of Jesus' cross in the early chapters of Acts is striking in two ways. The first is the absence of any positive value in Jesus' death; the second is the way in which his death is made a proof of his Messiahship.

The first of these contrasts notably with the Epistles of Paul, which insist on the redemptive effect of Jesus' crucifixion. From what Paul says here and there, especially in the opening chapters of 1 Corinthians, it appears that his emphasis on this motif was not usual in the gospel of the Apostles, but he makes it clear in 1 Corinthians 15 that he was by no means the inventor of it. It was part of the gospel he himself had been offered by those who were Apostles before him: Christ died for our sins, in accordance with the Scriptures (1 Cor 15:3). This interpretation of the cross therefore came early to the Apostolic gospel. But it did not necessarily come in the very earliest phase, the first days—or weeks, or perhaps even months—of the new proclamation. The gospel of the Apostles evidently claimed from the start that salvation and forgiveness of sins come through belief in Jesus, but not necessarily that they are effected by means of his crucifixion.

The second striking feature of the Acts' representations of the cross in the earliest Apostolic gospel, confirmed by other evidence as well, is the incorporation of Jesus' cross into specifically Messianic theology. The logic of this is not difficult to figure out. The cross was the most obviously un-Messianic aspect of Jesus' career; his ignominious death would apparently make it impossible to claim Messianic status for him. If the gospel of the Apostles would claim that he was Messiah, it must confront this problem directly. It is therefore not surprising that the ingenuities of Scriptural interpretation recorded in Acts' speeches are dedicated primarily to demonstrating that the miraculous sign of the resurrection had been predicted (albeit in a hidden way) as the Messianic feature *par excellence,* and that therefore a temporary death was inevitable and according to plan. Why *this* form of death, the scandalous cross? We are not told in any detail. We are simply told that the Messiah had to die, so as to be raised to glory. It was necessary. It has happened. Whatever temporary embarrassment and confusion the crucifixion had caused, it was in fact on the divine agenda and has been definitively overcome. But note that focusing on the specifically Messianic aspect of the cross changes the meaning of the theologizing about suffering that had been part of the gospel of Jesus. Suffering is no longer a general condition for the righteous, the Dominion of God, the Son of Man. It now becomes a special feature of the Messiah. However they had once understood the death of John the Baptist, the Apostles now concentrated their attention on the death of Jesus, and probably diverted to it the Scriptural interpretations and reflections by which they had digested John's death—not to assimilate Jesus to a pattern already confirmed by John, but to make Jesus *rather than* John (and the other sons of the Dominion) the fulfillment of prophecy. The suffering of the Son of Man is really the suffering of Jesus himself.

The earliest gospel of the Apostles was thus basically completed. The Dominion of God would come, presided over by Jesus as Messiah. The baptism by which we are to be made ready for that Dominion was to be received in Jesus' name.

The promised judgment would arrive, with Jesus as "the one designated by God as judge of the living and the dead" (Acts 10:42). Forgiveness of sins was available to those who enlist in Jesus' name. The Messiah had come, fulfilled what the Scriptures predicted of him, and now reigns in invisible glory. The great pre-gospelling of Scripture and the great news of John and of Jesus were now clarified in a new and definitive edition.

Almost all the major features of earlier gospels were recapitulated and reinterpreted in this new gospel of the Apostles. The baptism of John and the predicted greater Baptizer to come were reaffirmed and redirected; the impending Dominion of God was brought under the Lordship of the exalted Jesus; the suffering and glorification of the Son of Man was attached to the crucified and resurrected Messiah; the promise of forgiveness of sins to the repentant—indeed, the promise made to Abraham—was brought under Jesus' jurisdiction, available to, and only to, those who believed in him. The earlier gospels were recapitulated and reinterpeted—and utterly changed. Thus dismantled and reorganized, they became a new gospel—the gospel of the Apostles.

THE GOSPEL OF THE HELLENIST APOSTLES

Luke does not give us much help in the task of reconstructing the process by which the gospel of the Apostles came to be. He contradicts himself in his attempts to attribute it to the instructions of the risen Jesus, and even then leaves the disciples somewhat uncomprehending. Once the Apostolic gospel is received and launched, he prefers to put Peter in charge of proclaiming it and also leaves it to Peter to extend it to the Gentiles, with the Jerusalem Apostles giving their seal of approval. Somehow, the Apostles acquired their gospel and ushered it harmoniously into the world; any disagreements were temporary, and were authoritatively resolved. Such a smoothly continuous development from conservative roots by legitimately constituted leaders preserves the myth, but steals for the Twelve credit that belongs to others—for instance, to the anonymous evangelists who preached the gospel to Gentiles in Antioch (Acts 11:20). If those evangelists are to have their due, we must suspend the myth and unravel a few of Luke's seams in order to discover something about the gospel they preached—the gospel of the Hellenist Apostles.

The gospel of the Hellenists was a gospel of the Apostles in the sense in which this chapter generally uses the terms: a message by authoritative proclaimers of the truth revealed in Jesus, a public evangelizing on which a substantive number of Christians formed their understanding of the good news. Whether or not its proclaimers were regularly called Apostles, Paul may have used that title for them, for his catalogue of resurrection witnesses in 1 Corinthians 15 lists the order of appearances as having been to Peter, then the Twelve, then five hundred unnamed brethren at once, then James, "then all the Apostles," and finally Paul himself (1 Cor 15:5-8). Who are "all the Apostles"? Paul is not likely to mean the Twelve, both because he has just mentioned them and because his battles over the issue would certainly have led him to avoid using the terms interchangeably: for him, the Twelve are the Twelve, and the Apostles are the Apostles. He does not name names; but if Luke is right about the details of Paul's itinerary as Paul made his way to Jerusalem for the last time, to his imprisonment, then Paul was probably the houseguest of one of these unnamed additional Apostles. For Luke reports that "we came to Caesarea, and entering into the house of Philip the evangelist, one of the Seven, we stayed with him" (Acts 21:8). "Evangelist," or "preacher of the gospel," is about as close as one can get to saying "Apostle" without actually using the word. I think it likely that Philip and the rest of "the Seven" are among—if not identical with—those whom Paul so casually (or evasively) designates as the remainder of "all the Apostles."

THE ORIGIN OF THE HELLENIST GOSPEL

The main body of evidence by which we can follow through with this hint about "Philip the evangelist" comes likewise from Acts, but it requires some reading between the Lucan lines. The relevant story takes place mainly in Acts 6:

> But in those days, what with the disciples much increased in number, there arose a murmuring of the Hellenists against the Hebrews, about the overlooking of their widows in the daily ministry. Accordingly, the Twelve, having summoned the crowd of disciples, said: "It is not good for us to leave aside the Word of God to wait on tables. But, brothers, search out from your number seven men attested as full of spirit and wisdom, whom we will appoint to deal with this need, ourselves then keeping to prayer and the ministry of the Word." And this announcement was quite satisfactory to the whole crowd, and they chose Stephen, a man full of faith and Holy Spirit, and Philip, and Prochorus, and Nikanor, and Timon, and Parmenas, and Nicholas (a convert from Antioch), whom they presented to the Apostles—and after praying, they ordained them. (Acts 6:1-6)

On the surface, the story seems likely enough—a plausible account of a minor squabble and its sensible solution. But just below the surface, it begins to look curious. Why should the Twelve suppose that these community welfare ministrations would otherwise be their own personal responsibility? If they were already in charge of the services to "Hebrew" women, the same objections made here about distracting them from the ministry of the Word would hold in that case as well. Why specify the number of *seven* new administrators? And why insist on their being full of spirit and wisdom, rather than requiring practical efficiency, reliability, good reputation for fairness, or the like? Were these Greek-named Seven to take over the entire operation of the Jerusalem Christians, or only minister to the "Hellenist" community, whatever that might be?

These questions may properly arise from a close look at the account. If the verses I have just quoted were all we had, we might well conclude that the questions are irresolvable, though intriguing, and that there was perhaps a rationale that made evident sense at the time but has been lost to history. But the remaining verses in that same passage raise still starker questions.

For despite the carefully specified terms according to which the Seven were appointed, we never again hear anything about their "waiting on tables" or otherwise participating in the welfare operations in Jerusalem (or wherever). Two verses later, we find Stephen—already oddly emphasized in the quoted text as being full of faith and the Holy Spirit—described as being "full of grace and power, doing great signs and wonders among the people" (Acts 6:8). Signs and wonders are not the normal marks of a waiter on tables, but they are familiar in the New Testament as part of the credentials of an Apostle. The next verse announces that some of those to whom Stephen preached rose up in argument against him, "but they were not able to withstand the wisdom and the spirit with which he spoke" (Acts 6:9-10). The illusion of table-service has totally vanished. Stephen is obviously an evangelist. His gospel is powerful, but jarring to the conservatism of his hearers, who accuse him of blaspheming Moses and God. The indignant people, together with the elders and scribes, arrest him and haul him before the Sanhedrin (Acts 6:11-12). The charge is blaspheming against the Temple and the Law by claiming "that this Jesus of Nazareth will destroy this place and will change the customs which Moses delivered to us" (Acts 6:13-14).

Asked to answer to the charges, Stephen launches into a speech that can hardly be a record of his actual utterances at trial. It is too long and too little to the point: Luke has apparently taken a document related to the incident and made it into a fictitiously situated oration.[11] But in the course of doing so, Luke perhaps gives away more of the truth than he intended to do—probably even more than he realized to be the truth. The accusations against Stephen, Luke's narratorial voice has claimed, were made by suborned false witnesses (Acts 6:11,13). But if Luke had read carefully the speech he then places in Stephen's mouth, he would have realized that the witnesses had been at least partially justified: for Stephen clearly blames Solomon for building a Temple, the inappropriateness of which Stephen signals by arguments from reason, tradition, and Scripture (Acts 7:44-50). Stephen concludes by berating his judges about their being in a long tradition of religious blundering—the heirs of those who consistently persecuted the prophets, and the betrayers and murderers of the one whose coming those prophets had predicted (Acts 7:51-53). He then sees and announces a vision of the Son of Man, which is too much for his accusers: they stone him, and he calls upon "Lord Jesus" as he dies (Acts 7:57-60).

Finally, Luke shows some real information apart from the Twelve Apostles. He knows that in the early days there was a group of Seven, including Stephen, Philip, and five others (about whom he seems to have known only the names), who were called "deacons" and were important leaders associated with a group known as "Hellenists." True to his usual form, he subordinates the provocative Seven to the orderly Twelve, possibly because he (or his source) misguidedly supposed that "deacon" (i.e., minister of the Word, as in Peter's designation of the Twelve in Acts 6:4) meant what it had come to mean by Luke's time, a subordinate ecclesiastical title associated with table-service. But whether the subordination was Luke's work or pre-existed in his source, and whether it was an innocent misunderstanding or a deliberate falsification, it is too superficial in this account to disguise the truth behind it: Stephen was not an appointee of the Twelve, but represented a different early Christian group and a different gospel of the Apostles.

Who then were these "Hellenists" from whom the Seven emerged with a gospel so offensive to conservative Jews as to produce the first Christian martyr? Some suppose they were Greek-speaking Jews; but "Hellenists" (*Hellēnistai*) is not the plausible word for that (*Hellēnizontes* is the obvious term if the issue were language), nor is "Hebrews" the likely designation for speakers of Hebrew or Aramaic (which would be *Hebraizontes*). Nor is it a matter of distinction between Gentile converts and born Jews: a convert was a proselyte (*prosēlutos*), as in the case of Stephen's colleague Nicholas, who is thus distinguished from the rest of the Seven (Acts 6:5). I think it much more plausible that the clue to the meaning of these terms lies in the story of Stephen's trial, and that the Hellenists and Hebrews represent divisions within Judaism that go back two centuries before it, to the days of Antiochus IV. The books of Maccabees and Daniel deal with the urgent contention that took place then, between "reformers" who relaxed Jewish customs to adopt the cultural ways of the Greeks, and traditionalists who insisted that only the ancestral observances would do. The latter required that the Law be observed literally and without compromise; the former promoted forms of Greek enlightenment that entailed the abandonment of some of the Law's precepts, including circumcision. One of the most obvious ways of labelling them is to call them, respectively, Hebrews and Hellenists.[12]

I suggest accordingly that the Hellenists of Acts 6 were effectually "Protestant" Jews, who had suspended various observances and ideas through a reform movement which their opponents inevitably associated with the influence of the Greeks, while the Hebrews were their religiously conservative counterparts who would not compromise their ancestral ways. Luke's source points to two distinguishable, and perhaps not mutually communicative, groups within the Jews that became also distinct groups within the Christian body, one of them (the Hebrews) following the kind of conservative Jewish piety that Luke associates with the Twelve Apostles, and the other (the Hellenists) following a more liberalized path—and gospel—that was far more objectionable to the Jewish authorities.

Luke accepts and approves of both. He also uses traditions stemming from each. His governing myth is formed in the Hebrew image and supposes that it was the Hebrews who best understood Jesus and carried on his perfected work in the gospel of the Apostles and in a Church governed by religiously conservative principles. But Jesus' Hellenist disciples may have understood his liberties with the Law and his detachment from the Temple more adequately, and what Luke discloses about the Seven seems, despite his attempt to subordinate them to the Twelve, to point to Hellenist Christians, Hellenist Apostles, and a specifically Hellenist gospel.

Luke's account of the origin of the Seven is factitious and fictitious, derived from the assumption that the early Jerusalem Christians either were or ought to have been a unified community under the leadership of the Twelve Apostles. If the story of the ordination of the Seven was not Luke's invention, then it probably originated in the same manner as the rumors and assumptions that bedevilled Paul about the authenticity of his own Apostolic office. Those who did not like what they thought Paul was preaching preferred to believe that he was a secondary agent whose gospel and whose permission to proclaim it came from the leadership of the Twelve Apostles; any differences between their preaching and his could then be dismissed as the unauthorized liberties of an underling. So it must have been with the Seven: if they preached a gospel offensive to conservative sensibilities, their effect could be conveniently neutralized—either for the sake of un-Christianized Jews whose tolerance was desired, or for the sake of scandalized conservative Christians—by representing them as commissioned subordinates who had irresponsibly gone beyond their authorization.

Luke is probably not the inventor of the misrepresentations about the Seven, just as he is probably innocent in his subordination of Paul. He reports their accomplishments with pride and approval, never suggesting that they had overstepped their bounds or acted objectionably. By his day, the Temple was gone and the Jewish Law no longer governed Christian observance; Stephen was obviously a heroic pioneer of the gospel that had prevailed. If the ordination of the Seven is rooted in a distrust of their mission, it is not Luke's distrust but a relic of earlier and more troubled times. And that the times were troubled can scarcely be in doubt. The tension between the Hellenists and the Hebrews was not likely to have been founded on a squabble about attention to Hellenist widows. The issue was theological, having to do with a difference in gospel. And the difference was sufficient to inspire a persecution of the gospel of the Hellenist apostles.

Stephen's fate was not entirely an isolated incident. Some conservative Jews—possibly even some conservative Christian Jews—who were offended by what he had to say in Jesus' name against the permanence of the Temple and of the Law of Moses were evidently offended by all those who were of his party and held his opinions. The aftermath is reported by Luke immediately after his account of Stephen's death: "And there was in that day a great persecution against the Church in Jerusalem—all were scattered through the regions of Judea and Samaria, except the Apostles" (Acts 8:1). The verse reads plausibly until we reach the last phrase, at which point it becomes flatly incredible. Drive out the followers and leave the leaders in their places? No persecution was ever conducted thus. Luke has something quite wrong.

The persecution reported in Acts 8:1 was almost certainly real. The unreal part, Luke's report that the "Apostles" were exempted, indicates that Luke at this point had two major sources of information. One came from the group that operated under the leadership of Peter; and according to it, the Apostles continued to operate effectively, perhaps literally in Jerusalem, during and after the persecution that arose about the preaching of Stephen. Hence it was clear to Luke that the

"Apostles" (i.e., in terms of Luke's myth and his conservative sources, the Twelve) were not affected by the persecution. His other source originated in the community related to the Seven: it was their theology that was especially unacceptable to conservative Jews, and it was they and their followers who were driven from Jerusalem. From their perspective, the persecution drove out everyone, the whole Church. Luke blends the two sources of information with the clumsiness that belongs to dutiful innocence.

Those who were driven out by the persecution, Luke reports from his Christian Hellenist sources, wandered about gospelling the word (Acts 8:4). They did so in Judea and Samaria, according to Acts 8:1, and when Luke resumes his attention to the same sources in Acts 11:19-20, he adds, "Those who were scattered on account of the persecution that occurred about Stephen travelled to Phoenicia and Cyprus and Antioch, not speaking the word to anyone but Jews—but there were some of them, men from Cyprus and Cyrene, who, settling in Antioch, spoke to the Greeks, gospelling the Lord Jesus" (Acts 11:19-20). They were successful. Luke adds a few verses later that the title "Christians" (*christianoi,* i.e., Messiahists) was first used in Antioch (Acts 11:26).

This casual reporting offers an invaluable set of historical disclosures. First, it was the gospel of the Hellenist Seven that introduced the good news to a range of places outside the traditional Jewish homeland: Phoenicia and Cyprus and Antioch. Second, it was this gospel that was first offered to the Samaritans and Gentiles—not Peter's, not even Paul's, but one like Stephen's. Third, the gospel of the Hellenist Apostles evidently emphasized the title "Messiah" (*Christos*) in a way that brought its followers to be called accordingly. And a tentative fourth, derived from these and other evidences: the version of Christianity which Saul of Tarsus persecuted and finally accepted was founded on the gospel not of the Hebrew Twelve but of the Hellenist Seven. Luke knew that the gospel Saul had hated and persecuted was linked with Stephen (thus

Acts 7:58 and 8:1), but Galatians 1:13-24 permits us to go correctively further, to surmise that Saul met it in Damascus rather than Jerusalem, and that it was probably in fact the only Christian gospel he knew in his persecuting days.[13] His idea of Christianity was formed by, and his eventual conversion was to, the gospel of the Hellenist Apostles.

THE CONTENT OF THE HELLENIST GOSPEL

What was the content of the gospel of the Hellenist Apostles? The evidence is scanty. We know from pieces here and there that it was offensive to those who revered the Temple and the Law, that it proclaimed the Dominion of God, that it emphasized the title "Messiah," that it was founded on claims about Jesus of Nazareth (Acts 6:14, 8:5,12,16,35). We are told (and have no good reason to doubt) that it was effective with the Samaritans and the Gentiles, which tends to confirm its detachment from Temple and Law, which in turn explains why it was persecuted and suggests why it may have been objectionable to Christian Hebrews. Much of this content is in continuity with the gospel of Jesus, and to it may be added one more potentially significant hint. The last provocative words of Stephen before his stoning are reported to have been "Behold, I see the heavens opened, and the Son of Man standing at the right hand of God" (Acts 7:56).

This is the only instance in the entire New Testament of a reference to the Son of Man by anyone other than Jesus. It is not likely to have been Luke's invention. But Luke may be responsible for the narrator's description of what Stephen saw, as distinguished from Stephen's own words. The narrator says that Stephen saw the glory of God, and Jesus standing at his right hand (Acts 7:55). That may be the same thing, but not necessarily. Stephen reports a vision not of Jesus but of the Son of Man. At his own trial, Jesus is reported to have testified that the Son of Man will be seated at the right hand of God

(Mt 26:64, Mk 14:62, Lk 22:69). This was an apt affirmation of his own gospel: those who have given themselves over to the Dominion of God will, after their present sufferings, be glorified at his right hand. It is possible that Stephen's testimony, so obviously parallel, meant the same thing: Jesus' gospel of the Dominion of God and the *collective* glorified Son of Man was true; whatever the threat or the reality of present suffering for the sake of that gospel, those who enlist in the Dominion of God on Jesus' terms will triumph in the end.

If the Hellenist gospel used the title Son of Man at first, it was apparently not for long. It is not heard again. But there may be some important continuity between that title and another that Stephen is *not* said to have used, though it evidently became characteristic of the Hellenist gospel: Messiah, Christ. Luke reports that the name "Christians," Messiahists, was first used in Antioch after the Hellenist mission had established itself there (Acts 11:26). What did it mean, and why was it applied?

"Messiah" was not an unequivocal and settled term. To many traditionalists, it implied Davidic origin, Bethlehem birth, eventual kingship. It has these associations in the Synoptic Gospels, and probably among most Hebrew Christians, and became established early on as Jesus' title. But it did not necessarily mean the same things to Hellenist Jews or to Hellenist Christians. These are not Paul's favorite associations with the title, and I suspect that they were not the usual associations for those from whom he first learned what the "Messiahists" he persecuted were all about. One can easily imagine why the followers of Jesus might be called "Jesuists," but why *Christians*? Whether the term was applied derisively by others or piously by themselves, I suggest that it was applied because there was something more striking about their doctrine of Messiah than the mere claim that the term applied to Jesus.

Let me propose what it might have been. Suppose that Stephen and his colleagues had understood that Jesus had meant by the term Son of Man exactly what Daniel had meant—the collective of the glorified righteous—and that his fellow-believers continued to mean this when, outside Palestine and in a new mission field, they shifted away from it to the term Christ, Messiah. I suggest, that is, that the Antiochene nickname arose not exclusively because the Hellenists claimed that Jesus was the Messiah, but because they claimed that *they* were, that through Jesus they were now members of Christ, Messiah, formerly known as the Son of Man. The collectivity of the Dominion of God, with Jesus as its foremost member—Lord of the Dominion and head of the whole body of Christ—is a doctrine familiar from Paul's Epistles. I suggest that Paul may have learned it from those he once persecuted, and subsequently joined in their life "in Christ."

THE HELLENIST GOSPEL AND THE HOLY SPIRIT

There is one more theme—familiar also from Paul's writings—that must be considered in any account of the gospel of the Apostles: the Holy Spirit. Acts seems to make the Holy Spirit the single most important factor in the beginnings of the Apostolic gospel, and Luke would probably have preferred me to treat it in the section of this chapter entitiled "The First Gospel of the Apostles." But I suspect that Luke's tendency to centralize the Twelve and unify the story has got in the way in the case of the Holy Spirit too—and that the historical truth may be more precisely that the Holy Spirit was the single most important factor in the founding of the gospel of the *Hellenist* Apostles.

When I say that Acts makes the Holy Spirit the single most important factor in the beginnings of the Apostolic gospel, I mean that literally: it is more important than the resurrection of Jesus. Acts does not launch the new gospel with the resurrection, nor does it imply that the Apostles are sufficiently enlightened, despite the post-resurrection teachings of Jesus, to preach it. Jesus does not send them out to preach. He tells them to wait in Jerusalem "for the promise of the Father" (Acts 1:4), explaining that this is something "which you heard from me—that while John baptized with water, you will be baptized with Holy Spirit not many days from now" (Acts 1:4-5). When those days have elapsed, "you will receive power of the Holy Spirit coming down upon you," and then—and only then—"you shall be witnesses to me in Jerusalem, and in all Judea and Samaria, and to the ends of the earth" (Acts 1:8). With that, Jesus leaves them, and they return to Jerusalem to pray, to replace Judas in the college of the Twelve Apostles, and to wait obediently for the promise to be fulfilled.

What is especially notable about this opening is that it attests to the Pentecost event as the real point of departure for the gospel of the Apostles, and implies that it made such a dramatic and surprising difference that it had to be retrospectively anticipated by Jesus' predictions both before and after his resurrection, and grounded in Scripture. Whatever fancifulness may have gone into its particular details, the opening part of Acts bears witness to a memory that the Apostles did not preach their gospel, or even understand it yet, on Easter Sunday or a month later. It was, according to this memory, Pentecost's Holy Spirit that made the gospel of the Apostles possible.

But which gospel of the Apostles? On which Apostolic recollection does Luke here depend?

For Luke had two significantly different sources for Apostolic memories. One was rooted in the Synoptic tradition, with its intimate attachment to the Twelve; the other, to which his Synoptic colleagues perhaps had no access, came from those people who informed him that the activities of Stephen and the Seven inspired "a great persecution against the Church in Jerusalem, and all were scattered around the regions of Judea and Samaria . . . and those scattered by the persecution that took place about Stephen went on to Phoenicia and Cyprus and Antioch" (Acts 8:1, 11:19). Luke did not always know how to reconcile these two sources of information. The beginning of Acts shows an awkwardness that seems to derive from his attempt to conflate them.

The ending of Luke's Gospel represents Jesus' post-resurrection association with his disciples as lasting less than a day. To judge from what we learn from Matthew and Mark, this was the Synoptic tradition. Yet the beginning of Acts offers a period of forty days (Acts 1:3), a stylized figure that approximates the gap between the resurrection and Pentecost. The contradiction is blatant and unresolved. Behind it lies, I suggest, a pair of authentic memories, one from a group that recalled that the foundation of the Apostolic gospel was complete with the witnessing of Jesus' resurrection, and the other from a different group that remembered that it was completed only some weeks later. Matthew and Mark show nothing of the latter tradition, just as they show nothing of what Paul refers to as the final self-disclosure of the risen Jesus to "all the Apostles" (1 Cor 15:7). Luke's wider researches gathered in early memories from Christians who were not of the school of the Twelve; and it is this, I think, that led him away from the Synoptic tradition to have Jesus promise the Holy Spirit at the end of his Gospel (there is nothing that corresponds to this in Matthew and Mark) and to delay the completion of Apostolic understanding and the launching of the Apostolic gospel until this promise was fulfilled. I propose, that is, that the Hebrew side of the early Church traced its origins to Jesus' resurrection, and that the Pentecost experience was the foundation of the gospel of the Hellenists.

That is not, of course, the way Luke represents it. His myth was not hospitable to such a division. Indeed, he may have been entirely unaware that any such division had existed: naively receiving from his Hellenist informants that "the Church in Jerusalem" was persecuted and "all" were scattered, he extended the meaning more broadly and literally than was warranted. He was certainly capable of accepting a similar generalization about the outpouring of the Holy Spirit without realizing that what Hellenists called "all" did not necessarily include Hebrews or the Twelve. We know that he had information from the Jerusalem Hellenist Christians, we know that his sources about the Twelve were limited, and we know that he was inclined to harmonize his materials within the boundaries of his myth of Christian origins. He assimilated to Peter and the Twelve nearly everything that came to him from the earliest days. I do not think it unlikely that in his story of Pentecost, he has once more ascribed to them something that was not originally theirs.

Luke's portrayal of the Pentecost event is obviously full of stylized and implausible storytelling twists. The recipients of the Holy Spirit are seated within a house (Acts 2:2), yet their speaking in tongues draws a large and wondering crowd of witnesses (Acts 2:6). The witnesses are from various language groups and hear their own languages (Acts 2:6-11), yet somehow they know that the speakers do not know the languages and that others in the crowd are hearing different tongues. The improbability is obvious, expecially when Luke cannot make up his mind whether the speakers are miraculously gifted with other languages, or the hearers miraculously gifted to hear tongues not being spoken, or the speaking is an unintelligible babble that seems drunken (Acts 2:4,6-8,13,15). Luke has heaped together various versions of glossolalia and compacted them into an artificial setting in order to join the first dramatic reception of the Holy Spirit to the first dramatic proclamation of the gospel of the Apostles. In doing so, he has passed lightly over another feature of the scene: the rush of wind and the tongues of fire (Acts 2:2-3). These are transparently a way of characterizing the event as the fulfillment of the gospel of John the Baptist, which promised that his own baptism in water was only the shadow and the preparation of the greater baptism to come, in Holy Spirit (or holy wind) and fire. Whoever reported this to Luke was undoubtedly handing on a tradition in which this fulfillment of John was important, but Luke does not see to it that his reader will make the connection, nor does he have the Apostles report it to the crowds. It remains in his account as a fossil of a once-valued gospel fulfillment, a memory whose significance Luke does not seem to appreciate.

For Luke, neither the tongues of fire nor the miraculous foreign tongues remain important. The listeners forget the glossolalia and concentrate on the message they hear about "the great things of God" (2:11), and Peter's speech begins by insisting that the principal significance of all this is in the gift of vision and prophecy (Acts 2:16-18). The heart of it is the proclamation of a gospel that offers three dramatic pieces of news: first, God has raised the crucified Jesus from the dead, in accordance with Scriptural promises about the Messiah, and the Apostles are witnesses to this (Acts 2:23-32); second, Jesus has been exalted to God's right hand, in accordance with other Scriptural promises (Acts 2:33-35); and third, the exalted Jesus has received from the Father the promise of the Holy Spirit and has poured out what they may now see and hear (Acts 2:33). And then the grand summarizing conclusion: "Therefore, let the house of Israel know assuredly that God has made him both Lord and Messiah, this Jesus whom you crucified" (Acts 2:36).

Most of this is entirely familiar to anyone who has heard the Christian gospel at any time during the last nineteen centuries. But two features are not routine elements in the standard received gospel, and they are worth pausing over. One is that the gospel of Acts 2 does not say that Jesus *was* the Messiah: it says that he *has become* Messiah, that God made him Lord and Messiah—and it seems to imply clearly that God made him Lord and Messiah precisely in the act of raising him and exalting him to sit upon the heavenly throne. It does not claim that the Messiah was to have the throne of David, but, with a delicate ambiguity that is undoubtedly deliberate, claims rather that David, as a prophet, knew that God had promised that he would cause one of David's descendents to be seated upon "his" throne (Acts 2:30). But whose throne? The usual popular interpretation, of course, was that it referred to the presently vacant throne of David, but in this case it is clear that it is a heavenly throne, for the prophetic utterance of David cited in the following verse is interpreted as a reference to the resurrection of the Messiah (Acts 2:31), and the following three verses attest that Jesus has been resurrected and exalted and seated *at God's right hand* in Lordship (Acts 2:32-35). Unlike the emphasis of the Synoptic (or Hebrew) tradition, which wants to see Jesus as Messiah, albeit in a hidden way, all during his public ministry, the gospel of Acts 2 manifests a fairly well-tooled scheme of understanding, supported by Scripture, according to which the Messiahship was bestowed upon him through his resurrection, exaltation, and Lordly enthronement.

The second feature that is not entirely standard in the generally received Christian gospel is that the Holy Spirit which the resurrected and enthroned Jesus receives from the Father is emphatically promised to be bestowed upon others—not only upon the Apostles who preach the Apostolic gospel thus inspired, but upon anyone who repents and enlists in the name of Jesus Messiah (Acts 2:38). "For the promise is for you and for your children and for all those distant ones, as many as the Lord our God may call" (Acts 2:39). The promise of the Spirit releases the Apostolic gospel, and the Apostolic gospel in turn releases the Spirit to all who believe—to all who hear it well enough to see rightly. But the Spirit's role in the seeing and hearing bears scrutiny. Consider the enigmatic statement of Acts 2:33: "he poured out this which you see and hear." The obvious meaning is that they see the inspired Apostles and hear perhaps their miraculous tongues, perhaps their inspired prophetic gospel, perhaps both. I do not question that this is entitled to be taken as the essential meaning. But I observe that this formula appears intriguingly a little later, in the fourth chapter of Acts, when the spokesman of the Apostles, forbidden by the authorities to preach the Apostolic gospel, replies that they are not able to keep silent about the things they have seen and heard (Acts 4:20). Both texts are echoed in the following chapter, where Peter proclaims that Jesus, as prince and savior, has been exalted to God's right hand to give repentance and forgiveness of sins: "And we are his witnesses of these things, and the Holy Spirit which God gave to those submitting to him" (Acts 5:32). The grammar of the original text does not allow the verse to be read as if they are witnesses to or of the Holy Spirit. It requires that it be understood as meaning "We and the Holy Spirit are witnesses of the important truths about Jesus," including the truths that are invisible to the physical eye. I suggest that the underlying claim is that the gift of the Holy Spirit brought to the Apostles a revelation of the exaltation and enthronement of Jesus. They are witnesses not only of his resurrection but of his full glorification, which they see in the Holy Spirit. And their gospel offered the same gift of the Holy Spirit to obedient and repentant believers, so that they too might see and hear for themselves the truth proclaimed by that form of the Apostolic gospel that was born from above by what the Spirit had given.

By Luke's time, the place of the Holy Spirit in the Christian gospel was firm and general. So was the assumption that Gentile converts were free from the Jewish Law. These two achievements were interrelated, as Paul attests in arguing to the Galatians that their reception of the Spirit is the guarantee of their freedom from the Law. Luke's Hellenist sources took him back to the earliest days in Jerusalem, and if it was from them rather than from his other sources that he learned about the Pentecost event, it is understandable that Luke might either innocently or by mythic design ascribe the original gift of the Holy Spirit to the Hebrew Apostles whom he saw as the principle of steady continuity in the unfolding of Christian revelation, just as he did in the case of Gentile freedom from the Law. My conjecture that the gift of the Spirit belonged originally to the Hellenists rather than the Hebrews is an attempt to account for various phenomena: the differences between the general Synoptic tradition and Luke's special emphasis on the Spirit (as well as the place of the Spirit in the Fourth Gospel, which will be addressed in the last chapter of this book); the inconsistencies in Luke's timetable at the end of his Gospel and the beginning of Acts; some of the peculiarities of the gospels Luke places in the mouth of Peter; various confusions about the place and function of the Holy Spirit in Luke's representations of earliest Christianity;[14] the tensions and distinctions between Hellenist and Hebrew Christians; and the absence of a doctrine of the Holy Spirit in some of the early texts. Let us now consider some of these phenomena from the perspective of the gospel of the Hebrew Apostles.

THE GOSPEL OF THE HEBREW APOSTLES

The Hebrew Apostles, whom Luke identifies with the Twelve, play a prominent and conspicuous part in Acts as the leaders of the Church and the founders of its new gospel, but it is apparent that Luke is working with relatively little received information. We never hear a Hebrew Apostle except Peter preach (the closest we come is the remarks of James to the meeting in Acts 15). It is likely that some of what Luke placed in Peter's mouth was not originally Hebrew preaching at all, but came rather from the Hellenists. Luke obviously relied on their recollections in his story of Stephen, of the first extensive persecution, of the initial extension of the Church into the world outside Jerusalem, and probably relied on Hellenist accounts in his reports of other matters in the earliest Christian days.

But to admit that Luke had little information about Peter and his colleagues is not to say that he had none. Luke's myth of the Twelve Apostles, an extension of the Synoptic tradition's view of Christian origins, is not a mere fantasy but an overgeneralization of something that was undoubtedly true in substantial part. When Paul refers to a visit to Jerusalem and to his conference with "those appearing to be pillars" (Gal 2:9), he refers to the leadership of the Jerusalem Church whose approval was potentially critical to the continuation of the gospel he himself preached among the Gentiles (Gal 2:2). The meeting was successful. Paul submitted his gospel for scrutiny, and the Hebrew leaders acknowledged that he had been entrusted with the gospel for the uncircumcised while they, and especially Peter, carried the gospel to the circumcised (Gal 2:7-9). The gospel of the Hebrew Apostles was still alive and successful in its own mission field, and that field was made up of conservatively observant Jews.

This, according to Paul's testimony, was at least fourteen years after his own conversion (Gal 2:1). The expulsion of the Hellenist Christians from Jerusalem had long since taken place, carrying the Hellenist Apostolic gospel into new places and new forms. The Hebrew Apostles, and their gospel, were dominant in Jerusalem and evidently had powerful influence outside it. But fourteen years is a long time, capable of sheltering many changes. The gospel of the Hebrew Apostles had by now confronted a Hellenist gospel to the Gentiles, and had accepted its authenticity; years before, when the Apostolic gospels were in their infancy and Jerusalem was in an uproar over some of the things proclaimed in the name of Jesus of Nazareth, the Hebrew leadership was not likely to have been quite so hospitable to the gospel preached by Stephen. What was the gospel of the Hebrew Apostles in those days?

Its main outlines were probably those I have attempted to reconstruct in the section of this chapter entitled "The First Gospel of the Apostles": the Messiah has come in the person of Jesus, has suffered and been raised to God's right hand in accordance with the Scriptures, will come finally as judge to bring salvation and forgiveness and a share in the Dominion of God to all who believe and are baptized in his name. A few distinctive features emerge, I believe, from the hints of surviving evidence that confirm and clarify the distinctions between the Hellenist and Hebrew gospels.

THE PLACE OF THE LAW

First, the gospel of the Hebrew Apostles reaffirmed the Law and customs of conservative piety. In part, this reaffirmation was probably rooted in a basic difference between Hebrew and Hellenist Jews, but it was likely to have been intensified by the Hebrew reaction to the gospel of the Hellenist Apostles, which must have seemed to bring the movement surrounding Jesus into dangerous disrepute among conservative Jews. Luke reflects a knowledge of this emphasis in his portrait of Peter as a scrupulously observant Jew, keeping the dietary laws faithfully and refusing to mingle with Gentiles, and also in his association of the Jerusalem Church with attempts to impose such observances on Christians generally, especially in Acts 11 and 15. But it is Paul who provides the strongest evidence. His Epistle to the Galatians reveals three crises. One had taken place in Antioch, when certain persons came from James and influenced even Peter and Barnabas to give up their table-fellowship with uncircumcised Gentile converts (Gal 2:12-13). Another had taken place in Jerusalem, when the freedom from circumcision of the Gentile convert Titus had been called into question by what Paul calls "false brethren" (Gal 2:1-4). The third crisis is the occasion of the entire Epistle: the Galatians have been re-evangelized by a gospel that calls them to accept the observance of the Law.

Paul takes care to insist that this rival gospel is not an authentic gospel at all, and he introduces the other crises in order to drive his point home: this question has been tested out before and resolved in the proper manner; the conclusion reached was that the Gentile converts are not subject to the Law. What he opposes cannot therefore be what Peter was preaching. But it is entirely possible that it was what Peter *had been* preaching, an early form of the gospel of the Hebrew Apostles that had shifted with later experience but had before the shift become habitual in the understanding of the Hebrew Church in Jerusalem, who had not needed to keep up with such changes. The wavering of Peter and Barnabas under pressure of Jerusalem visitors suggests that this was probably the case, and so does the argument with which Paul faced Peter down on that occasion. Salvation comes simply on account of faith in Jesus Christ, and even conservative Jewish Christians must acknowledge that their observance of the Law has no worth except to the extent that it is based in a faith in the justification that comes through Jesus alone (Gal 2:11-16).

The wording of Paul's claim, imitated by my paraphrase, is important. He does not say that works of Law are of no significance for Jewish Christians. He says that righteousness can be founded only on faith in Jesus Christ, and that only on this condition is there righteousness in the works of Law—not for Gentiles, who are free from any Law but Christ, but for Jews, for whom the Law may remain efficacious if grounded in a faith in Christ. Paul obviously expects that Peter will recognize that this is the true gospel of the Apostles. But he has also seen Peter waver from it. The meaning of Peter's wavering is, I suggest, that the gospel of the Hebrew Apostles had enjoined fidelity to the Law upon Jews, and had only recently come to embrace a more sophisticated relaxation of this principle through a more radical understanding of how the Law was to be revalued in Christ. The Law was still a source of merit for Jews but no longer binding for those whose salvation came through the righteousness of Christ.

This is a distinction that probably did not need to be made by the gospel of the Hebrew Apostles as long as that gospel envisioned only the mission to Jews. Such a distinction is likely to have been a result of the success of the gospel of the Hellenist Apostles among the Gentiles. The difficulties the gospel of the Hellenists encountered with the Hebrew

Christians of Jerusalem are likely to have been due in part to early Hebrew rejection of the liberties with the Law taken by the Hellenist gospel of Stephen and the Seven. But now, at the level of Apostolic leadership, there was a convergence between the two. Paul's opponents in Galatia may have defended what once had been the gospel of the Hebrew Apostles, but they were not defending what it had come to be. If it was once a gospel of Law, it was now more precisely and thoroughly what it had been from the start, a gospel of salvation through Christ.

There is one other major relic of the gospel of the Hebrew Apostles preserved in the New Testament: the Epistle of James. It is a homily in the tradition of Jewish wisdom literature and does not set out to preach a gospel, but in the course of its homilizing it takes a clear stand in favor of "a royal law according to the Scripture" (Jas 2:8) and against the notion that faith can substitute for works done in accordance with the Law. It is in accordance with the Law that we will be judged, the Epistle of James insists (Jas 2:12). The insistence is patently a polemic against what the author takes to be a rival gospel that offers freedom from the Law through faith.

The Epistle of James embodies a contention between a version of the gospel of the Hebrew Apostles and a version of the gospel of the Hellenist Apostles, but the contention is probably at root the older battle between the Hebrew and Hellenist camps within pre-Christian Judaism. The main argument centers on the justification of Abraham. Did his righteousness derive from following the works enjoined upon him, or from his faith? The issue was an old one. More than two centuries before the Epistle of James, conservative Jews insisted on the practice of circumcision as an indispensable condition of entering into the inheritance of Abraham, in accordance with the prescriptions of Genesis 17, while their Hellenist rivals neglected circumcision and undoubtedly appealed, as Paul eventually appealed, to the assertion of Genesis 15:6 that Abraham's faith was the source of his righteousness. The Epistle of James takes its stand unequivocally: Abraham was justified by works rather than faith, and faith without the aid of works is simply dead and useless (Jas 2:17,26).

On the surface, it appears that the Epistle of James is in direct opposition to the gospel of Paul, who argued that the true heirs of Abraham are those who share Abraham's faith, not his circumcision (Gal 3:6-18), and that works of the Law are worth nothing apart from faith in Christ (Gal 2:16, 3:5). But the author of the Epistle of James, taking shelter under the name most thoroughly associated with Hebrew Apostles, has obviously not envisioned Paul's idea of faith. This Epistle uses the term *faith* to mean nothing other than *belief*, arguing that even demons have faith in the oneness of God and are no better for it (Jas 2:18-19). That is not at all what Paul had in mind. What the Epistle of James offers is a caricature of righteousness apart from the Law, in order to affirm what its author takes to be the authentic righteousness within the Law. Freedom is not apart from the Law but within it (Jas 2:12). The Epistle of James understands Christian faith as a believing that must enact the righteousness of the Law if it is to be complete. Jesus is Lord in glory, and the Christian is to trust in that truth (Jas 2:1); but the rest of the gospel is the Law.[15]

THE ABSENCE OF THE HOLY SPIRIT

In their conservative reverence for the Law, the Epistle of James and Paul's opponents in Antioch and Galatia were faithful to their Jewish heritage, but not merely out of habit. Fidelity to the Law was a part of their Christian belonging, not just their Jewish heritage: it was part of the gospel of the Hebrew Apostles because it was the vital and active principle of Christian life. The Epistle of James makes this explicit in a curious and significant way by drawing an analogy between body and soul, on the one hand, and faith and works on the other. How would you set up this analogy? Most of us would probably say that faith is to works as the soul is to the body, the former animating the latter in each case, and the latter concretizing the former. But that is not what the Epistle of James says. It claims rather that faith is to works as the body is to the soul (Jas 2:26).

In the Epistle of James, faith is equivalent to belief and is a less vital principle than in the writings of Paul; but it may have been so throughout the gospel of the Hebrew Apostles. The vital principle is works, the enactment of one's obedient trust and belief in God, the doing of the word of life. The significance of this is further suggested by the fact that the Epistle of James never mentions the Holy Spirit, and uses the term "spirit" to refer only to that which animates human beings—and gives them vicious leanings (Jas 4:5).[16] Law and spirit are therefore in opposition to each other to some extent, the Law being the necessary discipline and restraint for the unreliable spirit.

If the gospel of the Hebrew Apostles generally followed the pattern of thought found in the Epistle of James, the clash in Galatia becomes the more intelligible. Paul had proclaimed the gospel of the Hellenist Apostles, offering freedom from Law through the Holy Spirit received by faith in Christ; those who came after him had demanded observance of the Law, in the name of a gospel that did not recognize Paul's version of faith or the Holy Spirit it was purported to bring. From the Hebrew perspective, the spirit that would set aside the Law was not holy, and would bring not freedom but a new bondage. From Paul's point of view, to accept the Law is to reject the Holy Spirit—and it is not impossible that this is precisely what the countermissionaries thought too, and asked Paul's converts to do.

The Pentecostal happening of Acts 2 is of such startling power and exciting properties that it is difficult to imagine the gospel ever retreating from the state it achieves there. After such an event, one can understand Paul's dealings with the Galatians, but not those of his opponents. Unless, of course, the opponents were not heirs of that Pentecost, but belonged to another part of the Church that formed its gospel and its life in another way and from other resources. I have already indicated some reasons for thinking that this is the case—that Pentecost belonged to the Hellenist Apostles and not to the Hebrews, and that it therefore belonged to Paul and not to his opponents in Galatia. I wish now to point to one other indication, and to a text that may be an authentic memory of the early gospel of the Hebrew Apostles.

After the overwhelming transformation of Acts 2, it seems clear that from now on everything must be different, transmuted in the new start and new life given by the Holy Spirit. Anyone who has read attentively the ending of Luke's Gospel, the beginning of Acts, and the great fulfillment in Acts 2 is bound to have a sense of what Acts 3 will have to be like—but is bound also to be surprised. The character of Chapter 3 is simply not in continuity with what has gone before. It does not seem to have come from the same traditions at all. Peter works a miraculous cure and preaches a gospel to the onlookers, but there is no reference to the Holy Spirit in either the cure or the gospel. The healing has taken place through the power of faith in Jesus' name (Acts 3:16), and the promise of the gospel is that if they repent and turn, for the removal of their sins, "times of refreshment may come from the countenance of the Lord, and he may send you the foreordained Jesus Messiah" (Acts 3:19-20). There will be an indefinite delay before this fulfillment, since although Jesus has been raised and glorified (Acts 3:13,15), "it is necessary that heaven receive [him] until times of restoration of all things," in accordance with prophecy (Acts 3:21). The times of refreshment, the restoration, the sending of the exalted and commissioned Jesus will come in due course, but not yet. And what is given in the meantime? Faith in his name, which brings blessing and power to cure maladies (Acts 3:26) and leads to the forgiveness of sins for the repentant (though not necessarily before the time of that future fulfillment). But there is no Holy Spirit, no immediate change in life or expectation, no more direct consolation than had been offered by the gospel of John the Baptist. This is very like the sense of things engendered by the Synoptic tradition—Jesus having been invested with an unseen glory and a power that can aid the believer—but significantly unlike the Fourth Gospel or Acts 2. It is what one might expect from the early days of the Hebrew Apostles.

It is important to stress *early days*. The gospel of the Hebrew Apostles began with a leadership, an experience, a community, and a disposition different from those that situated the gospel of the Hellenists. These two gospels were at first probably as different (and as similar) as the gospels of John the Baptist and Jesus—one should hardly expect otherwise. It is entirely natural that the Hebrew gospel would be conservative about works of the Law and would see in the Law the principle of religious life until the reign of Jesus Messiah should begin fully. It is just as natural that the Hellenists would be more detached from the Law and ready to seize upon a spiritual principle that would diminish the Law's authority. Each group undoubtedly thought it important that its own views be imposed upon the process of incorporating Gentiles into Christian salvation. But it appears that the Hellenists got there first and established an extensive precedent in the conversion of Gentiles to their gospel. Hebrew Christians seem to have resented this liberty, but the Hebrew Apostles learned to make a crucial distinction: Peter and his colleagues would continue to preach to the Jews, while Paul and his colleagues were free to preach his gospel to the Gentiles (Gal 2:9). Thereafter, those who troubled Gentile converts about the Law were without authorization (Acts 15:24-29). They were out of date. The gospel of the Hebrew Apostles had been clarified and readapted to Hebrew Christians. What was essential to the gospel of the Apostles in all its forms was located in salvation through faith in Jesus Christ.

THE GOSPEL OF ALL THE APOSTLES

Even if the gospel of the Apostles was not uniform in its earliest days—even if there were forms that were sharply and contentiously different from one another—the Apostles eventually came to agreement about it. The pillars of the Jerusalem Church acknowledged the authenticity of what Paul preached among the Gentiles (Gal 2:7-9), and Paul in turn accepted instructive information from his predecessors and incorporated it into his gospel (1 Cor 15:1-8) so that he was able to say "Therefore whether I or they, thus we proclaim, and thus you believed" (1 Cor 15:11). The Apostolic agreement evidently did not instantly persuade all those who had been initiated into one gospel or another, for the habits of belief and the memories of bitter disputes continued to trouble the settlement that had been made. But the principal battle had been won over the essentials of the gospel of the Apostles.

The fundamental success of the settlement would take time to work its way through the Christian churches, but the security of its achievement is firmly represented in two illustrative cases that tested the diplomatic waters.

One of the test cases is that of Apollos. According to Acts, Apollos was an Alexandrian, an eloquent speaker and a powerful expounder of Scripture (Acts 18:24), whose original gospel was accurate but incomplete until he received further instruction in Ephesus (Acts 18:24-26), after which he preached in Corinth (Acts 18:27). Some of the Corinthians were evidently deeply impressed, for Paul berated them for forming factions—some of them considering themselves Paul's disciples, others disciples of Peter, still others disciples of Apollos (1 Cor 3:4,22). It was the latter group that most concerned Paul, for the lengthy disussion of foolishness and wisdom in the first three chapters of 1 Corinthians comes to focus on Apollos, who had evidently seemed exceptionally wise and learned by comparison with the doctrine that Paul had preached.

Paul's response is a jumble of indignation: he had been simple because they were still only babies (1 Cor 3:1-3), and yet what he preached is the truer and deeper wisdom next to which human intellectual ingenuity is foolish (1 Cor 1-3); he preached it in a manner that did not seem wise so that they might see that its wisdom is divine rather than human (1 Cor 2:4-5). Furthermore, Apollos was merely building on Paul's foundation (1 Cor 3:6-15), and the final judgment will reveal whether Apollos built well or ill (1 Cor 3:10-15). Besides, the accomplishments of the gospel are all God's; no one else can really take credit for them (1 Cor 3:5-9).

Paul's consternation arose in defense of his authority and his gospel, to which Apollos was evidently a potentially dangerous threat. But what is especially striking is that for all his defensiveness and annoyance, Paul never faults Apollos. Whatever the differences between their presentations and styles and arguments, Paul and Apollos did not preach different gospels. There is no other gospel, and there can be no other gospel (2 Cor 11:4; cf. Gal 1:6-9). Apollos and Paul built differently, but on the same foundation of the one Apostolic gospel of Jesus Christ. It is that foundation that matters. The additional eloquence and sophistication is permissible, and only the ultimate judgment of God will determine whether it is appropriate ornament or straw and stubble for the fire (1 Cor 3:10-15). But in the meantime, the gospel of the Apostles is one and the same, whether preached by Paul or by Peter or by Apollos or anyone else.

The other important test case is one to which I have adverted before, the occasion on which Paul visited Jerusalem in order to clear up problems arising from the interference of Hebrew Christians in his Gentile mission (Gal 2:1-9). There is no need to rehearse the particulars at length: Paul, recognizing the authority of the Hebrew Apostles as important (though not more important than his own), presented to them the gospel he preached among the Gentiles. They may have felt about Paul the way Paul felt about Apollos, but their judgment on the matter was like Paul's about Apollos: they added nothing, but recognized that Paul had been entrusted with the true gospel for the Gentiles. With that, they offered to Paul and Barnabas the right hand of friendship and sent them on their way. Neither the gospel of the Hellenist Apostles nor the gospel of the Hebrew Apostles was changed, but that handshake did more than settle the boundaries of their mission fields. It established that the differences between them were no longer to be considered of much importance when compared with what they had in common—the good news of all the Apostles that salvation was offered through, and only through, faith in Jesus Christ.

4

The Gospel of Demetrios

Demetrios was not an uncommon name in antiquity, but it is attached to only two persons in the New Testament. One is the rabble-rousing silversmith of Ephesus who according to Acts 19:23-41 preached a summary gospel proclaiming the goddess Artemis (whose greatest temple was one of the wonders of that city and of the ancient world) and succeeded in rallying opposition to the gospel of the Apostle Paul. His gospel is not the subject of this chapter. The gospel in question belonged rather to the New Testament's other Demetrios. It stood in much deeper opposition to that of Paul and all the Apostles, and has a much less spectacular but much more influential presence in the pages of the New Testament than the preaching of Demetrios the silversmith. The Demetrios with whom it is associated is mentioned only passingly in 3 John 12: "To Demetrios testimony has been given by all, and by the truth itself—and we also give testimony, and you know that our testimony is true."

I will argue in this chapter that this Demetrios was an agent—the only certainly nameable agent afforded by extant evidence, though by no means the only or even the chief agent—of a gospel that arose from the Christian movement but denied the place given to Jesus Christ in the gospel of the Apostles. Traces of this gospel are scattered and obscured and can be recovered only through patient and careful reconstruction, but I believe that the main outlines can be reconstructed. I believe, moreover, that they witness to a movement that constituted the greatest threat experienced by the gospel of the Apostles in at least one influential part of the world, and that the movement inspired polemical attitudes that colored the rest of the Johannine literature and helped to inspire the gospel which the next chapter will treat as the gospel of the Ultimate. And yet the gospel of Demetrios, although characterized by its opponents as the gospel of Antichrist, deserves a place in the sequence of Christian gospels. It arose within the Christian movement as an attempt to improve on the gospel that preceded it and (I will argue) eventually—in the third Epistle of John—left a legacy within the Christian scriptural canon.

THE ANOMALOUS CHARACTER OF 3 JOHN

3 John is the shortest book of the New Testament, barely over two hundred words long. Its language, rhetoric, and general manner align it with the rest of the Johannine literature—the Fourth Gospel and the First Epistle of John, as well as 2 John, which it resembles closely. Given these resemblances and the slightness of its own substance, 3 John has understandably been considered by New Testament scholarship to be little more than a minor appendix to Johannine thought, in the form of an occasional letter—standing in relation to the Johannine corpus rather as the Epistle to Philemon does to Paul's other surviving work.

Yet despite its brevity and its various resemblances to the other Johannine works, 3 John can be shown under close examination to be significantly different from the rest of the Johannine corpus and even to represent a counterposition.

The first clues are to be found in the positive values of this Epistle. These emerge most strongly in the eleventh verse: "Beloved one, do not imitate what is evil, but what is good. The one doing good is of God (*ek tou theou*); the one doing evil has not seen God (*ouch heōraken ton theon*)." If the first part of this advice is rather banal, the accompanying observations invest it with theological values that deserve to be carefully appreciated. It is evidently assumed that the addressee has a choice in the matter, since he is exhorted to define himself by imitating the good rather than the evil. But note the implicit equations that then follow: to be among the doers of good is evidently to be revealed as being of God and as having seen God; evildoers apparently are not of God and have not seen God. The underlying gospel presumes that we can be of God, and that we can see him.

Being of God is not an unusual theme in Christian literature; the rest of the Johannine books affirm this theological category repeatedly, and if in doing so they are bolder than some other writings, they are not very far away in spirit. *Seeing* God, however, is entirely a different matter. It is not uncommon as an eschatological category (it is, after all, one of the promises made by the Sermon on the Mount to the pure in heart), but as a category of present life it occurs in the New Testament only here. Or, to be more exact, it occurs as an affirmed present possibility only here: elsewhere in the Johannine literature, this category is mentioned in order to be explicitly and polemically denied. "No one has seen God at any time," claims 1 John 4:12, and the Fourth Gospel asserts with equal emphasis that "no one has ever seen God" (1:18). The contrast is stark and significant. What the Fourth Gospel and the First Epistle of John firmly rule out of possibility is casually assumed by the author of 3 John as the normal condition of those who do good. These works are not cut from the same theological cloth.

If we examine the ground of the polemical denial in the Fourth Gospel and in 1 John, it is easy to perceive that what is at stake is an affirmation of the mediation of Jesus. The Fourth Gospel's denial of direct seeing of God is followed immediately by an assertion of this principle: "No one has ever seen God; the only-begotten son, the one existing in the bosom of the Father—that one has made him known" (1:18). 1 John spins out a more involved chain of argument: though no one has seen God, ever, yet if we love each other, God abides in us; and we know this because of his having given us his spirit;

and we have seen and testify that the Father sent forth his son as savior of the world, and whoever may confess that Jesus is the Son of God, God abides in him and he in God (4:12-15). The inward abiding of God is a function of a public act of faith, namely, the confession of Jesus as Son (and therefore as savior); and the inward abiding that comes from the confession of Jesus is the closest we can come to God. But we do not see him: what we see is the mediating sonship of Jesus, and this is the highest reach of our seeing.

The First Epistle of John can consider seeing God as an eschatological event: it has not yet been made to appear what we shall be, but we know that if he [God] should appear, we shall be like him, because we shall see him just as he is (3:2). It is a specifically future event, and involves a deep transformation. To see God is to be perfected in his image, and although this may eventually come to pass, it cannot be yet. In the meantime, we can know God but not see him. We can know him by knowing his abiding spirit (3:24), and we can know his spirit by confessing faith in Jesus Christ (4:2). Against the sort of doctrine offered in 3 John, the rest of Johannine literature emphasizes consistently that it is impossible to see God but assures us that we can know God through, but only through, the mediation of Jesus.

One further affirmation in 1 John illustrates this difference, through a phrase that is interestingly and probably not accidentally parallel to 3 John's insistence that the evildoer has not seen God. 1 John too argues that the sinner is one who has not seen—but what the sinner has not seen is Jesus: "Everyone who abides in him does not sin; everyone who sins has not seen him nor known him" (3:6). It is he, Jesus, whom we have seen with our eyes, says 1 John (1:1); in him the eternal life that was with the Father was made manifest, visible, allowing us to see and bear witness (1:2). Jesus is the visible locus of what belongs to the transcendent divinity that no one has seen. Against the assertion of 3 John that it is a failure not to have seen God, the Fourth Gospel and 1 John urgently insist that no one has done so, and that seeing and confessing Jesus constitutes the highest reach of human possibility and the nearest approach to God.

The historical reason for the polemical insistence on the mediation of Jesus emerges clearly in 1 John 2:22-23: "Who is the liar, if not the one denying that Jesus is the Christ? This is the anti-Christ, the one denying the Father and the Son. Whoever denies the Son does not have the Father; the one confessing the Son has the Father also." To deny the Son, to deny the Apostolic gospel's insistence on Jesus as the One through whom God is mediated, is to cut oneself off from the Father. To enter into relationship with the Father, it is necessary only to acknowledge the gospel of the Son. Evidently this is not an academic issue but a practical response to a crisis situation. "Even now many anti-Christs have come about" (2:18). The deniers of Jesus are abroad. They are not the Jews who had never accepted Jesus, nor the Greeks who had never belonged to the Christian fold. They have arisen from within the movement with which the author of 1 John identifies himself: "They went out from us; but they were not of us, for if they were of us they would have remained with us" (2:19). 2 John picks up the same themes with the same urgency "Many deceivers entered into the world, those not confessing Jesus come in the flesh: this is the deceiver and the anti-Christ" (7). These are not outsiders, but those from inside who have gone too far: "Every one who goes too far, and does not abide in the teaching of the Christ does not have God. He who abides in the teaching has both the Father and the Son" (9). Accordingly, the Second Epistle of John greets its addressees with fervent reference to the mediating Christ: "Grace, mercy, peace be with you from God the Father and from Jesus Christ the Son of the Father" (3). The First Epistle of John similarly begins with a reference to Jesus and concludes with a resounding assurance that "we know that the Son of God has come, and has given to us understanding, that we might know the true one; and we are in the true one, in his Son Jesus Christ" (4:20).

And where does the Third Epistle of John pledge its allegiance to this threatened teaching, this indispensable confession? It never, in any way, mentions Jesus at all. It belongs, I believe, to the group of deniers who are the enemies of the rest of the Johannine writings.

The relationship between 2 John and 3 John has appeared so close, to the eyes of modern scholarship, that a leading introduction to the New Testament can casually refer to "the writer of 2, 3 John" without bothering to argue for identity of authorship.[1] Anyone who has read the two letters can readily see why. They are of similar length, language, and style, and both begin by identifying the author as "The Elder," *ho presbuteros,* and close with the same formula. The easy and plausible conclusion is that they emanate from the same hand and from essentially the same time and place. It seems fully appropriate, if not inevitable, that they should end up side by side in the New Testament.

But in fact they have not always been side by side. Their history of reception into the revered books of the Church is different despite their superficial resemblance. Adolf von Harnack built a case, subsequently supplemented by T. W. Manson, for the proposition that the Latin translation of 3 John was by a different hand from that which had translated 1 and 2 John.[2] The obvious inference is that 3 John was received into at least that part of the Western Church at a different—undoubtedly later—time than 1 and 2 John. This inference is confirmed by one of the earliest lists of canonical books, the Muratorian canon, which registers that only two epistles of John are accepted in the Catholic Church. One of these is clearly 1 John, since it is quoted earlier in the document. The other is undoubtedly 2 John, evidently translated into Latin at the same time and by the same person.[3] 3 John is not received.[4] Clement's witness suggests that the same distinction obtained in Alexandria, for he treats of 1 John and 2 John in his *Adumbrationes* but does not mention 3 John, and furthermore he cites 1 John on one occasion as "the larger epistle" (i.e., of two: *Iōannes en tē meizoni epistolē*). 3 John was resisted by some ecclesiastical authorities until well into the third century.[5] This oddity might by itself serve as a hint of hidden important dissimilarities between it and its eventual companion epistles. Unfortunately, the sources do not mention the reasons for the Church's early hesitations about the canonical appropriateness of 3 John, merely the fact of its omission or non-acceptance. However, if we move beyond the surface, we can construct a plausible explanation.

3 John complains of the behavior of one Diotrephes, who has been a thorn in the author's side:

> I wrote to the congregation; but Diotrephes, who loves the first place among them, does not receive us. On account of this, if I come I will remember his works that he performs, prating against us with malicious words; and as if this were not enough for him, he does not even receive the brethren—and forbids those who want to, and throws them out of the congregation. (9-10)

Some New Testament scholars have guessed that Diotrephes is one of those heretics denounced elsewhere in the Johannine literature—a proto-Gnostic, or teacher of false doctrine, or denier of Christ. But this opinion does not really square with the evidence of the complaint. 3 John does not accuse Diotrephes of false teaching of any sort. He is represented as arrogant, full of pride of place, churlishly refusing to receive the author of 3 John or his brethren, speaking maliciously against them and imposing sanctions on others of his congregation who are more hospitably disposed. There is not a word about Diotrephes' orthodoxy, only complaints about his abuse of power. And yet if we want a model by which to measure the meaning of Diotrephes' reported behavior, 2 John will indeed supply it. It is offered not in 2 John's description of the deceivers and anti-Christs, but rather in that Epistle's recommendations concerning how the faithful should respond to anti-Christs and deceivers:

> Everyone who goes too far, and does not abide in the teaching of the Christ, does not have God; he who abides in the teaching has both the Father and the Son. If anyone comes to you and does not bring this teaching, do not receive him into the house and do not wish him well [i.e., greet him]—for whoever wishes him well shares in his wicked works. (9-11)

The pattern is precisely what 3 John criticizes: a stark and total inhospitality. If the pattern is applied in the way that serves the evidence best, then false teaching is not to be associated with Diotrephes but—at least in Diotrephes's opinion—with those whom he has rebuffed. Ironically, Diotrephes has been reputed a heretic on account of the criticism attached to him by 3 John, but the chances are that he was, according to the principles upheld by 2 John, a paradigmatic defender of the faith. 2 John and 3 John do indeed belong together, but not as two members of the same gospel: they are type and antitype. Their resemblance comes not from common authorship, but from deliberate imitation. The author of one of them—or perhaps the authors of both—wished to exploit the authority of the anonymous Elder (whom tradition has associated with John). 3 John does so in order to discredit Diotrephes and those of his disposition, and to commend Demetrios and the unnamed brethren. It is likely enough a direct imitation of 2 John, which itself may well have been a contrivance to use the authority of the Elder in order to promote steadfast opposition to the gospel of Demetrios. (Possibly, both letters merely imitate epistolary formulae known by the authors to have been characteristic of the casual letters of the revered Elder, but no other example has survived.)

The Muratorian canon does not explain why only two rather than three epistles of John "are accepted in the Catholic Church." No early writer tries to account for 3 John's not always being readily received in circles that accepted 2 John as sound Scripture. I suggest, however, that the explanation can be reconstructed: it is, as 2 John prescribes, that the churches should not receive those who fail to bring with them the Apostolic gospel about Jesus. 3 John shows no glimmer of a gospel about Jesus. For all the emphasis in the rest of Johannine literature on the importance of this one criterion of authenticity, the Demetrios whom 3 John commends is not praised for being faithful to the teaching of Christ, and in the light of the rest of Johannine literature the absence of this particular commendation is conspicuous. The implications of its absence coincide with other indications, including not only the controversy about seeing God but even 3 John's lament about the success of the policy of opposition enjoined by 2 John. 3 John is a fossil remain of an alien gospel. Whenever and wherever in antiquity it was known to be such, it was not received by those who stood by the gospel about Jesus Christ, the gospel of the Apostles. The fact of its non-reception long survived the memory of the reasons why and was eventually overridden by a later Church that could no longer discern any grounds for exclusion, nor recollect this gospel's reputation for keeping bad company. Luther complained of the unevangelical nature of the Epistle of James, was unhappy with the Book of Revelation, and would gladly have excluded both from the Bible. But the canonization of 3 John is by far the greatest irony and anomaly of the New Testament.

It is ironic and anomalous, that is, with respect to what the Christian good news finally came to be, and especially with respect to 3 John's misleading specious resemblance to the rest of the Johannine writings that so fervently opposed its doctrine. But the ironic anomaly did occur. Although the gospel of Demetrios did not succeed, and although it was regarded as anathema by some of its contemporaries within the Christian fold, neither the historian nor the theologian is entirely free to dismiss it as a pernicious and contemptible distortion, despite the urgings of 1 and 2 John. Historically it has a claim, since it arose from within the Christian movement and exerted what seems to have been a considerable, even if not extensive, influence—enough to stir up the polemical energies of three other books of the New Testament. It even succeeded in insinuating itself into the Christian canon through 3 John. That, depending upon one's theories of Scripture and revelation, may give it theological as well as historical credentials. But that issue aside, the gospel which 3 John associates with the name Demetrios was once offered within the Christian body as a serious proclamation of good news. It deserves to be considered not merely from the perspective of its ultimately triumphant rivals, but in accordance with its own intents and purposes. I shall later argue that those who triumphed over it learned something from it in the process, and that it did indeed enter into the formation of the gospel of the Christian Church. But for the time being, the task is to understand and appreciate it for itself.

THE CONTENT OF THE GOSPEL OF DEMETRIOS

What then was the gospel of Demetrios?

The brevity of 3 John permits few positive points of reconstruction, but these can be augmented by a careful assessment of the critique which appears to be made against the gospel of Demetrios by other early Christian documents. My attempt at reconstruction will proceed accordingly.

THE CENTRAL ROLE OF THE TRUTH

The dominant motif by which 3 John would seem to characterize the gospel of Demetrios is that it is a gospel of Truth. The word *truth, alētheia,* occurs six times prominently within the brief text: the salutation styles Gaius, the addressee, as one "whom I love in truth" (1) and expresses the author's joy that the brethren have testified to his truth, just as he walks in the truth (3)—for nothing gives the author (or implied author) greater joy than to hear of his children walking in the truth (4). Those who receive the brethren who bring this gospel become co-workers in the truth (8). Thus far, the word *truth* carries a highly ambiguous value. It is not clear what tradition it most belongs to or what its precise meaning is, but dim patterns begin to emerge. It has overtones of integrity, righteousness, piety, fidelity, but not much hint of philosophical speculation. The center of gravity is close to the moral rather than the intellectual life. The likelihood is that this usage of the word had recently derived from a Hellenized way of formulating the essential values of Jewish religious tradition as it was practised and revered in the "enlightened" parts of the Diaspora, wherever semi-conservative Jews took a middle course between the terminology of the Holy Scriptures and that of Greek rationalism.

But in verse 12 the usage takes a different turn. "To Demetrios, testimony has been given by all, and by the truth itself." It is of course possible to interpret this statement in a number of ways, by making use of various forms of metaphor. The dominant style of 3 John, however, does not lead us to expect a rhetorical flourish. The statement is more probably close to being quite literal. The writer believes that the Truth to which he and his community have access is objectifiable and in some sense self-manifesting—a theological analogue of the general Christian (and Jewish) doctrine of the Holy Spirit, from which this usage is probably derived. The gospel of Demetrios is a gospel of Truth, a truth that is at once the standard of right conduct and a power that reveals that which is approved.

THE ABSENCE OF JESUS' ROLE

The gospel of Demetrios is not, however, a gospel of Jesus Christ. This may be inferred when we contrast 3 John's total silence about Jesus with the polemic of the Fourth Gospel and the other two Johannine epistles against their doctrinal enemies. To appreciate just what the gospel of Demetrios did or did not say, one must move beyond its own neglect of the subject to the statements of its opponents. What is the false gospel envisioned by the rest of Johannine literature?

A few verses elsewhere in the Johannine writings seem to suggest that the key issue was (as we know it to have been for other early Christian writers, notably Ignatius of Antioch) the humanity of Jesus—the opposition between the ultimately orthodox insistence that Jesus was truly human, having real body and flesh, and the doctrine of the Docetists that Jesus only appeared to be of mortal stuff but had really come in an unfleshly form. Thus the received text of 2 John establishes a creed of Jesus' humanity: "Many deceivers entered into the world, those not confessing Jesus come in the flesh: this is the deceiver and the anti-Christ" (7). 1 John gives the same specification:

> Many false prophets have gone out into the world. In this you know the spirit of God: every spirit which confesses Jesus Christ come in the flesh is from God, and every spirit which does not confess Jesus is not of God—and this is the one [i.e., the spirit] of the anti-Christ. (1 John 4:1-3)

Similarly, the Fourth Gospel climaxes its prologue with the confession that "the Word became flesh" (John 1:14). From these clues, we might well suppose that the gospel of Demetrios was essentially a Docetic gospel, possibly acknowledging Jesus but denying his humanity.

I do not think that these clues should be so read. There is no doubt whatsoever that these verses oppose themselves to the Docetists—that is not in question. But they do not belong to the main thrust of the documents in which they are found: these are later additions to the texts, adding an anti-Docetist polemic to the one that originally stood there.[6] Nothing else in the Fourth Gospel celebrates the flesh of Jesus, except the brief passage on the literal fleshliness of the Eucharist in 6:51b-58, which is generally conceded to be a later insertion,[7] out of keeping with the tonal and conceptual drift of the chapter at large, and in some ways inconsonant with the Fourth Gospel overall. Aside from these two brief passages, the Fourth Gospel works consistently in another direction: "flesh" is a negatively valued term, opposed to spirit. There is no account of Jesus' birth or infancy, no institution of the Eucharist, and considerable mystery about where Jesus has come from. The emphasis is not upon his genuine humanity but upon his celestial origin and his apartness from humankind.

Close attention to 1 John reveals a similar distinction between the one clearly anti-Docetic verse and the general drift of the rest of the text. Despite the insistence upon the flesh of Jesus in 4:2, the following verse expresses the negative side of the proposition without reference to this touchstone, speaking merely of the confession of Jesus: "Every spirit which does not confess Jesus is not of God." It is clear which of these confessions is textually primary. The rest of the epistle repeats frequently the necessity of acknowledging that Jesus is deserving of a heavenly title and of special honor, but never elsewhere insists that his flesh is of any importance.[8] "Who is the liar, if not he who denies that Jesus is the Christ?" (2:22) "Whoever denies the Son does not have the Father" (2:23). "This is his commandment, that we should believe in the name of his Son Jesus Christ" (3:23). "By this the love of God was manifested in us, that God sent forth his only-begotten Son into the world" (4:10). "And we have seen and we testify that the Father sent forth the Son as savior of the world" (4:14). "Everyone believing that Jesus is the Christ is begotten of God; and everyone loving the begetter loves his only begotten" (5:1). "Who is the one who overcomes the world, if not the one believing that Jesus is the Son of God?" (5:5). "This is the testimony of God, which he has testified concerning his son: the one believing in the Son of God has the testimony in himself" (5:9-10). "And this is the testimony, that God gave to us everlasting life, and this life is in his Son" (5:11). "Whoever has the Son has the life; whoever does not have the Son does not have the life" (5:12). "I have written these things to you that you may know that you have eternal life, you believers in the name of the Son of God" (5:13).

The original writer of 1 John was not concerned about Docetism: that was the luxury of a later interpolater after the basic battle of 1 John had already been substantially won. The struggle of the Epistle in its original state was on more radical grounds: the sheer question of the acknowledgment of Jesus as Son, as Christ, as the one through whom we are saved and come to a relationship with God, the Father. The original text of 2 John 7, formed in the context of this more essential struggle, was probably two or three words shorter, and said simply: "Many deceivers entered into the world, ones not confessing Jesus Christ." Such anti-Docetist touches occur in the Fourth Gospel, 1 John, and 2 John, which were received together and kept together by the Church; but they do not occur in 3 John, because it was not the companion of the other Johannine writings. To see how far apart from them it was, one has only to move beyond the superficial anti-Docetist insertions into the deeper currents of the texts, to see what the original polemic was about and what the original issue had really been. Once the anti-Docetist inserts are pared away, the remainder starkly outlines an important part of the gospel of Demetrios. Evidently, what the Fourth Gospel and the first two Epistles of John were reacting to was their opponents' willingness to do without the central mediation of Jesus, and their failure to acknowledge him as the Son or the Christ.

A parallel sin of omission can be found envisioned and resented by the Epistle of Jude, which complains of those who "reject lordships and blaspheme glories" (Jude 8). A plain reading of this verse in the context of the gospel of Demetrios shows it to be a complaint like that of the Johannine literature, but cast in a language that picks up different themes from the gospel of the Apostles. Jude is affirming the Lordship and glorification of Jesus against a group which has dismissed the whole idea of Lordship and the concomitant idea of hidden glory.[9] Jude, like the Johannine writings, observes and resists a gospel that negates. This gospel of Demetrios withholds from Jesus special offices or titles or conditions that have been accorded by the gospel of the Apostles.

SEEING GOD

But such withholding cannot have been the main message of the gospel of Demetrios, however much it may have been its by-product. Jude and the Johannine writings register with indignation the implications of a gospel that offered a way to God without the mediation of Jesus—without acknowledging that he was the Son, or the Christ, or glorified, or the Lord. The offense of this gospel lay precisely in this omission, but that was not the gospel itself. The gospel of Demetrios evidently offered this offense by claiming that we have immediate access to God, that we can see God, without the mediation of Jesus. Its good news was not the denial of Jesus, but the claim that, whatever other parties might allege, it was possible to see God and be of God without subscribing to others' notions of the glorification of a risen Jesus, without believing that Jesus is now Lord of the world, and without presuming that God had interposed a mediating Son or an official Christ between himself and the world. The gospel of Demetrios offered a simpler way of belonging to the truth, and more immediate access to God, without the scenario that elsewhere required Jesus in various roles.

3 John supposes that those who are firmly on the side of the Truth, and who walk in the Truth, have seen God. This does not imply a crude conception of God's literal visibility, nor does it suggest that 3 John had fallen under the influence of Hellenistic mystery cults, where the eyes of initiates actually

beheld what they took to be manifestations of divinity. The verb referring to seeing is hopelessly ambiguous, capable of covering many situations.[10] Philo, who insists pointedly that God is invisible, nevertheless takes "seeing God" to express the closest one can come to God, the fullest grasp of the spirit, not in the eschatological future but in the present. One of his favorite false etymologies is the interpretation of "Israel" as "he who sees God."[11] There is a probable connection between this interpretation and the circles that eventually produced both the gospel of Demetrios and the Johannine literature (although it obviously need not have been from Philo that these circles had learned it). 3 John's original idea of seeing God resembles the Fourth Gospel's later (and perhaps imitating) idea of seeing Jesus: this seeing consists in a fullness of understanding and belief through which the beholder is partially transformed into the likeness of the beheld. The gospel of Demetrios had transferred this normally eschatological category into present experience. With it were perhaps also transferred other of its former eschatological implications such as the transfiguration of the beholder into the image of God—1 John 3:2 assumes that this will accompany our future seeing of God. But on this, 3 John is silent. We cannot in fact determine just what the seeing itself was for 3 John, or what its theological implications were taken to be. It was probably a form of experience and thought that derived from native Jewish traditions, however, rather than from Greek pagan ones. Or, more specifically, it derived from recent Christian traditions, for the gospel of Demetrios was not a foreign invasion or an alien movement but a development from within the Christian body.

HIGHER KNOWLEDGE

1 John characterizes the false missionaries—those who bore the gospel of Demetrios—as defected Christians, not outsid-

ers: "They went out from us, but they were not from us [or "of us"]; for if they were of us they would have remained with us; but that they might be manifested, that they are not all of us" (1 John 2:19). The "us" evidently carries a general reference to authentic Christians and a particular reference to the group whose gospel is reflected in 1 John. The gospel of Demetrios was apparently an offshoot of 1 John's style of Christianity, but (in the judgment of the author of 1 John) something of a parody and hence also a warning to the world that not all who seem to represent the truth really do so.

The succeeding verses in 1 John set up the indictment of the rival gospel:

> And you have an anointing from the Holy One, and you know all things. I did not write to you because you do not know the truth, but because you know it and [know] that every lie is not from the truth. Who is the liar, if not the one denying that Jesus is the Christ? (1 John 2:20-22)

Truth is an important category in the thought of 1 John, just as it is in the thought of 3 John. But to 1 John, the claim of the gospel of Demetrios to be the truth's manifestation is an outrageous distortion; far from being the truth, it is a lie. This, 1 John maintains, can be demonstrated in two ways. Denial of the axiomatic Christhood of Jesus is self-incriminating, simply because that was the doctrine from the beginning. In addition, those who really have the truth will automatically perceive the falsity of a denial of Jesus.

The first of these arguments of 1 John perhaps requires an answer from proponents of the gospel of Demetrios; if so, then the obvious reply is that we have now advanced beyond the beginning and seen more clearly. The second argument is not really an argument at all, and the gospel of Demetrios, claiming a special intimacy with the truth, could dismiss it out of hand. Indeed, 1 John's instructions to its addressees could be taken as an implicit recognition that they do not yet know the truth. The gospel of Demetrios undoubtedly claimed just that: the unreconstructed believe what they believe because they do not yet know, have not yet seen the truth—have not yet seen God. Against such views, 1 John instructs its addressees (while carefully insisting that they already know all this): be confident in the original doctrine and believe that the anointing from above has really taught you all things, and abides in you, and makes it unnecessary for anyone to teach you, and is true, and is not a lie, and requires that you remain in it just as it taught you (1 John 2:27).

This anointing (2:20,27) is apparently identical with the Spirit of God which has been given to authentic Christians (3:24, 4:13), a spirit that confesses Jesus (4:15): it is the functional counterpart of what 3 John refers to as the Truth, though of course the gospel of Demetrios would claim that the Truth does not give the testimony of the gospel of the Apostles, does not confess Jesus. 1 John is perhaps responding to some such claim when it says "the spirit is the one testifying, because the spirit is the truth" (5:7). Did the gospel of Demetrios also have a place for the Spirit as such? Possibly; but the likelihood is perhaps stronger that "Truth" was its invariable term, that in the streamlining of the gospel by which the mediation, the titles, and the glory of Jesus were eliminated, the Spirit too was set aside as being too odd or primitive, or parochially Jewish, its offices entrusted rather to the more absolute and universal term "Truth."[12]

MORAL FREEDOM

Another dimension of the gospel of Demetrios may be visible through 1 John's glancing references that link the deceivers with the world and with sin:

> Children, let no one deceive you: the one doing righteousness is righteous, just as that one [i.e., Jesus] is righteous. The one doing sin is from the devil, because from the

> beginning the devil sins. For this was the Son of God manifested, that he might destroy the works of the devil. Everyone begotten by God does not do sin, because the seed abides in him; and he is not able to sin, because he has been begotten by God. By this is shown the children of God and the children of the devil. Everyone not doing righteousness is not of God. (3:7-10)

The main thrust of the argument is the opposition between the Son and the devil: those who follow the way of the Son are following righteousness, whatever anyone may say to the contrary, and those who do otherwise—no matter what they may claim—are of the devil's party. "Righteousness" seems to be a code word for the received standards of comportment within the Johannine community (the claim of 5:17 that "all unrighteousness is sin" would otherwise be oddly tautologous and pointless), and the opposing gospel to which this passage refers probably contained an accusation that to follow those standards is to be in sin. We have an earlier analogue in Paul's threatening admonition to the Galatians: if you persist in subjecting yourselves to the Law, you condemn yourselves as sinners; the righteousness of the Law is sin. The gospel of Demetrios claimed an analogous enlightenment, an attunement with the truth from whose perspective the conservative Johannine "righteousness" may have seemed to be a significant lack of freedom, a symptom of sinfulness. 1 John reacts defensively: the feelings of guilt that normally accompany a preoccupation with righteousness should not be taken as an indication that such accusations are true, for "if our heart should condemn us, God is greater than our heart and knows all things" (3:20), and we can therefore have a confidence based on the knowledge that "we keep his commandments and do the things that are pleasing in his sight" (3:22; cf. 5:2-3). The deceivers, the deniers of Christ who do not keep these commandments—i.e., do not "do righteousness"—are not from God. They are of the devil.

These deniers are also of the world. After warning his addressees once more about the anti-Christ character of the gospel of Demetrios, 1 John adds:

> You are of God, children, and you have overcome them: because he who is in you is greater than the one who is in the world. They are from the world: on account of this, they speak of the world and the world hears them. (4:4-5)

The "world," for 1 John, is preeminently the place of lust, *epithumia*:

> Love not the world, nor the things in the world. If anyone love the world, the love of the Father is not in him: because all that is in the world—the lust of the flesh and the lust of the eyes and the pomp of life—is not from the Father but from the world. And the world passes away, and its lust—but he who does the will of the Father abides to the age. (2:15-17)

And thereupon immediately follows a warning about the anti-Christs who went out from us but are not of us. It seems that the gospel of Demetrios is associated with forms of "unrighteousness" that are especially connected with the world and its lusts, and that the appeal of that gospel was thought by its enemies to have something to do with this: ". . . they speak of the world and the world hears them" (4:5). The world, the devil, and the flesh stand over against God, his Son, and the commandments of righteousness.

The pattern emerges in various ways but remains the same in essence: to be of God or know God, says 1 John, one must have faith in his Son, who is diametrically opposed to the world and its lusts. Belief in the Son overcomes the world (5:5). Yet one does not know the Son unless one keeps his commandments and walks just as he walked (2:4-6). The enemy gospel accommodates to the ways of the world, with its lusts and darkness, and shows its league with the devil and its ignorance of God by denying Jesus and taking liberties with the commandments and examples that derive from him. The gospel of Demetrios, then, was evidently a gospel of liberation from the restraints of traditional righteousness as well as a gospel of direct contact with God.

RECAPITULATION: THE EVIDENCE OF JUDE

The Epistle of Jude perceives a similar pattern but is much more blunt in stating it: "Some men have covertly entered, previously marked out for this judgment, impious, changing the grace of our God into licentiousness and denying our only sovereign and Lord Jesus Christ" (4). Jude admits reluctantly that such people are indeed within the fold, and tries to explain this away by a crude bit of theologizing: they came in covertly, and are preordained for an example at the judgment (which is an exact analogue, bent to the form of Jude's cruder thought and style, of 1 John's contention that they are from us but not of us, and are allowed to exist in order to reveal that not all who are from us are truly of us). They still join in the Christian love-feasts (12). But they are "murmurers, complainers, walking in accordance with their own lusts; and their mouth speaks swollen words, courting favor for the sake of gain" (16); they are "scoffers, walking according to their own impious lusts" (18), "feasting together without fear, feeding themselves" (12), "dreamers" who "pollute the flesh, rejecting lordships and blaspheming glories" (8) but blaspheming what they do not understand while they are corrupt in their animal ways (10).

If one can peer beyond Jude's indignation, one can make out the lineaments not of mere backsliding and impiety, or sheer crude-mindedness, but rather of a rival gospel—the gospel of Demetrios. These internal enemies deny Jesus Christ, rejecting the claim of his lordship and speaking against the supposition that he is now glorified. But undoubtedly they suppose that this is in the service of a higher truth: the revelation of the grace of God, which releases those who can rise to it from the obligation of keeping the commandments which were once associated with his name—perhaps never rightly, but at any rate no longer rightly. They behave as if liberated, feasting without fear, at ease with their appetites, evidently enjoying sexual freedoms. Jude thinks them unenlightened blasphemers, dreamers, and self-indulgent animals; they undoubtedly consider themselves enlightened critics of a mistaken theology, authentic visionaries, and morally liberated pioneers of a truth that transcends obsolete commandments. They are evidently critical of the unenlightened ways of those about them (murmurers, scoffers, and complainers, says Jude); and their bold, and perhaps grandly stated, message is gaining a certain success among some of the more prominent and influential people (courting favor for the sake of gain).

The picture that emerges from the delicate language of 1 John coincides neatly with Jude's rougher and more candid sketch. Together they show a gospel of Demetrios in which Paul's Apostolic gospel was being both confirmed and inverted—for Paul had claimed freedom from the Law through divine grace, precisely in the name of Christ. Christ was for him a new Law as well as a source of freedom. Now, in the gospel of Demetrios, a still bolder freedom was being reclaimed precisely in the rejection of Christ.

CERINTHUS AND THE "HERESY" OF DEMETRIOS

It is possible that one other name from antiquity might be attachable to this gospel besides that of Demetrios. Admittedly, by the time members of the Catholic Church came to catalogue the heresies repudiated by themselves and their orthodox forebears, the earlier days were ill remembered: it is painful and confusing to attempt to construct sound history from the scattered fragments of legend, hearsay, invention, and fourth-hand reminiscence that appear in the works of Eusebius, Hippolytus, Epiphanius, and others who wrote their works two centuries and more after the fact. But there is one figure about whom some intriguingly relevant rumors were in circulation during the early centuries: Cerinthus.

The earliest notice of Cerinthus is in the *Adversus Haereses* of Irenaeus, who claims that the Johannine writings were primarily dedicated to refuting the doctrines of Cerinthus, which included the denial of Jesus' intrinsic Sonship and Christhood (III.11.1). Cerinthus, according to Irenaeus's account, evidently held Jesus in respect as unusually wise and just, but considered him a man born of Mary and Joseph who became the vehicle of a higher power that permitted him to proclaim the high and hidden God. Cerinthus taught that this power departed from Jesus before the crucifixion and left him to die as ordinary men do (I.26.1).

This teaching is strikingly consonant with the main outlines of the gospel of Demetrios, and there is no strong reason to doubt that Irenaeus had access to at least some reliable information. Later accounts make of Cerinthus a Judaizer, a circumcizing enemy of Paul, and a millenarian, but this may be because of a tendency to confuse Cerinthus with the Ebionites (Epiphanius, for instance, clearly confounds the two, and may have inherited a general tendency to do so).[13] The Ebionites were Judaizers indeed, but they had another doctrinal quirk that might have been still more notorious in the eyes of the post-Apostolic Gentile church and could account for Cerinthus's being muddled with them: like Cerinthus, the Ebionites were rejected by the main body of the Church, especially because of their insistence that Jesus was a man only, invested for a time with a higher power. This, the arch-heresy of the first Christian century, would have been enough to link and blend in undiscriminating memory two movements which had been alike in virtually no other respect, especially when one had disappeared from the scene.

Later witnesses than Irenaeus write of Cerinthus's devotion to the pleasures of the flesh, feasting, and sex, and although this is not attested by Irenaeus, it could also be authentic memory—and another link with the gospel of Demetrios. Irenaeus' account of the great antipathy between Cerinthus and John includes not only the claim that John wrote to refute Cerinthus but also the charming story in which John bolts from a bathhouse in Ephesus upon hearing that Cerinthus has entered, supposing that the bathhouse might collapse once that enemy of the truth were within (III.3.4.). The story is an interesting parabolic analogue of the firm opposition between the Johannine literature and the gospel of Demetrios which is still imbedded in the texts.

But there was also another curious piece of gossip linking Cerinthus and John. According to a dialogue by one Caius, no longer extant but available to Eusebius, Cerinthus was the author of the Fourth Gospel.[14] The notoriously untrustworthy Epiphanius attributes the same opinion to a heretical group whom he calls the *Alogoi*; and although there is some doubt as to whether he had any evidence other than the dialogue by Caius,[15] in any event it is curious that the Fourth Gospel was claimed in antiquity to have been written both against Cerinthus (thus Irenaeus) and by him (thus at least Caius). The historical ground of these contradictory opinions has been lost in both cases. The one exception is the text itself. I will argue, in the next chapter, that the Fourth Gospel makes most sense if read as a corrective response to the gospel of Demetrios that nevertheless appropriated or exploited various elements of that gospel. Those who could perceive the corrective intent might well suppose that the Fourth Gospel was written in opposition to Cerinthus's version of the gospel of Demetrios; those who were slightly more distant from the scene and more scandalized by what they knew of Cerinthus's teachings might with equal ease mistake the appropriations as a thinly disguised insinuation of Cerinthian teaching into the Christian stream, and suppose that Cerinthus lay behind the enterprise in a more substantial way.

The facts of the matter are lost in the mists of a confused history, mainly recorded long after the issue had become a curiosity of the past, and the paternity of heresies could be shuffled among various candidates. We know that such historically irresponsible attributions were made, and that the historians of the era on whom we must unfortunately depend for the evidences tended to be inventive and careless. Cerinthus was eventually branded as a Judaizing millenarian. I suspect that this is a gross mistake, deriving from a conflation of the two most notorious movements that questioned the prevailing Christology, that of the Ebionites and that of Cerinthus himself. I think that Irenaeus, who was first on the reporting scene, was probably more accurate in styling Cerinthus a protognostic and in remaining silent about any Judaizing tendencies within his teaching. Later witnesses, however, may be reporting the truth. I mean only to offer Cerinthus as a plausible candidate, as an important—and possibly even the major—originating agent of what was probably a variety of gospels that denied the lordship of Jesus, appealed to the salvific value of a relationship with the ultimate God, and claimed a moral liberty in his name. It is this message, in however many varieties it may have been offered, or under however many auspices, that constituted the gospel of Demetrios.

CONCLUSION: VALUING THE GOSPEL OF DEMETRIOS

The moral dimension of the gospel of Demetrios helps to explain its appeal, perhaps especially among those with "face" (i.e., status). Critics will inevitably accuse such a gospel of debasing life, capitulating to animal desires and undisciplined impulses, and betraying the sternness and strictness of divine truth into the hands of human weakness. Paul, after all, had been accused of such things—of promoting a gospel of lawlessness and sin, of trying to please men instead of God. Undoubtedly, many who responded to these gospels of release and liberty did so for reasons that would not pass the scrutiny of a discerning spiritual director. But Paul should not be faulted in the way his detractors offered to fault him, and neither should those who preached the gospel of Demetrios. In both cases, the liberation from the Law was theologically grounded on a more encompassing principle: in Paul's case, on an elaborate theory of the accomplishment of the cross; in the gospel of Demetrios, on a simpler theory (and experience) of a Truth which could be used to pare away unnecessary suppositions and obsolete customs and regulations of uncertain authority. Not everyone considers the proclamation of such freedom to be good news, as Dostoevski's Grand Inquisitor pointedly reminds us. The discerning spiritual director could probably find as many faulty resistances to the gospel of Demetrios as faulty acceptances of it. But the theme is inevitably recurrent: wherever there is a ritual, or a text, or a moral rule that is claimed to have divine sanction, there must always arise voices to challenge the claim—and some will hear the challenge as good news of liberation while others will hear it as impiety and threat.

I think that the case is similar with the larger theological aspects of the gospel of Demetrios. Part of the appeal of the gospel of the Apostles had undoubtedly been its concreteness, its graspable story, and its offering of a past and future king to mediate between troubled humanity and the incomprehensibly invisible divine. Christian apologists have frequently celebrated these firm contours and spoken of their advantages over the wispy qualities of myth and the remoteness of philosophical abstractions. But not all persons are temperamentally predisposed to see history as the proper form in which good news should be published, or ready to find it thoroughly congenial after the fact. For every religious thinker who supposes that God is managing a mysterious plan which he will occasionally hint about through special signs, there is probably another who believes that there is and should be nothing new under the sun, that God's ways are already in the public domain.

For those who fall into the latter group, the gospel of Demetrios had another special kind of appeal. The mentality that had led many Jews to contrive symbolic readings of Scripture in order to deliteralize commandments and give rational meanings to rituals and harmonize the whole as a systematic wisdom was essentially the same mentality that had led many Greeks to syncretize cults and allegorize rites and interpret religion into the terms of the philosophers. Those Christians who shared in this mentality were ripe for responding to—and originally for founding—the gospel of Demetrios, with its rejection of hidden lordship and of invisible glory and of what it considered a curious drama of purportedly saving events that had, in fact, taken place pretty much in a corner.

The gospel of Demetrios is as much in the Jewish tradition as in the Greek. But what is more to the point, it is in the Christian tradition. It arose from the Christian movement and appealed to those within it. It was evidently offered not as a mere alternative but as a higher and more perfected form of the liberating news. And if it was in some respects quite unlike the gospel of the Apostles, in some of the same respects it was strongly reminiscent of the gospel of Jesus. It was vigorously resisted, as all previous gospels had been. If much of the resistance was from Christians rather than outsiders, the same is true of the gospel Paul preached. If it failed to survive on its own terms, so did the original gospel of the Hebrew Apostles. The value of its place in the development of the gospel lay partly in the reaction it inspired, but also in the positive contribution it made to the gospel that followed it, which will be the subject of the next chapter. Yet it should not be thought of only in terms of its contribution to development. The gospel of Demetrios was an answer and a statement of its own, and still deserves as sympathetic a hearing as its rivals. What it offered may still be thought good news.

5

The Gospel of the Ultimate

PRELIMINARY:
SITUATING THE GOSPEL OF THE ULTIMATE

It is the basic argument of this book that the Christian good news as we know it was formed in five successive stages. In the gospels proclaimed by John the Baptist, Jesus, the Apostles, the movement associated with Demetrios, and, finally, another movement associated with the Gospel of John. The development was neither smoothly organic nor simply cumulative: each stage made dramatic shifts in the content and character of the good news by adding and subtracting, altering emphases, and variously changing the ways in which earlier stages were remembered and presented. The final version of this process is found in the Gospel of John, for it contains representations of the first four gospels, and adds a fifth—the gospel of the Ultimate—in a dramatic reinterpretation of the gospel, an attempt to give the definitive good news.

The gospel of the Ultimate is not identical with the Gospel of John but occurs within it. The Gospel of John is a highly complex and composite work, built out of various strata of sources and editing, probably the most literarily complicated of all the books of the New Testament.[1] Contemporary scholarship generally recognizes that its present state is the result of a process by which a variety of materials became incorporated, expounded, rearranged, altered, and reedited.[2] Just how and where and by whom all this took place is still unsettled, and it is beyond my ambitions to attempt a solution.[3] I will be primarily concerned in this chapter with the most novel phase of that complex process, the insertion of the gospel of the Ultimate; but in order to situate this new and most ambitious version of the good news, it will be necessary to give extensive background consideration to earlier stages of the Fourth Gospel's formation—and to one final corrective stage by which the daring of the gospel of the Ultimate was itself modified and made less startling. The Fourth Gospel is itself built out of the struggle with five gospels, and this chapter will attempt to suggest how the fifth came to be, and eventually came to be modified, in relation to the other four.

My basic working hypothesis about the main stages of the Fourth Gospel's origin derives the Fourth Gospel from a combination of all the gospels treated in this book, some absorbed in separate written stages, some remembered in conjunction with others.

- The foundation of the Fourth Gospel was *the gospel of Jesus*—the same gospel that lies behind the Synoptics, but as heard and remembered by people other than those who founded the Synoptic tradition, and largely in circumstances and places different from those reflected in the Synoptic recollections. In some respects, those who brought Jesus' gospel to the foundation of the Fourth Gospel probably understood it more adequately than did the founders of the Synoptic tradition, though that understanding was inevitably colored by their own presuppositions and was partially obscured by the later layers of interpretation that made their way into the Fourth Gospel—especially
- *the gospel of the Hellenist Apostles,* in accordance with which the remembrances of Jesus were filtered through the conviction that it was only in and through the Holy Spirit that Jesus' gospel could be finally understood, particularly as Jesus had promised that gift of the Spirit with its new disclosures concerning his own exaltation and glorification. This was a written stage, which I will call the *gospel of the Beloved*

Disciples. Seeing Jesus as the Messiah and Son of God who was destined for exaltation and glorification, the author or authors of this level of the Fourth Gospel also incorporated

- *the gospel of John the Baptist*—not as John had actually preached it, and not even his acutal preachment as read through Christian lenses, but rather a revisionist version of John's gospel formed not among Christians but among followers of John who had surrendered the apocalyptic expectation of the judgment by the Coming One, and reinterpreted John's message accordingly. These revisionists were perhaps the Jewish Hellenist counterparts of those Hebrews who preserved John's apocalypticism for the Synoptic tradition, and may have brought this revised gospel of John into the Christian fold in two different forms, the more radical of which had some resemblances to
- *the gospel of Demetrios,* which was threatening and unacceptable to the main Christian community on account of its refusal to accord to Jesus the sort of glory and Lordship that had formed an important aspect of the Apostolic gospel and on account of its overbold claims about God's immediate accessibility and the believer's moral freedom. While it therefore inspired polemical opposition from the Christian camp, it also, like the more radical revision of John the Baptist's gospel, had suggestive affinities with the Hellenist Christian doctrine of the Spirit, and its main attractive features could be coopted in a revised reinterpretation of the Christian gospel, which took form as
- *the gospel of the Ultimate,* which reaffirmed the traditional Apostolic understanding of Jesus as glorified Lord, unique savior, final revealer, and true King of the heavenly world, but raised all of this to a more theologically ambitious level by insisting that these things are true on a far grander scale and in a much more immediate way than had previously been realized. This view was brought out through a rewriting of the then-existing stage of the text, adding and adjusting so as to show that the Apostolic gospel had been a partial and inadequate formulation of the deeper truth available through

bolder and more startling claims (that will be discussed later in this chapter). The great distance of this gospel from the basic Apostolic gospel eventually motivated its partial re-writing by an author or authors who were loyal to

- *the traditions of the gospel of the Hebrew Apostles,* not simply in their Synoptic form, but *as they were believed and lived out in Christian circles in the latter part of the first Christian century.* This rewriting was not systematic or thorough (the text it corrected may have by then been too well established to permit that, which may also have been the case in the previous stage of revision), but it did manage to restore a place for more traditional Christian religious practices and ideas that had been shunted aside by the gospel of the Ultimate—and with that restoration, the Fourth Gospel was complete in the form that has come down to us.

This is a working hypothesis. I will not undertake to offer proof that it describes the historical truth. I offer it as a plausible conjecture, a likely description of how the Fourth Gospel was formed, because it seems to me to make helpful sense of what the Fourth Gospel now is, and to help account for the place and nature of the gospel of the Ultimate within it. The first step at explaining all this is a consideration of the background of the Fourth Gospel and therefore of the gospel of the Ultimate.

THE BACKGROUND OF THE GOSPEL OF THE ULTIMATE

THE FOURTH GOSPEL AND THE SYNOPTIC TRADITION

The Fourth Gospel is not a Synoptic Gospel. Matthew, Mark, and Luke all draw from a common pool of resources, varying from one another like brothers with a common background and interesting shades of difference in the stories they tell together, and with interestingly independent gleanings and leanings that supplement what they share. The Fourth Gospel is not from the same family. Its incorporation of the gospel of the Ultimate, which addresses questions that the Synoptics simply do not attempt, makes it significantly different in one respect, as will be seen later in ths chapter. But there is another fundamental difference in their very roots. The Synoptic Gospels deal with the career of Jesus as seen primarily from the perspective of the Galilean disciples, the Twelve, the predominantly Hebrew point of view. The basic stratum of the Fourth Gospel comes, I believe, from the perspective of other disciples whose geographical base was not Galilee but Judea, and whose religious base was not Jewish Hebrew but Jewish Hellenist.

If the Fourth Gospel had not survived, and our understanding of Jesus' career had therefore to be based on the Synoptics alone, we would necessarily conclude that Jesus' public mission began in Galilee after the baptism and imprisonment of John (and after a period of obscurity, during which the Synoptics place Jesus alone in the desert) and that it was conducted in Galilee, with a few excursions northward and eastward, in the company of the twelve Galilean disciples, until the fatal trip to Jerusalem eventuated in his crucifixion. We might well have suspected that the Synoptic account is stylized and oversimplified in its representation, perhaps compressing a longer time into the single Synoptic year, and that it is possibly misleading in its minimizing of Jesus' connections with Judea before the final week of his life[4] but there would have been little reason to doubt the basic historical accuracy of the overall pattern.

But the Fourth Gospel did survive, and it offers a very different set of assumptions. In the first place, Jesus' mission lasts longer in the Fourth Gospel. The Passover of his crucifixion is preceded by two others (Jn 2:13, 6:4), amounting to a period of over two years. In the second place, the Fourth Gospel claims that Jesus' mission began before John was imprisoned, while he was still actively baptizing (Jn 3:24). And in the third place, Jesus' mission is not, in the Fourth Gospel, primarily to Galilee. Indeed, Galilee figures relatively little in it.[5] After the wedding feast at Cana, Jesus spends a few days in Capernaum (Jn 2:1-12) and then goes to Jerusalem (Jn 2:13); he returns briefly to Galilee and heals the royal official's son (Jn 4:43-54), but he is received in Galilee on account of what the Galileans had seen of his work in Jerusalem, not in their home territory (Jn 4:45), and shortly afterward he goes back to Jerusalem (Jn 5:1). Chapter 6 and the first nine verses of Chapter 7 show Jesus in Galilee for an uncertain length of time, after which Jesus once more returns to Jerusalem; and that is the end of his Galilean mission.[6] All the rest of the time is spent in Judea or on its fringes, with an excursion through Samaria, until the afterthought resurrection appearance in the appended Chapter 21 gives us one more glimpse of Galilee.

Had the Fourth Gospel been the only survivor, we would have assumed that Jesus, though a Galilean, had concentrated his activities mainly in Judea, missionizing Galilee only for a time after Judea had become dangerous, but then returning to Judea, despite the danger, for the remainder of his public life.

Who were the companions of Jesus' missionary activity, the disciples who might have been in a position to remember and report it? The automatic instinct is to think of the Twelve, but this is an instinct arising primarily from our experience of the Synoptic Gospels. In the Fourth Gospel, we meet the Twelve as such only once in the course of Jesus' mission, and in suspicious circumstances. At the end of Chapter 6, a hard saying by Jesus brings about his desertion by "many of his disciples," who then "were walking with him no longer" (6:66). Jesus then speaks to "the Twelve," asking whether they too intend to desert him. Peter replies movingly and with conviction that they will not, whereupon Jesus replies "Did I not choose you, the Twelve? And one of you is a devil" (6:70). Did he not choose them? In the Synoptic tradition he most certainly did; but in the Fourth Gospel it is by no means clearly so. No such choosing is otherwise mentioned; the Twelve are not previously referred to, but suddenly appear here as if well known, and there is no further mention of the Twelve in the course of the remaining public ministry. On the surface of it, these few verses, Jn 6:67-71, look rather like a piece of editorial special pleading, designed to confirm for the Twelve a place as the ultimate loyalists—a place that is not offered elsewhere in the Fourth Gospel's account of Jesus' mission. I think this a late corrective addition to the text, making its mark on the surface only.

Beneath the surface of it, the picture tends to look even more un-Synoptic with respect to the followers of Jesus. We hear of "the disciples," but (apart from one more glancing reference in Jn 20:24) not of the Twelve, nor of the apostles—the latter term is used only once, and in a casual and untechnical way (Jn 13:16). Of course, the Twelve are not all individually prominent even in the Synoptic tradition. There, some of them are named only in the list of members, and only Peter, James, and John play especially forward roles. But in the Fourth Gospel, James and John are never named at all, and are referred to in only one indisputable instance—and even then anonymously, as "the sons of Zebedee"—in the postscript Chapter 21, which clearly constitutes a special pleading of another kind. And Peter? Apart from his acting as spokesman in the suspect verse 6:68, Peter appears only once in the entire course of the Fourth Gospel's representation of Jesus' public ministry, and that is in the very first chapter, where in three verses Andrew reports to him that they have found the Messiah and then conducts him to Jesus to receive his nickname (Jn 1:40-42). We are not even told how Peter received Andrew's testimony. Thereafter (6:68 once more set aside), Peter remains invisible until the Last Supper, when Jesus' public ministry is over.

Whenever Peter appears in the Fourth Gospel, it is clear that his importance is assumed: he receives his name from Jesus in 1:42, Andrew is introduced as his brother in 1:40 and again in 6:8 (though Peter is not said to be present), and he figures substantively at the Last Supper and throughout the subsequent account of the passion and resurrection of Jesus. But during Jesus' public ministry, the Fourth Gospel gives Peter no role whatsoever except for the special moment at the end of chapter 6. Verse 68 obviously assumes that the reader will readily recognize the signal importance of both Peter and of the Twelve whose spokesman he is; but the Fourth Gospel does not itself provide the basis for this recognition. The author of 6:67-71 was appealing to traditions very like those of the Synoptic Gospels, but very unlike those that form the bulk of the Fourth Gospel.

There are, of course, brief appearances by other members of the Synoptic Twelve. Andrew and Philip and Thomas play small parts, Judas and Jude appear along with Peter in the Last Supper scene. But none of the Twelve is prominent within the cast of characters met during Jesus' public ministry, at least not by comparison with other figures unmentioned by, and perhaps unknown to, the Synoptic tradition—Nathaniel, Nicodemus, Lazarus, and still others only barely noticed in Synoptic Gospels: Martha, her siser Mary, the man born blind. Nathaniel is identified in the appended chapter 21 as being from Cana in Galilee (Jn 21:2); the others just mentioned are all Judeans.

All in all, then, the balance of geographical and personal references seem to suggest that the traditions underlying the Fourth Gospel are not only largely independent of the Synoptic tradition, but derive mainly from a different locale and a different set of disciples. The Synoptic tradition is associated with the Galilean Twelve; the Fourth Gospel's memories seem to come from followers in Judea.

The differences between John and the Synoptics have led, almost inevitably, to the theory that the Fourth Gospel was written precisely to supplement and complement the Synoptics by showing the traditions they had omitted and the deeper meanings they had not brought fully forward. The theory seems quite plausible at first: if the Fourth Gospel's author was assuming familiarity with the Synoptic Gospels, he would not need to repeat the materials they had collected, and could concentrate on supplying what they had omitted and pressing for a more theologically ambitious interpretation of the entire story. One might thus account for the Fourth Gospel's omission of the institution of the Eucharist and of Jesus' work as an exorcist, and for the substitution of lengthier and more explicit discourses for the parables that figure so importantly in the gospel of the Synoptic Jesus. But scholarly attempts to establish this theory have resulted in the conclusion that the Fourth Gospel does not in fact behave in quite this way. It shows clear contacts with some of the materials of the Synoptic tradition but does not indicate a knowledge of any of the Synoptic Gospel texts as we have received them. The Fourth Gospel appears to be a largely independent undertaking, arising from Christians who were not familiar with Matthew, Mark, or Luke as such.[7] It retells the foundational stories of John and Jesus with an eye to theological purposes of its own, occasionally correcting what it takes to be errors or misunderstandings but never attempting to address the Synoptic picture as if it were either a rival or a more modest predecessor.

The Fourth Gospel's differences from the Synoptics have also resulted in the suspicion that it is a fanciful construction, without historical reliability. In my reconstruction of the gospels of John the Baptist and Jesus, I made little use of the Fourth Gospel, on the grounds that the Synoptics offer evidence that is almost certainly closer to the original historical reality. To be sure, Matthew, Mark, and Luke all show telltale symptoms of interpretive interference with the raw material of history. We could hardly expect otherwise. They wrote their accounts of John and Jesus as Christians writing to Christians, reporting the gospels of Jesus and John from a viewpoint within the gospel of the Apostles. But the memories from which they wrote still carried much of the shape and texture of those earlier times and those earlier gospels, and had not yet been extensively revised in the image and likeness of the Apostolic news. Thus they can tell us much—probably more than they were meant to do—about pre-Apostolic gospelling.

The memories behind the Fourth Gospel have been pushed farther away from John and Jesus, toward the later news. This is especially evident in the treatment of John the Baptist. His Synoptic portrait is not generally convenient for Christian purposes. Although there are individual touches that bend John toward the Apostolic gospel (like Matthew's having John ask Jesus for baptism, or Luke's report of Mary's visit to Elizabeth), the overall Synoptic John the Baptist remains an independent figure whose gospel does not point to Jesus. But in the Fourth Gospel, John the Baptist has been almost totally refashioned for Christian purposes. His mission, his baptism, and his gospel all have as their primary and virtually exclusive task the preparation of Jesus' way, as that way was understood during the Apostolic period. Similarly, the Jesus of the Fourth Gospel carries far more of the stamp of later Christian belief than does the Synoptic Jesus. In Matthew, Mark, and Luke, Jesus points continuously to the Dominion of God; in the Fourth Gospel, he points rather to himself as the true and proper object of faith, as Apostolic Christianity had encouraged. In short, when it turns to the backgrounds of the specifically Christian gospel, the gospel of the Apostles, the Fourth Gospel shows a deep interpretive bias. The gospels of John and Jesus are portrayed as anticipating from the start the content of the Apostolic gospel.

This does not mean, however, that the Fourth Gospel simply disregards the historical John or the historical Jesus, as if real memories of them had faded and they could be made to say or do whatever the evangelist might find convenient. In both cases, the outlines of their gospels, as they can be reassembled from Synoptic evidence, are present in the Fourth Gospel. But where the Synoptics concentrate on reporting what the historical John and Jesus said and did, with occasional interpretive asides or adjustments, the Fourth Gospel is especially concerned to disclose more clearly just what their sayings and doings were finally understood to have meant, whether or not this had been adequately understood at the time, and characteristically places these bolder messages on the lips of John and Jesus. Matthew 12:40 has Jesus interpret his own reference to the Sign of Jonah as a statement about his coming resurrection, although this interpretation is absent from the parallel texts and is intrinsically improbable; Luke 9:45 claims that the disciples simply did not grasp Jesus' prediction of his own passion, though the prediction itself is made clearly. Here and there, the Synoptic tradition thus brings explicitly into the gospel of the pre-crucifixion Jesus overt and explicit elements of post-resurrection belief, to have him define the meaning of statements and parabolic sayings in accordance with their later interpretation. The Fourth Gospel uses this technique throughout, making John and Jesus speak plainly what the community of the Fourth Gospel eventually had come to believe. It gives us memories of the historical Jesus and the historical John, but it gives us their gospels not as they had preached them, but as they were thought to have meant them—that is, as they were subsequently reassessed within the boundaries of intense new convictions about what had really happened and about who Jesus really was. The foundation of the Fourth Gospel is highly interpreted historical memory, and largely non-Galilean memory, but historical memory nevertheless.[8]

THE FIRST STAGE OF THE FOURTH GOSPEL'S COMPOSITION: THE GOSPEL OF THE BELOVED DISCIPLE

THE PLACE AND PURPOSE OF THE BELOVED DISCIPLE

The text of the Fourth Gospel as it has come to us closes with a brief discussion of the rumor that "the disciple whom Jesus loved" was not going to die (Jn 21:20). Then verse 24 sums up by saying that "this is the disciple who bears witness about these things, and wrote them up." As it stands, the Fourth Gospel seems to present itself as the work of an eyewitness of Jesus' career, and indeed a most important and intimate eyewitness: the disciple whom Jesus loved.

This appearance diminishes with a second look. Jn 21:24 may be read as if it were written by a disciple speaking about himself, but it is couched in the third person rather than the first. Its concluding words are "and we know that his witness is true." More tellingly, the whole of the final chapter seems, on various grounds, to be a late addition to the Fourth Gospel, a sort of appendix to a text that originally ended with Chapter 20; and the discussion of the rumor that "the disciple Jesus loved" was not going to die takes place primarily to make it clear that Jesus never made such a promise—the purpose for its inclusion in Chapter 21 is almost certainly apologetical, to deal with the fact of that disciple's death. "The disciple whom Jesus loved" was not likely to have been the author of Chapter 21.

But even if Chapter 21 is an afterthought, it may still be able to tell us something usefully true about the sources and authorship of what had gone before. For this is not the first time the Fourth Gospel has laid claim to being derived from eyewitness testimony. Just after his report of the death of Jesus, the narrator's voice breaks out with a similar testimony: ". . . and he who saw has borne witness, and his witness is true, and he knows that he has said the truth so that you too may believe" (Jn 19:35). The witness in question is not named or identified further; but the only person who has been mentioned in the scene who might fill the role is "the disciple whom he loved" (Jn 19:26). Again, the narrator refers to this disciple in the third person. The disciple whom Jesus loved is evidently not the author of these words. But the narrator claims that this disciple is the source of the information.

We do not know the identity of the one who is referred to as "the disciple whom Jesus loved."[9] The title is first introduced into the Fourth Gospel at the Last Supper, where Jesus reclines with "one of his disciples . . . whom he loved" (Jn 13:23); it recurs in the crucifixion scene (Jn 19:26) and in the account of the disciples' discovery of Jesus' resurrection (Jn 20:2) and is used twice more in the appended final chapter (Jn 21:7,20). No name is ever directly attached, and it is impossible to know whether the title applies to someone whom we meet by name earlier in the Fourth Gospel, or another who is never named, or perhaps one who first enters the Fourth Gospel's scene at the Last Supper. But in any event, the Fourth Gospel places this disciple in a position to witness some extremely important events in the career of Jesus, and claims that this is the witness whose testimony is true and is given so that we may believe (Jn 19:35). That claim is echoed once more at the end of Chapter 20, in what was probably the original conclusion to the Fourth Gospel: "And these things have been written so that you may believe that Jesus is the Messiah, the Son of God, and that, believing, you may have life in his name" (Jn 20:31).

This last statement is of a kind unparalleled in the Synoptic Gospels and is an important clue to the unravelling of the Fourth Gospel's compositional history. Luke prefaces his Gospel by assuring its addressee, Theophilos, that he intends to present an account that will assure Theophilos that he had been accurately instructed about Jesus (Lk 1:1-4). Matthew and Mark say nothing about their purposes. The Fourth Gospel embodies the claim that it is written to inspire belief in Jesus as Messiah and Son of God. This is evidently the same purpose for which the testimony of the disciple Jesus loved had been given, "so that you too may believe" (Jn 19:35). Evidently, whatever the Beloved Disciple has reported or written is understood as directed at awakening belief in Jesus as the gospel of the Apostles saw him.

I remarked a paragraph ago that the end of Chapter 20 was probably the original conclusion to the Fourth Gospel. That is somewhat misleading. More precisely, the last verse of Chapter 20 is probably the original conclusion of the first major stage of the Fourth Gospel's composition, not of the Fourth Gospel as we have it. The latter is the product of further stages of additions, alterations, and editorial adjustments, building on the legacy of the former—and the former was evidently a written account formed in the Apostolic image. Behind the Fourth Gospel as it has come to us is a written Gospel of the Beloved Disciple, a form of the gospel of the Apostles built primarily upon memories of Jesus from the days of John the Baptist until the exaltation of the risen Lord.

Was the mysterious Beloved Disciple the author of this non-Synoptic Gospel, or only the witness on whose testimony it was built? We cannot be sure. It is not likely to make much difference. The Fourth Gospel remembers Jesus and John the Baptist in ways that are deeply colored by the Apostolic beliefs, and it is of relatively little moment whether the narrator's voice is that of a later believer interpreting the reminiscences of the Beloved Disciple, or that of the Beloved Disciple reformulating those reminiscences in the light of the Apostolic faith in which they had been reunderstood and transformed. In either event, the story is told from the perspective of a later illumination—and the main source of that illumination is the Holy Spirit.

THE ROLE OF THE HOLY SPIRIT IN THE GOSPEL OF THE BELOVED DISCIPLE

The narrator of the Fourth Gospel is clearly aware of differences between the disciples' understanding of Jesus during his public career and their later understanding after his triumph over death. After Jesus' brief discourse on the sheep and the shepherd in Chapter 10, the narrator admits "Jesus spoke this parable to them; but they did not know what it was that he had said to them" (Jn 10:6). As Peter and the Beloved Disciple behold the empty tomb, the narrator remarks that "they did not yet know the Scripture, that it was required that he be raised from the dead" (Jn 20:9). Similarly, near the beginning of the story, the narrator similarly observes about Jesus' difficult saying concerning the Temple that "when he was raised from the dead, his disciples remembered that he said this, and they believed the Scripture and the word that Jesus had spoken" (Jn 2:22). From the perspective of Jesus' resurrection, both Scripture and the gospel of Jesus were understood in a new light, interpreted in a new way. "Now, his disciples did not know these things at first; but when Jesus was glorified, then they remembered that these things had been written about him and they did these things to him" (Jn 12:16). The gospel of the Beloved Disciple was written from the time when they knew these things—when they read the Scriptures in a new way and therefore remembered and interpreted what they had witnessed accordingly.

The Synoptic Gospels offer parallels to these admissions—the disciples' inability to comprehend Jesus' predictions of his passion and resurrection, their need to have the Scriptures expounded by the risen Jesus in order to read them rightly. But there is one note introduced into the Fourth Gospel that is not paralleled in the Synoptics. At the Last Supper, Jesus foretells the coming change in their understanding, not by a prediction of his resurrection but by a prediction of a significantly different kind. "These things I have spoken to you, while abiding with you: but the Paraclete, the Holy Spirit, which the Father will send in my name, he will teach you all things, and will recall to you all the things which I told you" (Jn 14:25-26). It will be the gift of the Holy Spirit that will make all the difference in their ability to remember and grasp the meaning of Jesus' gospel, and it will be through the Holy Spirit that they will receive further illumination about matters which Jesus may not necessarily have revealed even in parables. This sense of the Holy Spirit belongs to the times of Apostolic realization, after a further stage beyond even Jesus' resurrection, and is reminiscent especially of the gospel of the Hellenist Apostles.

This stratum of the Fourth Gospel is deeply saturated with the recognition that the reception of the Holy Spirit is the key to the Apostolic gospel, the turning point of Apostolic understanding. It is this event, rather than Jesus' resurrection, that is repeatedly foretold in the course of Jesus' misunderstood career. In the course of the Feast of Tabernacles, Jesus makes an elliptical promise that rivers of living water will flow out of those who believe in him (Jn 7:38). There is no indication that any of his hearers could understand the meaning of this at the time, but the narrator explains from his later perspective: ". . . but he said this concerning the Spirit, which those believing in him were going to receive." Then the narrator adds "for there was no Spirit as yet, because Jesus was not yet glorified" (Jn 7:39). At the Last Supper, Jesus promises that after he goes away to the Father, he will send the Spirit to his disciples (Jn 16:7)—or, in another passage, he will pray the Father to send the Spirit (Jn 14:16)—and then the Spirit will be in them (Jn 14:17) and will glorify him (Jn 16:14). "When the Paraclete comes, which I will send to you from the Father—the Spirit of Truth, which will come forth from the Father—he will bear witness to me" (Jn 15:26). It is the Spirit of Truth that will lead them into all truth, even about the things that are to come (Jn 16:13). It is then, and only then, that they will bear witness concerning him (Jn 15:27). That is, both the understanding and the proclamation of the Apostolic gospel will be based, not on the resurrection of Jesus but on his glorification as known through the gift of the Spirit. This is a theme of the gospel of the Hellenist Apostles, of which the gospel of the Beloved Disciple is a concrete instance.

The Synoptic Gospels, however, arise from the tradition of the Galilean Hebrew Apostles. Some of that tradition is correctively insinuated into the Fourth Gospel as well, for instance in the special tribute to the Twelve that appears, and disappears, so abruptly at the end of Chapter 6. But I believe that the main body of the Fourth Gospel, the stratum that I have labeled "the gospel of the Beloved Disciple," derives from Judean Hellenists, and that it is this derivation above all that accounts for a range of significant differences from the Synoptics even at this stratum of the Fourth Gospel's composition, quite apart from the later addition of the gospel of the Ultimate. I will attempt later to show that it is also this Hellenist origin above all that makes the gospel of the Ultimate possible; but for the moment, I wish to pursue some of the significant features that appear at this stage of composition.

The gospel of the Beloved Disciple arose from Christians' experiencing of the Spirit as it illuminated memories of Jesus and the reading of Scripture (and, to a considerable extent, the remembrance of John the Baptist as well), and it accordingly points forward to that culminating experience at various stages of its narrative, from the preaching of John to the discourses of the Last Supper.

The extent to which the experience of the Spirit transformed the understanding of the Hellenist Apostles should not be underestimated. At the Last Supper, Jesus foretells this change: "These things I have spoken to you, while abiding with you; but the Paraclete, the Holy Spirit, which the Father will send in my name, he will teach you all things and will recall to you all the things which I told you" (Jn 14:25-26). Both parts of the statement are important. They will remember things that Jesus had said and will understand their meanings in an entirely new way, as in the case of the saying about the Temple; and they will be taught through the Holy Spirit additional things that Jesus had not necessarily talked about, even parabolically. "These things I have spoken to you in figures; an hour is coming when I will speak to you no more in figures, but I will tell you plainly about the Father" (Jn 16:25); the Holy Spirit, in glorifying Jesus, "will take from what is mine, and declare it to you" (Jn 16:14). That is, Jesus' revelations will not cease with his departure from this world. Through the Holy Spirit, he will reveal still more after his glorification. Just before the original conclusion at the end of Chapter 20, there is a summary verse that hints in the same direction: ". . . and then Jesus even did many other signs in his disciples' presence, which are not written in this book" (Jn 20:30). What are these additional signs? They may be earlier events in Jesus' career, omitted for economy, but the curious word "then" (*oun*) invites an alternative reading. After that—after his final moments in this world—Jesus revealed many other things to the disciples, being present to them through the Spirit. The gospel of the Beloved Disciple was, by all these indications, preeminently a gospel about Jesus as he was understood through the gift of the Spirit. If the Synoptic Gospels' recollections are sometimes reshaped to fit Jesus as he was known in the gospel of the Hebrew Apostles, the authentic memories contained within the Fourth Gospel can be expected to be reinterpreted even more, so as to release to the reader the faith-inspiring revelations that the disciples had not received during Jesus' career, and could not receive until the Spirit came to show them all the truth. The belief to which the gospel of the Beloved Disciple is meant to lead us is the belief the Spirit had brought about.

In the Fourth Gospel, the remains of the original gospel of the Beloved Disciple lie intermingled with the next major stratum of rewriting, which presented the gospel of the Ultimate to press the understanding of Jesus to even more daring lengths. It is not easy to tell what belongs to which stratum of composition. Any attempt at reconstruction is further hampered by the degree to which the gospel of the Beloved Disciple has already adjusted its memories of Jesus in the light of the Spirit's illumination. But though the gospels of Jesus and John the Baptist show up in the Fourth Gospel filtered through these two phases of reinterpretation, the recognizable outlines of their forms are still discernible. Before considering the gospel of the Ultimate, it remains then to attend to the gospel of Jesus as it was remembered by the community of the Beloved Disciple, then the content of the gospel of the Beloved Disciple as it reinterpreted Jesus, then the way the gospels of John the Baptist and Demetrios made their mark and prepared the way for the radical reinterpretation that was the gospel of the Ultimate.

THE GOSPEL OF JESUS IN THE GOSPEL OF THE BELOVED DISCIPLE

The Dominion of God is at hand, the gospel of Jesus had proclaimed. The Fourth Gospel refers explicitly to the Dominion of God only twice as such, but in both cases it is mentioned as if it is a familiar notion, and as if it is taken for granted that Jesus' hearers hope to see and enter into that Dominion. "I tell you solemnly, if one be not begotten from above, he cannot see the Dominion of God" (Jn 3:3); "I tell you solemnly, if one be not begotten by water and Spirit, he cannot enter into the Dominion of God" (Jn 3:5). There is no attempt at explaining what "the Dominion of God" is; speaker and listeners alike appear to assume that it is understood, and indeed that the news of its accessibility has already been published—for the drift of Jesus' teaching here is that becoming members of the Dominion of God will not be as simple a matter as his audience supposes: more is required in a way that they have not anticipated. In short, these references presuppose the gospel of the Dominion of God as it was proclaimed in Jesus' gospel. This is the advanced course, for which the basic course is prerequisite. The basic course as known through Jesus' Synoptic preaching insisted that the Dominion of God was at hand, and that we are called to enter into it by becoming sons of God. The advanced course takes one further interpretive step: becoming a son of God is less metaphorical and more literal than you may have suspected; it involves being begotten from on high, through the Spirit. Though obviously colored by a post-Pentecost interpretation, this is recognizably based upon the gospel of Jesus.

Elsewhere in the Fourth Gospel, the term "Dominion of God" does not appear, but the general notion is present. Jesus' own gospel seems to have been quite free of national and political hopes concerning what or who is to come into the world, and the Fourth Gospel shares this detachment much more than the Synoptics. The Kingdom (i.e., Dominion) that is in question is not of this world, and Jesus' own kingliness is therefore not from here but from heaven (Jn 18:36). He comes in the name of the Father, seeking not the glory mortals can give but the glory of God (Jn 5:41, 7:18), which is the only glory worth seeking and having (Jn 5:44), just as the Dominion of God is worth the loss of all else. Jesus' gospel comes from God (Jn 7:16), and whoever truly cares to do the will of God will recognize that this is so, and will know that Jesus imitates the works of God by doing what God empowers him to do, and that he is sent to lead others to do the same. As in the Synoptic accounts, Jesus' cures are among the significant works by which the inbreaking of God's merciful rule is made manifest. For the true works of God are not the works of the Law, but works that imitate the divine mercy and manifest human obedience. The true worshiper of God is not the keeper of the Law of Moses, but the keeper of the Law of God—one who does God's will by imitating a righteousness that is deeper and more complete than the righteousness of the Law. To be *merely* a disciple of Moses is to be blind to the light that comes from God, even to the light that comes from Moses' Scriptures. True righteousness must exceed the righteousness of the Scribes and Pharisees, claims the Jesus of the Synoptics. Theirs is the righteousness of the Law only. The Fourth Gospel likewise shows Jesus insisting that he who sets aside the Law of Moses to cure on the Sabbath is in fact seeking and imitating the ways of God, the mercy of God, the glory of God—and there is no unrighteousness in him (Jn 7:16-24). Those who belong rightly to God, in the gospel of Jesus, combine this obedient reenactment of God's mercy with a love of neighbor, exemplified so perfectly by Jesus that it is an imitation of his love as well (Jn 13:34-35, 15:12,17).

In the gospel of Jesus, the Son of Man is essentially the same as the Dominion of God. In the Fourth Gospel too, the Son of Man, like the Dominion of God, comes ultimately from heaven, and gathers into heaven all those who abide in him. They who remain in him, keeping not the law of Moses but the true commandments by which God's own righteousness is imitated and secured, will share in the glory when the Son of Man is glorified. The Son of Man is the perfect Son of God, the locus of the truest worship of God, and thus the true Temple;[10] the Son of Man is also the authoritative judge, capable of forgiving or retaining sins. And this judgment, this glory, this truth of worship is not only a matter for future fulfillment: the Son of Man has already begun coming from heaven and giving new life of a kind different from the life of this world. All those who keep the commandments of the Son of Man and abide in him will see and share in his glory, given him by the Father; they become members of the Son of Man, and God's true children, begotten from heaven and not just from men.[11]

This sketch of the gospel of Jesus as it appears in the Fourth Gospel is, of course, incomplete. Virtually all of these statements are there given additional values and twists that accommodate Jesus' gospel to the gospel of the Spirit that succeeded it among the Hellenist Apostles. The contours of Jesus' gospel are there sufficiently to make it credible that the Beloved Disciple knew and reported what Jesus had said and done. But these reports speak with a special accent. It is plausibly an accent of Judean Hellenists in part, but the other part is no less important. These reports speak correctively, to say that the gospel of Jesus was not only this, but that as well—not only the proclamation of the Dominion of God, but special news about the conditions for entering it; not only the offer of sonship to God but particular information about the form it takes; not only a message about the Son of Man but further secrets about who and what he is. The gospel of the Beloved Disciple appears to have been written not merely to inspire belief in Jesus, but to inform its readers that the right kind of belief, and the most adequate understanding of Jesus, can be reached only through what the Spirit has shown in the gospel of the Hellenist Apostles, and that other understandings of Jesus have either missed or fallen short of the mark. Whenever the gospel of the Beloved Disciple may have been finally set down, I suspect that its initial thrust and motivation came from the days in which the Hebrew Christians and the Hellenist Christians contended about the right way of interpreting what had happened among them.

What then was this interpretation? What did the gospel of the Beloved Disciple intend in telling its story so that "you may believe that Jesus is the Messiah, the Son of God, and that, believing, you may have life in his name" (Jn 20:31)? Just what does this confession mean?

THE GOOD NEWS OF THE GOSPEL OF THE BELOVED DISCIPLE

From the beginning, the insight into Jesus' Messiahship is pivotal to the gospel of the Beloved Disciple, as it evidently was in all forms of the gospel of the Apostles. Andrew announces to Peter that in Jesus they had found "the Messiah (which is, translated, Christ)" (Jn 1:41), and four verses later, Philip tells Nathaniel that they have found the one "whom Moses wrote about in the Law, and the Prophets—Jesus, the son of Joseph, from Nazareth" (Jn 1:45). These two confessions are parallel with each other and with the climactic testimony in which Martha (not Peter!) testifies that "I have believed that you are the Messiah (*Christos*), the Son of God, the one coming into the world" (Jn 11:27).

The Messiah, the Son of God, the one whom the Law and the Prophets predicted, and the Coming One are apparently alternative ways of referring to the same figure. The last of these titles is undoubtedly related to the recurrent allusion to Psalm 118:26, "Blessed is he who comes in the name of the Lord," which was widely understood to be a promise of an agent of divine intervention. As I have previously shown, some Jews aligned this verse with their hope of a Davidic political Messiah; but that was not the way in which John the Baptist had understood the Coming One, *ho erchomenos*, nor is it the understanding of the gospel of the Beloved Disciple. The Fourth Gospel never suggests that Jesus is descended from David, nor that he is to have a kingdom of this world. He is indeed the fulfillment of the the Scriptures, and the fulfillment of John the Baptist's gospel of the Coming One—"everything John said was true about this man" (Jn 10:41)—but he is not the Messiah hoped for by militant nationalists. In the gospel of the Beloved Disciple, the very notion of Messiah has undergone a reinterpretation that conforms it to a different expectation.

Nathaniel's confession, "You are the Son of God; you are the King of Israel" (Jn 1:49), may seem at first to refer to a political figure, but I suggest that the latter title participates rather in the same reinterpretation, and should be understood in a more metaphorical way. Jesus' kingdom is not of this world (Jn 18:36), and the Israel whose king he is, is not a political or ethnic entity. The Dominion he proclaimed was of a different order: the Dominion of God, which one may see and enter not through political liberation but only through a begetting from above by the Holy Spirit (Jn 3:5). After thus instructing Nicodemus, Jesus expresses surprise that he does not know these things when he is "the teacher of Israel" (Jn

3:10). This is a rather odd expression if taken literally, but I think it makes more likely sense if this expression, like Nathaniel's "King of Israel"—or, for that matter, Jesus' epithet for Nathaniel, "an Israelite in whom there is no deceit" (Jn 1:47)—is read in accordance with another clue to the meaning of Jesus' Messiahship. Jesus tells Pilate "You said it, that I am a king. I was born for this, and for this I have come into the world, that I may bear witness to the truth" (Jn 18:37). The meaning of his kingship, and his purpose as the One Who Comes, is to bear witness to the truth. This is not a kingship of a literal sort. If he is King of Israel, then Israel seems to be a metaphor for the truth, an Israelite is one who belongs to, or seeks, the truth, and the teacher of Israel is a teacher of truth.[12] It is not merely coincidental that the Fourth Gospel's account of Jesus' entry into Jerusalem makes no reference to Davidic descent, but has the crowds proclaim, with deeper meaning than they knew, "Blessed is the one who comes in the name of the Lord—the King of Israel" (Jn 12:13). When some members of the earlier crowds had boldly identified Jesus as the Messiah, his lack of conventional credentials had proved a stumbling block for others, who murmured, "Surely the Messiah does not come from Galilee! Didn't the Scripture say that it is from the seed of David, and from Bethlehem, the village where David was, that the Messiah comes?" (Jn 7:41-42). As is so often the case in the Fourth Gospel, those who are puzzled have simply missed the point. The answer to their question is implicitly a flat no. That is not what Scripture said at all. The Scriptures, properly read, indeed point to one who is to come—that is what Moses and the Prophets were all about (Jn 1:45; cf. 5:39, 46; 8:56; 12:41); and the appropriate title for this Coming One is indeed "the Messiah (which is, translated, Anointed)." But this title has nothing whatever to do with descent from David or the restoration of this dynasty to power in the land; it has to do with the revelation of the truth. The Samaritan woman has a clearer understanding about what is rightly expected: "I know that Messiah is coming (the one called Christ); when he comes, he will disclose everything to us" (Jn 4:25).

Messiah, or Christ, is thus essentially a title for a revealer, whose kingship is not of this world but rather of the transcendent order of heavenly truth. The Coming One comes to bring light, to disclose the truth that makes us free (Jn 8:32). Yes, he will be King of Israel—but not in the commonplace literal sense. Yes, he will bring rescue—but not from the Romans. Yes, he will save those who recognize his kingship—but not from political oppression. Yes, he will liberate us and make us free—but with the truth, not the sword. And yes, under his dominion, all the Israelites who have been scattered about the world will again be gathered into unity—but not in a new earthly kingdom. It is in these shifted senses that the gospel of the Beloved Disciple proposes to win the reader's belief that Jesus is the Messiah, in whose name we may have life.

The reinterpretation of Messiah is rich and thorough, and I think it likely that this is not the invention of the gospel of the Beloved Disciple, but rather part of its general Hellenist inheritance. Those who had become somewhat detached from the letter of the Law, and had learned to read its rules symbolically, saw in it "the shape of knowledge and of truth" (Rom 2:20), empowering one who grasps its deeper meaning to be "a guide to the blind, a light to those in darkness, an instructor of the simple, a teacher of beginners" (Rom 2:19-20).[13] The true Messiah promised by such Scriptures would plausibly have been understood as the greatest teacher of all, one whose instruction would finally make plain the real meanings of the texts that over-literal conservative interpreters had misunderstood. It is likely that Hellenist Jews, in their contentions with their Hebrew counterparts long before the time of Jesus, had already formed the expectation that the Messiah who was to come would alter the conventional understanding of the Law of Moses and make possible a purer and more spiritual form of worship than was practised in the sacrificial cultus of the Temple. Stephen was accused of proclaiming that just such changes were being brought about through Jesus of Nazareth. The accusation was probably accurate: he, like the gospel of the Beloved Disciple, had seen in Jesus the Messiah of Hellenist hope and had labored to communicate his realization to others.

The title "Son of God" may have been alternative and equivalent to "Messiah" in Hellenist circles, as it seems sometimes to have been among the Hebrews. But it probably carried the other usual metaphorical overtones as well—the one preeminently favored by God, the righteous one. On the literal level, the gospel of the Beloved Disciple appears to have held Jesus to be the son of Joseph (Jn 1:45), but a more important truth lay in his calling God "Father" in an intimate way. This brought about the accusation that he was claiming to be divine (Jn 10:33), but to the gospel of the Beloved Disciple the accusation was false and was based on a misunderstanding of an authorized metaphor. The Scriptures give him precedent: "Is it not written in your Law, 'I said you are gods'? If he called them gods, to whom the word of God came . . ." (Jn 10:34-35). Well, if this is the case, then only the dullest and most literal-minded of his hearers could possibly be offended by Jesus' readiness to call himself God's Son, especially when his gospel invites all to become children of God (Jn 1:12—cf. 11:52) by receiving the begetting from above through the Spirit (Jn 3:3,5). Jesus is of course Son of God in a higher and more thorough way: if the Spirit bestows divine Sonship, it is especially significant that Jesus is the one who sends the Spirit, or brings the Father to send it, and that it was upon Jesus that John the Baptist saw the Spirit descend and rest, marking him as the baptizer in Spirit whom John had proclaimed without knowing him (Jn 1:33)—and therefore marking him in a unique way as the Son of God (Jn 1:34). "Son of God" and "Messiah" are not identical terms in the gospel of the Beloved Disciple, but they converge. The former relates especially to the Spirit, the latter to the truth; but as the Spirit is finally the Spirit of Truth, these two titles finally coincide.

The good news of the Beloved Disciple is that those who believe that Jesus is, in these senses, Messiah and Son of God will have life in his name (Jn 20:31). There is no direct explanation of precisely what that means, and the matter is complicated by the interpretive additions of the gospel of the Ultimate, but I suggest that the gospel of the Beloved Disciple promised that believers would be given *zōē aiōnion,* "eternal life" or "life of the eon," and that this meant "life that will last forever." Within the boundaries of the gospel of the Beloved Disciple, that is, the term probably meant essentially what it means in the Synoptic Gospels (see Mt 19:16,29; 25:46; Mk 10:17,30; Lk 10:25; 18:18,30). It is that which more conservative Jews hoped to obtain through the Scriptures (Jn 5:39). It is not the life of this world, but of the next—hence Jesus' admonitions to his disciples not to be too protective of this world's life, since whoever loves it too much will eventually lose it, while whoever has a proper detachment from it, and dies spiritually to this world, will gain a life that can be kept forever (Jn 12:25) and will bear the good and abundant fruit that comes about only on condition of the death of the seed (Jn 12:24). It is in this sense that those who hear the word of Jesus and believe that it is the good news of the Father who sent him have eternal life, and will evade judgment; they have already made the transition from this death-bound world to the new world that lives undyingly (Jn 5:24). The kind of life that is sustained by earthly bread is doomed, along with the rest of this world, and therefore one should not be anxious about the sort of food that nourishes it; the important food is that which the Son of Man will give, the food given through the One whose signs show him to be the authentic agent of the Father, the food that remains and sustains life forever (Jn 6:26-27). This is why God sent his Son into the world—not to judge but to save, and to make it possible for believers not to perish but to live forever in the new age (Jn 3:16-17). For judgment is not itelf part of the gospel. It is not news at all.

The death that belongs to this world is readily perceivable all around us; judgment is already here, in the regular process. The real news, the gospel, is that one may evade this seemingly inexorable and inevitable doom by believing in Jesus as Messiah and Son of God, and thus enter into the life of that other dominion over which he presides.

That life is given through the Spirit, and the Spirit is given by or through Jesus to those who accept that he is the revealing Messiah of the truth, and the intimate Son of the Father. Such acceptance entails living out the truth he has revealed, keeping his commandment, which is his Father's commandment, that we love one another, and following the example of his Sonship in complete obedience to the Father's will and in loving one another as he has loved us. If one thus enters into the life that does not perish, the life of this world no longer matters. Jesus' own death is therefore the surrendering of a trivial form of life. From the perspective of this world, it may appear to be a condemnation, a disgrace, a scandal; but to the eye of the believer, it is his final and perfect obedience to what the Father had commanded (Jn 14:31) and his way of returning to the Father (Jn 14:28), leaving this world and the evil power that rules it (Jn 14:30), to accept from the Father the glory that was promised to the obedient Son of Man (Jn 17:24). That is, it is ordained that the Son of Man must suffer and die in order to enter into his glory. We do not ask why. It is the will of the Father, and the true Son obeys. As the ultimate sacrifice it is also the ultimate act of love, laying down his life in behalf of his friends.

It is not clear just how, in the terms of the gospel of the Beloved Disciple, Jesus' death is "in behalf" of those he loved. The High Priest remarks that it is "appropriate that one man should die in behalf of the people rather than have the whole nation perish" (Jn 11:50), and the narrator observes that this was a privileged but unwitting truth (Jn 11:51). But in what sense is his death in behalf of the people, and a protection against the perishing of the whole nation? It is possible that the gospel of the Beloved Disciple assumed that this was a sacrifice by which the Lamb of God takes away the sin of the world (Jn 1:29), but if so, it is a well-hidden assumption. The question is simply left unresolved, left as unclear as Peter's meaning when he claims willingness to die in behalf of Jesus (Jn 13:37). It is entirely possible that the gospel of the Beloved Disciple never reached a settled conclusion, but was content with a scattering of suggestions—the death of Jesus was the only way of obtaining the glory promised to the Son of Man and those who belong to him, the only way of returning to the Father to receive and transmit the gift of the Spirit, the only way of completing for our benefit the work which the Father had mysteriously given him to do as Son and Messiah. One way or another, the death of Jesus was somehow appropriate, necessary, and, in its own mysterious way, revealing.

The most surprising omission from the possible range of explanations is that the death of Jesus was necessary in order for the miraculous sign of his resurrection to take place. The Fourth Gospel does not attempt to make this claim. What was the stance of the gospel of the Beloved Disciple?

This too is unfortunately obscure. The last two chapters of the Fourth Gospel are full of compositional complications that show various layers of differing notions about Jesus' resurrection. At first, it appears that it took place in an ethereal and somewhat hidden manner: Mary Magdalen alone sees Jesus, and is not permitted to touch him, and is sent to inform the brethren that he will not appear to them in any physical way, or provide clear physical evidence to anyone at all. Two verses later, he appears miraculously in the midst of the disciples, and shows them his—presumably wounded—hands and side (Jn 20:19). Eight days later, he appears similarly in order to persuade doubting Thomas (Jn 20:26-29). Some time later, he appears, at first unrecognizably, on the shores of Lake Tiberias (Jn 21). The emphasis in the main body of the Fourth Gospel on Jesus' eventual glorification (rather than resurrection) and return to the Father (rather than return to the disciples) may reasonably awaken the suspicion that the gospel of the Beloved Disciple originally spoke not of resurrection but of some form of exaltation, and relied not on witnesses to the risen Jesus but on witnesses to the Spirit's disclosure of his glorification. It is, after all, possible that the gospel of the Hellenist Apostles emphasized the gift of the Spirit, rather than the resurrection, as the great turning point not because it seemed more decisive but because the Hellenists' evidence for Jesus' triumph over death consisted exclusively in the revelation through the Spirit.[14]

The gospel of the Beloved Disciple thus bore witness to Jesus as that Messiah and Son of God whose credentials can be discerned retrospectively, as the Beloved Disciple witnessed them not only during Jesus' ministry but from the later vantage point given by the Spirit, who bestows life in his name. But to the gospel that proclaimed this retrospective witness was added one other witness of almost matchless authority, whose testimony was not retrospective but prophetic: John the Baptist. By reinterpreting the gospel of John the Baptist, there was a way to show that Jesus was the object and the promise of the message with which gospelling had begun. Enlisting John in this way complemented and completed the witness of the Beloved Disciple—but it may also have set the stage for a quantum leap through the gospel of Demetrios to the gospel of the Ultimate. At any rate, the Fourth Gospel came to incorporate a new look at what was hidden in the gospel's beginning, in the work and proclamation of John the Baptist.

THE GOSPEL OF JOHN THE BAPTIST IN THE GOSPEL OF THE BELOVED DISCIPLE

In the Synoptic tradition, the Christian good news evidently began with John the Baptist. Hence each of the Synoptic Gospels begins its account of the public ministry of Jesus by turning first to John's mission, introducing Jesus in that context.

The result is slightly awkward for Christian purposes, since although the gospel of John the Baptist effectively stirs up a climate of fervor and reform and eager expectation—a climate apt for the gospel of Jesus—it is not helpful for the promotion of the gospel of the Apostles. The content of John's gospel simply does not look like what Jesus turned out to be.

The Fourth Gospel too begins the Christian story with John the Baptist, and gives him a more prominent and extensive role than the Synoptics do. But the result is not quite the same. The awkwardness is not there. The Fourth Gospel's version of John the Baptist and his gospel is dramatically and radically different from the Synoptic version. And the nature of this difference offers an efficient clue to how the gospel of the Ultimate could build upon the first stages of the Fourth Gospel.

Those who know the gospel of John the Baptist from the Synoptics will readily note familiar touches in the Fourth Gospel. John is the voice of one crying in the wilderness, "Make straight the way of the Lord" (Jn 1:23). He baptizes in water (Jn 1:26,31), but there is one coming after him (Jn 1:26,30), whose sandal-strap John is not worthy to loosen (Jn 1:27), who will baptize in Holy Spirit (Jn 1:33). These are authentic recollections of John the Baptist's gospel, but they come here with omissions and additions that change their meaning entirely. The main omissions have to do with the details of the Coming One as judge: the Fourth Gospel says nothing about the fire in which the Coming One will baptize, and nothing about the fan in his hand, the axe at the tree's root, the imminent harvest in which chaff and trash will be consigned to the flames. Nor does it mention any connection between John's baptism and the confession of sin, or the forgiveness of sin, or an ordeal by water analogous to a much greater ordeal to come. In short, John's gospel has been completely purged of its apocalyptic and eschatological elements, even though these were originally the heart of the matter! Whatever in the gospel of John the Baptist was bound up with such a judgment is reinterpreted or simply omitted from the Fourth Gospel's accounts.

The elements that are retained are accordingly shifted so that they no longer point to the judgment to come. More important, whatever is retained of the Baptist's gospel is made to point directly, specifically, and exclusively to Jesus. The Coming One whose sandals John is unfit to untie is reported, because he is de-eschatologized by being identified with Jesus (Jn 1:29-30), who is the one that will baptize in Holy Spirit (Jn 1:33). This identification requires a litte maneuvering, since a future spectacular judge is being transformed into a present figure of a very different sort, but the task is performed: the one who is to come after John is already standing in their midst, unknown by them (Jn 1:26); he had even been unknown by John, though it was simply for the purpose of manifesting him to Israel that John had undertaken his baptizing mission (Jn 1:31), but he had finally been disclosed in a vision (Jn 1:32-33) in which John saw the Spirit come down like a dove from heaven and rest upon Jesus. The essential object of John's gospel is Jesus, and Jesus has arrived.

In short, from the Synoptic evidence it appears that the gospel of John the Baptist was about an eschatological judgment shortly to come in power and glory, and that this judgment would be administered by an unnamed Coming One; there is no good evidence that John knew Jesus. In the Fourth Gospel, all this is turned a full 180 degrees: John not only knows Jesus, but identifies him as the One who was to come, fulfilling the purpose of John's baptism and the message of his gospel. It is plain that John's gospel has been ruthlessly reedited to make it a gospel about Jesus. To understand better the climate that produced the gospel of the Ultimate, it is potentially useful to consider how and by whom the reediting was done.

If we puzzle into the origin of the Fourth Gospel's portrait of John the Baptist, the most obvious fact appears to be that it passed through Christian hands at the end of its journey. The simplest solution would be to propose that it is nothing more or less than a thoroughgoing Christian reworking of the original gospel of John the Baptist. But such a solution is too simple. Who, and what purposes, can be held responsible for the elimination of the eschatological dimension? As the Synoptics attest, early Christianity had no great difficulty accepting the kind of apocalyptic espoused by John's gospel. A Christian editor attempting to exploit the gospel of John the Baptist might be expected to represent John's eschatological judge in terms that would point to Jesus, but there was no need to eliminate entirely the threshing and fire of John's Coming One. Some early Christians evidently believed that Jesus was he. Why does the Fourth Gospel so alter this aspect of John's gospel, rather than simply redirecting it to Jesus?

Two explanations readily suggest themselves, both perhaps true and mutually influential. One is that the gospel of the Beloved Disciple was not apocalyptic in its views. The gospel of the Hebrew Apostles was decidedly so, and envisioned Jesus coming in glory to conclude this world in judgment; but the gospel of the Hellenist Apostles placed its emphasis elsewhere, and quite likely either a branch of it or the main stream itself maintained that the work of Jesus, and therefore the work of John's Coming One, was substantially complete when the promised baptism in the Holy Spirit took place. When the Spirit comes, Jesus tells his disciples at the Fourth Gospel's Last Supper, "he will convict the world concerning sin, and concerning righteousness, and concerning judgment" (Jn 16:8). And with that, the promised judgment is complete. The unbelievers will be caught in the sin of their unbelief and will not receive the Spirit; the believers will receive it and will be assured of their righteousness; and this world and its ruler will have been overcome (Jn 16:9-11). The harvest is not to take place in fire and wind, but in the reaping of believers through the gospel (Jn 4:35-38) and in the Spirit that then gives life. The gospel of the Beloved Disciple could readily accept an interpreted version of John's coming baptizer with Spirit, for that was the essence of the gospel of the Hellenist

Apostles; but there was no room for a cosmic catastrophe. The judgment of this world was to take place more quietly and immediately. The conscripting of John's witness worked best if the eschatological themes were muted.

The second explanation for the deapocalypticizing of the gospel of John the Baptist in the Fourth Gospel is that the information about John came from followers who had already, without the influence of Christian beliefs, reinterpreted their memories of John's preaching to do without the great judgment that had not come, emphasizing rather what was stable and permanent in John's legacy. I suggest that the gospel of John the Baptist that was absorbed into the Fourth Gospel was not the one remembered by the Hebrew Apostles or by the Synoptic tradition, but was rather an already somewhat de-eschatologized version that meshed much more conveniently with the gospel of the Hellenist Apostles and may even have influenced that gospel. It is entirely possible that Baptist disciples who lived with a gospel already shorn of its cataclysmic judgment could have seen in the gospel of the Hellenist Apostles the fulfillment of what John had promised.

With the absorption of the witness of John at the beginning of the story to complement the witness of the Beloved Disciple at the end, the Gospel of the Beloved Disciple was essentially complete. It offered to show the reader that Jesus was the true revealing Messiah and the elect Son of God, the only one who could fully bring light and truth and new life into a world fumbling in darkness, falsity, and death. In doing so, it undoubtedly appeared to its believing community to take the Christian claims as far as they would go, and to reveal for the first time the full truth about what had unfolded through the work and the gospels of John the Baptist, Jesus, and the Hellenist Apostles. Had it remained in that state, the gospel of the Beloved Disciple would undoubtedly have been a powerful and compelling witness to the Christian gospel. But it was not to remain in that state. It was rather destined to become the point of departure for a still more daring gospel, the focal point of this chapter—the gospel of the Ultimate.

THE CONTENT OF THE GOSPEL OF THE ULTIMATE

THE EMERGENCE OF THE GOSPEL OF THE ULTIMATE

The gospel of the Beloved Disciple, in its written version, was a gospel that consolidated a community's sense of the good news, bringing the gospel of the Hellenist Apostles to a finished form. But it did not remain in that form: it was rethought and rewritten, with expansions and changes that took its message in a new direction that formed the gospel of the Ultimate. Why was this done?

One motivation came from the internal character of the gospel of the Beloved Disciple itself. This gospel maintained that the words and works of Jesus had been signs pointing to meanings deeper than had been grasped at the time, revelations that could emerge fully only when the gift of the Holy Spirit enabled Jesus' followers to understand in a more illuminated way. But this illumination was not necessarily limited to the stage that formed the Apostolic gospel. The Spirit had been sent to abide, and to instruct the believers in both old things and new. The invitation to see more deeply had not necessarily expired. As the community lived in the Holy Spirit, pondering and living out the gospel in which it had been formed, new insights emerged that assisted the transformation of the Apostolic gospel in the same way in which the gospel of Jesus had itself been transformed. The gospel of the Beloved Disciple offered the principles for its own revision.

A second motivation may have come from transformations in the gospel of John the Baptist. Baptist followers who had joined the Christian fold could transfer their understanding of John's message to the content of the Christian gospel, and see in Jesus the one whom John had promised, the baptizer in Holy Spirit and the final judge. But what of the non-Christian Baptist followers? I indicated in the first chapter of this book two ways in which disciples of John appear to have adjusted their beliefs in the light of the absence of a cataclysmic judgment, understanding his gospel according to a non-eschatological interpretation. I suggest that there is one more piece of evidence that may indicate yet another non-apocalyptic interpretation of John elaborated by his followers apart from Christian influence: the Prologue to the Fourth Gospel. In its present form, of course, the Prologue concludes by making Jesus the object of John's preaching. But although this conclusion is obviously the work of a Christian writer, the main body of the Prologue is not necessarily so. It represents John as bearing witness to the light that is the effulgence of the divine life and the divine word. Underlying this, I propose, is a reinterpretation of the One Who Comes, the heart of John's gospel. For although John appears to have meant the One Who Will Come as the definitive baptizer and judge, the title is grammatically susceptible of being understood in terms of the continuous present—the One Who Comes *constantly* into the world, the light and life and divine word by which all things were made, now continuing to shine in a darkness that cannot comprehend it. The principal motifs of the Prologue are not simply reshufflings of the main preoccupations of the rest of the Fourth Gospel: the emphases on the Word as God and on its creative origination of all things are not to be found outside the Prologue. It evidently had a somewhat different literary origin from the rest of the Fourth Gospel. If that origin was among followers of John the Baptist, restating his gospel as a witnessing to the true light by which all authentic illumination comes, a gospel of deliverance from darkness and death into divine light and life, then a Christian reincorporation of this gospel of John the Baptist would have provided a means for a dramatic reinterpretation of Jesus as the completion of John's work.

A third motivation for recasting the Apostolic gospel came from the gospel of Demetrios which, like the revised interpretations of John the Baptist's followers, set aside the eschatological expectations in favor of a higher self-disclosure of the Truth that brought the Absolute into immediate contact and offered freedom from conventional moral restraints. As a gospel growing out of the Christian movement, the gospel of Demetrios could claim to be a purer and more advanced version of the gospel of the Apostles, and its rejection of elements that must have seemed folly to the Greeks—a Jewish Messiah raised from a criminal's death into invisible glory and Lordship—enhanced its appeal and deeply threatened the foundations of the Apostolic gospel. The more obvious way to respond to the gospel of Demetrios—the way taken by 1 John, 2 John, Jude, 2 Peter, and Revelation—was simply to reaffirm the gospel of the Apostles and denounce as renegades those who offered an "improved" edition of it. But there was an alternative and bolder way. The gospel of Demetrios posed serious questions about the credibility of Christian beliefs and offered attractive alternatives. There were alternative ways to reinterpret the gospels, including the gospel of the Apostles, so as to reaffirm the centrality of Jesus in God's relationship to the world in a more systematic and sophisticated fashion.

In such a climate was born a reassessment of the gospel of the Beloved Disciple similar to the way in which that gospel had reassessed the message of John the Baptist. What John had said was true, but had not been adequately understood until later, under conditions of greater illumination, and must be adjusted in its presentation to bring out the new understanding. The cherished gospel of the Beloved Disciple was on the right track, but had not gone far enough to bring out the full truth that was hidden in it in an oblique and shadowed way. The words, the work, the person of Jesus were not exactly what they had been supposed to be. They were immeasurably greater, altogether ultimate. On the scaffolding of the gospel of the Beloved Disciple was accordingly built, through expansions, alterations, shifts of emphasis and interpretation, a new gospel that would disclose this deeper truth about what had taken place, the news about Jesus that is the gospel of the Ultimate.

THE MOTIFS OF THE GOSPEL OF THE ULTIMATE

The gospel of the Ultimate is a strikingly new gospel, but it is based on the familiar gospel of the Hellenist Apostles. Its novelty comes through a series of brilliant interpretive strategies. Elements that had metaphorical meaning in the earlier gospel are now taken literally, and earlier literal meanings are given metaphorical twists; events that were previously expected to take place in the future are reinterpreted as having already happened; favors and powers and offices that had been understood as graciously given by God to Jesus are represented as belonging intrinsically to him; and the good news that God has initiated a plan of salvation for us becomes the good news that our salvation has already been fully accomplished and may be lived now. The basic motifs are not new, but they have been completely redefined and reorganized.

The gospel of the Apostles had proclaimed that *Jesus is the Son of God,* for example. The title apparently had a metaphorical value that made it roughly equivalent to "Messiah"—one especially chosen and favored by God to do work in his name. In the gospel of the Beloved Disciple, Jesus' literal sonship is evidently to Joseph (Jn 1:45) and is of little importance: it is his metaphorical sonship to God that establishes who he really is. The gospel of the Ultimate keeps the title but denies the metaphor. The metaphorical understanding had only hidden the deep and startling truth that Jesus is far more than had been dreamed—not merely the specially favored and elected one, but the intimate and only-begotten child of the Father (Jn 1:14,18, 3:16,18), who enacts both the work and the presence of God, so much so that he can be called "the Son" in the absolute sense, as the complement of "the Father."

The Father loves the Son (Jn 3:35, 5:20) with such completeness that he shows the Son everything he does (Jn 5:20), and the Son, lovingly obedient to the Father who sent him, does only what he sees the Father doing (Jn 5:19). The Father not only gives the Son all judgment (Jn 5:27; cf. Jn 5:22) but gives him to have life in himself (Jn 5:26) so that he can give life to others (Jn 5:21). The intimacy between Father and Son is so complete that one must honor the Son as one honors the Father (Jn 5:23); the Father is in the Son so thoroughly that anyone who has seen the Son has seen the Father (Jn 14:9-10), who abides in him and works through him (Jn 14:10). Thus is the Father glorified in the Son (Jn 14:13), and those who wish to glorify the Father must do so by fulfilling his will that they discern the true Sonship of Jesus and believe in it. The Sonship that believers are called upon to see is absolute: Jesus and the Father are one (Jn 10:30; 17:11,22).

The *glory that belongs to Jesus* is therefore not the sort that the gospel of Demetrios appears to have rejected, a glory bestowed upon him at God's right hand. For in the gospel of the Ultimate, Jesus goes not to the right hand of the Father but into his very bosom (Jn 1:18), and his glory is not bestowed but *restored*; it is the glory that belongs to the only-begotten of the Father (Jn 1:14), in which God glorifies the Son with himself (Jn 17:5) in a glory given him because God loved him before the foundation of the world (Jn 17:24), a glory which the Son had with the Father before the world existed (Jn 17:5). If the glorification of a Jewish Messiah may have seemed a foolish notion to Greeks or to revisionists, they could hardly deny the glory of God's absolute Son: this is a deeper and more intrinsic glory than what the scoffers had rejected. If question can be raised about the Lordship of a man who is claimed to have been promoted to an office obviously beyond human powers, no equivalent question can stand with respect to the natural Lordship of the only-begotten of God, whose authority over all flesh is not in spite of, but because of, who he is (Jn 17:2). This is he who comes from above and is therefore over everything, as John the Baptist is made to acknowledge (Jn 3:31). This is he whose glory and Lordship may be appropriately and simply confessed in the finally discerning words of Thomas: "My Lord and my God" (Jn 20:28).

The *absolutizing of Jesus* by the gospel of the Ultimate does not merely assert his oneness with God, his identity with the Word that was with God, and was God, from the beginning (Jn 1:1-2). It assimilates to him all the important religious categories. Do the Jews search the Scriptures looking to obtain eternal life? Then let them understand not only that the Scriptures witness to him (Jn 5:39), that he is what Moses and the Prophets are all about (1:45, 5:45-46), but also that he *is* the life they seek (Jn 14:6). Do they hope in the eventual resurrection of the righteous and the life it will bestow? He *is* the resurrection and the life (Jn 11:25). Do they seek the truth, and try to follow God's way? He *is* the way and he *is* the truth (Jn 14:6). He *is* the light of the world (Jn 8:12, 9:5), the door of salvation (Jn 10:9), the true vine in which one must abide (Jn 15:1), the bread of life (Jn 6:35,48), the savior of the world (Jn 4:42). He replaces the Temple (Jn 1:51, 2:21) and the Law (Jn 1:17). In him is the fullness of grace and truth (Jn 1:14,16) that renders religiously obsolete all that is not he.

If the gospel of the Beloved Disciple, like the gospel of the Apostles in general, saw in Jesus *the final mediator between God and humankind,* the gospel of the Ultimate presses a large step farther: he is the only way in which God has *ever* been accessible to us, and the only way he ever will be. And therefore the gospel of the Ultimate can reassert the claim of the Apostles against the gospel of Demetrios more thoroughly and in a higher key. No one can come to the Father except through him (Jn 14:6). The Father has given all things into his hands (Jn 3:35), and without the Son the Father cannot be found (Jn 5:23). Without the Son, one can do nothing (Jn 15:5) except succumb to the darkness and death from which he offers to rescue us. For this world is blind and moribund; its apparent life is ephemeral and unreal, and its apparent wisdom is as false as its glories. Our condition is far more desperate than we had dreamed. Only Jesus, because he is not of this world (Jn 8:23), can rescue us from it. No one within it can see God or hear his voice (Jn 1:18, 5:37), but Jesus as the Son sees him and hears him (Jn 8:26,38,40) and is the only way he can be revealed (Jn 1:18). Jesus as the Son is the Father made visible and audible (Jn 14:7,9). That is the ultimate revelation. If the gospel of the Beloved Disciple celebrated the cure of the blind and the raising of Lazarus as signs of divine power and favor in Jesus, the gospel of the Ultimate sees in these signs not the miraculous restoration of physical sight or earthly life, for these are finally as trivial as the miraculously multiplied loaves that may sustain them briefly. The true meaning is what these things symbolize: that only from Jesus can we receive the vision, the sustenance, and the life that are not of this world.

How can we know whether these extravagant claims are true? The gospel of the Beloved Disciple tried to awaken belief in Jesus by reporting the signs he performed. His words and deeds appeared to be enough to establish that he is the one we were awaiting, the one whom the Scriptures and John the Baptist had led us to expect. But the gospel of the Ultimate makes a deeper claim: Jesus is not at all what we expected. Our expectations were too trivial, too benighted, to allow us to grasp who he really is. The recognition given him by the Apostolic gospel was true as far as it went, but it could barely offer a beginning. We can see him as the Ultimate only if it is given to us to see. If we have the word of God in us, and faithfully follow that beginning by abiding in Jesus and keeping what he commanded us from the Father, then the true realization may be *given* to us. There is no proof beyond the realization itself. If the Father has given us to the Son, then we will hear and follow him (Jn 10:27), and he will keep us, in accordance with the Father's will (Jn 6:39). But no one comes to the Son unless drawn by the Father (Jn 6:37, 10:29), and those who are not thus given to him will simply not believe

(Jn 10:26). Those who believe can do so only because the Father has given them to the Son (Jn 17:2,6,9) and the Son has accordingly chosen them (Jn 15:16). Embedded as we are in a world of sin and darkness, we can definitively disqualify ourselves from grasping the truth. If the love of God is not really in us (Jn 5:42), we will pursue the false glories of this world (Jn 5:44, 12:43) and the evil works of this world (Jn 7:7), serving the father of lies and lusts (Jn 8:44), and loving the darkness more than the light (Jn 3:19). Then we will surely be lost. If we seek the will of the Father obediently, we have a chance to love Jesus and perceive that he bears the true word of God (Jn 7:17, 8:42, 8:47). But the ultimate discernment comes only by gift. The gospel of the Ultimate confronts us starkly with its astounding claims, and finally announces that if we are God's, we will believe them—and if we do not believe, we are not God's.

And that is why the threat of *judgment,* so important a part of earlier gospels, is dispensable in the gospel of the Ultimate. It is not a future event, presided over by Jesus. Judgment is already here, in the darkness, sin, and death of this world, which will inevitably overwhelm us if we fail to seize the one chance of rescue brought by the Son of God. Jesus does not judge (Jn 3:17, 8:15, 12:47), because it is unnecessary for him to do so. The unbeliever is judged already (Jn 3:18). Jesus comes not to condemn but to save (Jn 3:16-17); condemnation is simply the automatic alternative (Jn 3:36, 5:24, 5:29, 12:48).

The transference of judgment from its usual eschatological place to the immediate present is not the only way in which the gospel of the Ultimate revises the ultimate events promised by the gospel of the Apostles. Its message throughout is twofold: *ultimacy is Jesus,* and *ultimacy is now.* If it answers the gospel of Demetrios in one way by reaffirming the glory and Lordship of Jesus in a far more dramatic way than the gospel of the Apostles had envisioned, it answers it in another way by acknowledging that what the Apostolic gospel promised for the Last Day is not really to be expected—not because the doctrine is false, but because the Last Day has arrived. The promises have already been kept.

The gospel of the Apostles proclaimed that those who reject Jesus will remain in their sins and be condemned, while those who believe in him will be forgiven and will be ushered into eternal life when he comes in glory from heaven to preside over the resurrection of the dead and the judgment. The gospel of the Ultimate resumes each of these particulars, but with reinterpretations that shift their meanings and values and make them present now.

As might be expected, the transvaluations extend not only to ideas of forgiveness and condemnation but to *the notion of sin* itself. The traditional conception of sin as a violation of the Law is present in the Fourth Gospel, but is mentioned only by the unenlightened, as a sign that they have not yet understood deeply enough. Consider the story of the man born blind. Jesus' disciples ask whether the man born blind is suffering punishment for his own sinning or that of his parents (Jn 9:2), and of course the answer is that it is neither (Jn 9:3). That sense of sin has nothing to do with the meaning of his blindness. Jesus' opponents accuse him of being sinful because he violates the Sabbath by restoring the man's sight (Jn 9:16,24), and when the man himself protests that a sinner could not do such a work, they denounce him as one born in sins (Jn 9:34). The gospel of the Ultimate then presses the story to a deeper sense both of sin and of blindness. The man had been born blind, Jesus had told his disciples, so that the works of God might be shown in him (Jn 9:3). The cure of his physical blindness may at first seem to fulfill that promise, but not from the perspective of the gospel of the Ultimate. The real cure comes only later, when Jesus invites the man to believe in him and the man responds with worshipful belief (Jn 9:35-38). Jesus then announces that this is his mission, this is how the work of God is shown: "I came into this world for judgment, that those not seeing may see and those seeing might become blind" (Jn 9:39). The man had shed his real blindness and sin when he saw who Jesus really is; the grumbling Pharisees, because they claim to see when they do not, remain in sin (Jn 9:40-41).

Sin is disobedience to God, not by specific deeds but by the blindness of *unbelief.* "If you do not believe that I am the One, you will die in your sins" (Jn 8:24). It is in believing in Jesus that one does the work of God (Jn 6:29). The will of the Father is expressed not in the commandments of the Law but in the mission of Jesus, which is for the purpose of allowing us to see the Son and believe in him (Jn 6:39). Those who escape their blindness by seeing the Son are saved; those who fail to do so are plunged into a deeper blindness and will die in sin, for they have rejected the will and work of God. The very presence of Jesus is judgment. He takes away the sin of the world for those who believe, and those who do not are self-convicted and remain in the world's sin.

What becomes of the unbelievers? They die. There is no thought of hellfire or of any other punishment except the one for which the world already destines them. And the believers? They live. "The one who hears my word and believes him who sent me has eternal life, and does not come to judgment but has passed out of death into life" (Jn 5:24).

This seems to have a ring of metaphor about it, but in the gospel of the Ultimate it is literally true. *Eternal life* is not something that will be given to the believer; it has already been given. Jesus has been empowered to give life not later, but now (Jn 5:21,26); those who receive it will never perish (Jn 10:28). "Everyone living and believing in me may not die, ever" (Jn 11:26). Those who have died in this world will hear his voice and live (Jn 5:25), rejoicing as Abraham rejoiced to see Jesus' day (Jn 8:56). Anyone who believes in him, "even though he die, shall live" (Jn 11:25).

The evident inconsistency of this last remark with what went before is a problem. Which is it: that believers will not die at all, or that they will live in spite of having died? The gospel of the Apostles, grounded in the doctrine of resurrection, was willing to admit that physical death may take place even in the case of believers, but that life would be restored at the end. This hope is expressed by Martha in the Fourth Gospel when she responds to Jesus' assurance that her brother Lazarus will rise by saying "I know that he will rise again, in the resurrection in the last day" (Jn 11:23-24). But from the viewpoint of the gospel of the Ultimate, this is another of the misunderstandings that occur throughout Jesus' attempts to make his gospel known, along with Nicodemus's failure to understand the meaning of rebirth (Jn 3:4), the Samaritan woman's misunderstanding of the metaphor of living water (Jn 4:15), and the disciples' failure to grasp his meaning when Jesus speaks of Lazarus's being asleep (Jn 11:11-13). According to the gospel of the Ultimate, *resurrection* is not a physical or a future event: eternal life is given now, and that is the true meaning of resurrection. Resurrection *is* Jesus. "I am the resurrection and the life; the one who believes in me, even though he die, shall live" (Jn 11:25). That is, the life that one has in this world may be lost, but the eternal life that is one's participation in the next world has already begun and will continue. The rising that is important is the exaltation out of this world into the eternal.

Several texts in the Fourth Gospel insist on the eventual physical resurrection. In Chapter 6, Jesus makes a series of pronouncements about those who will be saved, and in four instances he adds the refrain "and I will raise him [or it] up on the last day" (Jn 6:39,40,44,54); in the previous chapter, he announces that the hour is coming in which those in the tomb will hear his voice and come forth—those who have done good things coming to a resurrection of life, and those who have done evil things coming to a resurrection of judgment (Jn 5:28-29). It is highly unlikely that these texts belong to the gospel of the Ultimate. I think it most probable that they were added later, in conjunction with the last stage of corrective editing, which I will discuss at the end of this chapter. But for the moment, consider the instance from Jn 5:28-29.

What it formulates is a recognizably familiar glimpse of the last judgment, in terms which might be considered apt for the gospel of the Apostles. But it is not easy to believe that the gospel of the Ultimate, with its insistence that belief in Jesus is the indispensable condition of salvation, could settle for the mild notion that "doing good things" will assure one of a physical resurrection some day. The ring of the gospel of the Ultimate can be heard rather a few verses before: "An hour is coming—and is now here—when the dead shall hear the voice of the Son of God, and those who have heard will live" (Jn 5:25). Coming immediately on the heels of the saying that the one who hears and believes evades judgment and "has passed out of death into life" (Jn 5:24), this is surely another instance of the ultimization of the present: the time is now, and the expectation is not the restoration of life to the physically dead, but the rising of believers out of the condition of spiritual death into the life that belief bestows. The reliteralization of this metaphorical resurrection in Jn 5:28-29 belongs to another gospel and another stage of composition. The same is true, I believe, of the refrain in Chapter 6, "and I will raise him [or it] up on the last day." One of its instances, in Jn 6:54, is a verse that is generally conceded by commentators to be a late addition to the Fourth Gospel. The others sound odd and uncharacteristic because they are attached to motifs that occur with some frequency elsewhere in the Fourth Gospel, but never in association with resurrection. The refrain inserts the assumption that those given to Jesus by the Father, those believing and receiving eternal life, and those drawn to Jesus by the Father will nevertheless die. That is not only uncharacteristic of the gospel of the Ultimate; it is virtually contradictory to its assumptions. I suggest, therefore, that the references to physical resurrection in the Fourth Gospel belong to a later hand than that by which the gospel of the Ultimate was added, and that the gospel of the Ultimate reinterpreted the traditionally expected resurrection of the last day in terms of a present spiritual passage from death to life.

The present ultimacy and completeness of that passage from death to life is underlined by another of the transformations wrought by the gospel of the Ultimate on the gospel of the Beloved Disciple—its interpretation of *the gift of the Spirit.* A cornerstone of the gospel of the Hellenist Apostles, the gift of the Spirit was the moment of great illumination by which the hidden truth of Jesus' work and words could finally be understood. But according to the later gospel of the Ultimate, the understanding that was final in the gospel of the Beloved Disciple was still short of the mark, and the text of the Fourth Gospel interweaves two correspondingly different representations of what that event really was and meant.

One representation, probably that of the gospel of the Beloved Disciple, depicts the culmination of Jesus' work as coming after his return to the Father, when he will send the Spirit to his disciples (Jn 16:7) by asking the Father, who will give the Spirit permanently at his request (Jn 14:16). This is the Spirit of truth, who will be in them and remain with them (Jn 14:17) and remind them of what Jesus had told them (Jn 14:26), will glorify Jesus (Jn 15:26, 16:14) and teach them all things (Jn 14:26), including the things yet to come (Jn 16:13). Then they will see Jesus no more (Jn 16:10), but the Spirit will take the place of Jesus as another advocate or comforter (*paraklētos*), giving them assurance and conviction, not arbitrarily or groundlessly but by taking what truly belongs to Jesus and declaring it to them (Jn 16:14), speaking not of itself but according to what it hears (Jn 16:13).

The other representation of the gift of the Spirit, that of the gospel of the Ultimate, interweaves among these testimonies a still more daring claim: *the Spirit* is not really "another Comforter" but *is Jesus himself*! In this gospel, Jesus goes away to the Father not permanently, sending the Spirit in his stead, but temporarily, soon to return as the Spirit. He will not leave them orphaned, but will come to them (Jn 14:18,28). For a little while they will see him no more; but again a little while and they will see him (Jn 16:16). He will manifest himself to those who love him (Jn 14:22). He will prepare a place for them and will return to them and receive them to himself, so that where he is they may be also (Jn 14:3, 17:24). They will then behold him, because he lives and they too will live (Jn 14:19) with a life that shows them that he is in the Father and that they and he are in one another (Jn 14:20), that as he and the Father are in each other, so they are in the Father and in him, and that he and the Father have come to them and abide with them (Jn 14:23). In that day they will be one as he and the Father are one (Jn 17:11), he in them and the Father in him (Jn 17:23). What will dwell in them will be not another Comforter, but the ultimate Paraclete—Jesus himself and the very love with which the Father has loved him (Jn 17:26).

The gospel of John the Baptist had proclaimed a mighty Coming One whose judgment would put the finishing touch on this world. The gospel of Jesus had reaffirmed the main outlines of John's gospel, announcing that the collectivity of the Son of Man would come in glory from heaven to judge. The gospel of the Apostles had identified that glorified heavenly judge as Jesus himself, who was to return from the heavenly Lordship in which he had been installed, with the glory that had been given him. The gospel of Demetrios had set all this aside in favor of a more immediate and non-apocalyptic transformation. But the gospel of the Ultimate combined these visions, blending the non-apocalyptic immediacy of the gospel of Demetrios with a reinterpreted version of *Jesus as the glorified Son of Man* coming from heaven to end the power of this world and gather believers together into another.

In the gospel of the Ultimate, it is not the Spirit only who comes to the believers: it is Jesus himself, returned to abide with them as the Messiah was expected to do, and to bring them to where he lives with the Father. It is then that they see and share in the glory of the Son of Man. For the gospel of the Ultimate, like the gospel of Jesus, associates the title

"Son of Man" with glory and with judgment. It is because he is the Son of Man that Jesus has power to judge (Jn 5:27); and when he speaks of his impending glorification, it is in terms of the same title: "the hour has come that the Son of Man may be glorified" (Jn 12:23) and "the Son of Man is now glorified, and God is glorified by him—and God will glorify him in himself, and will glorify him forthwith" (Jn 13:31-32). After that, he will be raised up as the Son of Man (Jn 3:14, 8:28, 12:34) and as the Son of Man will ascend to heaven (Jn 6:62), whence he descended (Jn 3:13). But he will return and receive the believers to himself (Jn 14:3) so that they may see the fulness of his glory (Jn 17:24) and share in it (Jn 17:22), he abiding in them and they in him (Jn 17:23,25), so that they all may be one in the same glory that God has given him (Jn 17:21-23), the glory of the Son of Man.

And with that, everything has been given. All that remains is for the disciples to receive it faithfully and abide in it by keeping the commandments of Jesus as he had obeyed the commandments of the Father (Jn 15:10). If they love Jesus, they will keep his commandments (Jn 14:21), keep his word (Jn 14:23), which is the word of the Father (Jn 14:23), and love one another as he has loved them (Jn 13:34, 15:12). Unified in love, loving Jesus as the Son of God—and therefore loving the Father whom he makes manifest—they will know the truth at last and be made free (Jn 8:31-32), passing now out of this sin-bound world into eternal life, to abide forever in Jesus and in the Father. This is everything. There is nothing else. Apart from this there is only darkness and death. The gospel of the Ultimate is the good news that all four of the previous gospels converge in a still higher truth: in Jesus, the Ultimate has come into the world and shown itself, and has invited us to live in the Ultimate, now and forever.

POSTSCRIPT: THE FINAL CORRECTIONS

With the gospel of the Ultimate, we come to the end of the sequence of five gospels through which the Christian good news was formed. But we do not come to the completion of the formation itself. The gospel of the Ultimate is not itself the Christian gospel as it was proclaimed ever after. Nor is it even the finishing touch on the Gospel of John. The gospel of the Beloved Disciple had been reworked to provide a platform on which the gospel of the Ultimate could be constructed and displayed as the last word. But the gospel of the Ultimate was not allowed to have the last word. The Fourth Gospel was to be subjected to yet one more stage of editorial readjustment before it reached its present form.[15] The effect, and probably the purpose, of that final redaction was to put the gospel of the Ultimate out of the place it had commandeered as the definitive interpretation of the previous gospels, and to restore some of the aspects of those earlier gospels to authority—in short, to tame the gospel of the Ultimate into the service of those proclamations it had attempted to reform and replace. The final corrections in the Fourth Gospel do not offer a new gospel, but a compromise with an older one.

The perspective from which these adjustments were made may be guessed from the closing verses of Chapter 6, where, after some disciples have responded to Jesus' hard and scandalous sayings by abandoning him, Jesus turns "to the Twelve" (Jn 6:67) to ask if they too will leave, and receives from Peter their declaration of fidelity and belief (Jn 6:68-69). We have not met the Twelve before in the Fourth Gospel, yet they are presented as a readily recognizable inner circle, chosen by Jesus (Jn 6:70). Clearly parallel to Peter's confession in Matthew 16 and Mark 8, this vignette is a blossom from another garden, a remembrance cherished in the Synoptic tradition as a foundation for the gospel of the Hebrew Apostles. The insinuation into the Fourth Gospel of the recollection that the Twelve were specially selected by Jesus, that it was their spokesman who first arrived at a true discernment of who Jesus really was, and that it was they who remained faithful when others' loyalty was compromised, seems likely to be a late redactor's way of staking a bold claim for the Hebrew Apostolic leadership on territory that is not otherwise readily receptive to it. The final editorially corrective hand that finished the Fourth Gospel's compositional history was, I believe, dedicated to accommodating a fundamentally Hellenist document to the views of a more Hebrew Christian way.

I say "way" rather than merely "memory," because the issue at stake is not simply who is to have the place of honor, nor is the mode of editorial alteration simply the importation of Synoptic material: Peter's confession here is not the Synoptic testimony that Jesus is the Messiah and the Son of God, but an acknowledgment with a more Johannine ring—that he has the words of eternal life and is the holy one of God. Behind the insertion is not static recollection but a living religious tradition that understood itself to be rooted in the faith and work of the Twelve. The redactor intended to moderate the extreme views of the gospel of the Ultimate by realigning it with the Christian mainstream.

It is this same intent, I suggest, that sponsored another insertion just a few verses before. Jesus has discoursed on the true bread from heaven, insisting that it must be understood as a metaphor for himself (Jn 6:41,48), and that by contrast with the literal eating of manna, which sustains only temporarily the life of this world (Jn 6:49), this true bread is to be metaphorically eaten by believing in Jesus and thus receiving eternal life (Jn 6:40,47,50): "I am the bread of life—the one coming to me may not hunger, and he who believes in me may not ever thirst" (Jn 6:35). The life of this world, and the flesh that inhabits it, count for nothing: true life comes from the Spirit, and Jesus' words are accordingly spirit and life (Jn 6:63). But in the midst of all this, there is an abrupt interruption and shift in the message: suddenly, the bread of life is the flesh of Jesus (Jn 6:51), and the murmurers who balk at the literal meaning are not, as elsewhere in the Fourth Gospel, informed that they must take his words metaphorically and symbolically, but are assured that the meaning is indeed literal.

> Unless you eat the flesh of the Son of Man and drink his blood, you have no life in you. He who eats my flesh and drinks my blood has eternal life, and I will raise him up on the last day. For my flesh is truly food, and my blood is truly drink. He who eats my flesh and drinks my blood abides in me and I in him. (Jn 6:53-56)

Some of the key terms—having eternal life, abiding in me and I in him—are familiar landmarks of the gospel of the Ultimate, but the insistence on physical literalness is uncharacteristic not only of that gospel in general, but of the statements surrounding this passage in particular. The result, and undoubtedly the purpose, of this turn of affairs is to tie the promises of the gospel of the Ultimate to a physicalized understanding of the Christian Eucharist. The gospel of the Ultimate, with its disdain for flesh and blood (Jn 1:13) and its concentration on the spiritual order, could hardly find such a eucharistic understanding congenial. The Fourth Gospel, unlike the Synoptics, does not report an institution of the Eucharist in its account of Jesus's final gathering with his disciples. But just as the Twelve are thrust into Chapter 6 despite the Fourth Gospel's never having mentioned their appointment, so here a particular doctrine of the Eucharist is made an indispensable condition for participation in the Ultimate. The bread of heaven, originally as much a metaphor as the living water of Chapter 4, has been transformed into identity with the Eucharist, not simply as it had been instituted in the Synoptic accounts but as it had become in subsequent Christian religious life: a sacrament of the Church.

A parallel adjustment takes place with respect to baptism as well. In the Fourth Gospel's account of the Last Supper, Jesus washes his disciples' feet as a demonstration of how they are to love and serve one another. Peter, initially reluctant to receive such service, invites Jesus to wash his hands and head as well (Jn 13:9), but Jesus replies that this is unnecessary: those who have already bathed have no further need of washing, and the disciples are clean (Jn 13:10). Implicit in this may well be a rejection of Jewish ritual purifications, but I suggest that there is also a rebuff to Christian baptism. The disciples are clean not through baptism, but through the word Jesus had spoken (Jn 15:3). A short time later, he will send them into the world to extend that word that others may believe (Jn 17:20), but the Fourth Gospel does not say that he commanded or authorized them to baptize. In the Fourth Gospel, Jesus is the one who baptizes in the Holy Spirit. His words are spirit and life (Jn 6:63), and no other washing is needful. And so in his conversation with Nicodemus Jesus had insisted that one must be born again (or "from above"), that whatever is born of flesh is flesh and whatever is born of the Spirit is spirit. The Spirit is the consistent focus of the passage—except for one turn of phrase. In Jn 3:5, entrance into the Dominion of God is made conditional on being born again "of water and the Spirit." The mention of water is, I believe, a corrective insertion to reestablish within the Fourth Gospel the baptism in water which the gospel of the Ultimate was ready to leave behind with the preparatory work of John the Baptist, but which another part of the Christian community insisted was an indispensable part of belonging to Jesus.

I suppose that it was in the same process of editorial readjustment that the Fourth Gospel acquired its references to the resurrection on the last day. As I indicated earlier, these references are distinctly alien to the doctrine of the gospel of the Ultimate, which reinterprets the last day as being already present, and understands resurrection in an essentially metaphorical way as a present movement out of the death of this world into the life that belongs to eternity. But while the gospel of the Hellenist Apostles had tended to identify the great Scriptural promise and hope with the gift of the Spirit, and was followed in this by the gospel of the Ultimate, the Hebrew Apostolic gospel looked rather to the promise and hope of resurrection, which was to take place in conjunction with the judgment that had been envisioned by previous gospels. The resurrection to life and the resurrection to judgment mentioned in Jn 5:29 cannot be easily reconciled with the gospel of the Ultimate, but correspond well with the final wave of corrective alterations.

It seems to me quite likely that the final correcting hand was also active in imposing on the Fourth Gospel a version of the resurrection of Jesus that had not been there before. Jesus' appearance to Mary Magdalen was patently not written as the first of a series of demonstrations that his physical body was risen from the dead. He tells her that she is not to touch him, and sends her to the brethren to tell them that he is ascending to the Father (Jn 20:17). The assumption is clearly that they are to learn from her testimony that he is gone, and where, and that they themselves will not see his risen form before his ascension. The subsequent showing and touching of his wounds (Jn 20:20,27) and the meal beside the lake (Jn 21:1-14) do not come from the same stratum of composition as Jesus' words to Mary. Resurrection appearances like those of the Synoptic Gospels have been substituted for the original conclusion of the gospel of the Ultimate.

What that original conclusion had been cannot be determined. But there is some reason for supposing that it involved a communication to the disciples by the exalted Jesus, and that editorial reworking has placed in the Fourth Gospel's depiction of the Last Supper some discourse material that had earlier belonged to the concluding portion. That some editorial tampering has taken place is indisputable: in the last verse of Chapter 14, Jesus terminates this gathering to go to his death in obedience to his Father's command: "But that the world may know that I love the Father, and as the Father commanded me, so I do—arise, let us go hence" (Jn 14:31).

Yet the next verse simply resumes his discourse, without explanation. In the remainder of his discourse, there are hints that the original context was not the Last Supper but some post-crucifixion setting. Jesus informs them that he is making disclosures which he had previously not made "because I was with you" (Jn 16:4). He has finished the work which God had given him to do (Jn 17:4) and has conquered the world (Jn 16:33). It is now time for him to be glorified with his original glory (Jn 17:5). "I am no longer in the world," he announces (Jn 17:11), though his disciples still are. "When I was with them, I kept them in your name" (Jn 17:12). The proper position for such statements is after Jesus' death, not just before it, for his work is now complete and successful, and he is no longer with them or in the world. They do not yet quite understand, since the Spirit has not yet been given; they receive his words with puzzlement and uncertainty, in a state of sorrow and confusion, but Jesus promises that his joy will be awakened in them by a gift of the Spirit, which he will send now that he is returning to the Father (Jn 15:26-27; 16:7,17,20-22).

Some or all of this material has, I believe, been shuffled into this setting from an original post crucifixion discourse to make room for a more Synoptic-conventional telling of the resurrection. The gospel of the Ultimate was not to have the last word in the ultimate Gospel. Even if Thomas' succinct confession, "My Lord and my God" (Jn 20:28), is an authentic echo of the gospel of the Ultimate, the visible and tangible wounds of Jesus were not likely to have been the original inspiring occasion, but are probably another example of the way in which the final finishing touches of the Fourth Gospel's composition brought the gospel of the Ultimate within the boundaries of the gospel it had sought to replace.

These editorial changes were neither extensive enough nor ambitious enough to hide the gospel of the Ultimate, or to protect the Fourth Gospel from being rejected on its account, in some quarters, as too unorthodox. But the changes did anchor the rarified and volatile otherworldliness of the gospel of the Ultimate in the life and traditions of the broader Church, and perhaps made a significant difference in securing for it a permanent place in the Church's memory. Modified within the Fourth Gospel and counterpoised by the Synoptics, the gospel of the Ultimate no longer overwhelms its hearers as thoroughly as it must once have done, when it stood alone as a dazzling and total reinterpretation of the Apostolic gospel, meeting both the challenge and the example of the gospel of Demetrios. But its principal features still shine through, proclaiming a good news arrestingly different from any of the gospels that had gone before. If it was tamed to the service of the universal Church, it nevertheless remained—and still remains—the unique gospel of the Ultimate.

Epilogue

"Great abilities," said he, "are not requisite for an historian; for in historical composition all the greatest powers of the human mind are quiescent. He has facts ready to his hand; so there is no exercise of invention. Imagination is not required in any high degree; only about as much as is used in the lower kinds of poetry. Some penetration, accuracy, and colouring, will fit a man for the task, if he can give the application which is necessary."

—Boswell's *Life of Johnson*

"It is one of those cases where the art of the reasoner should be used rather for the sifting of details than for the acquiring of fresh evidence. The tragedy has been so uncommon, so complete, and of such personal importance to so many people that we are suffering from a plethora of surmise, conjecture, and hypothesis. The difficulty is to detach the framework of fact—of absolute, undeniable fact—from the embellishments of theorists and reporters. Then, having established ourselves upon this sound basis, it is our duty to see what inferences may be drawn, and which are the special points upon which the whole mystery turns. . . . See the value of imagination," said Holmes. "It is the one quality which Gregory lacks. We imagined what might have happened, acted upon the supposition, and find ourselves justified. Let us proceed."

—*The Memoirs of Sherlock Holmes*

If we suffer from a plethora of surmise, conjecture, and hypothesis, I acknowledge that I have not alleviated the suffering; nor have I made any new contribution to the pool of absolute undeniable facts. This book was not written to Johnson's prescription, nor to all of Holmes's. I have tried to discern the special points on which this historical mystery turns, to imagine what might have happened, and to act upon the supposition, in order to see what patterns then suggest themselves among the evidences that survive. Imaginative conjecture is not the enemy of history but its indispensable ally; and if science is the attempt to make systematic rational sense of the relevant evidence, that attempt nevertheless takes place within the boundaries that imagination provides. What is discovered by the rigorous examination of facts often challenges imagination to reconsider and reorganize; what is proposed through an act of reimagining often challenges the usual sense of what the facts really are.

The evidence relevant to the subject of this book is a set of facts of one sort or another, all of them clamoring to be heard on terms that are not quite justified, each of them deeply involved with surmises and imaginings that are not quite sound. I have tried to be fair to what they are—not to what they pretend to be, or to what others have claimed them to be, but to what they should say to this inquiry. The authority is ultimately theirs, however. I have merely cross-examined them with questions drawn from a combination of their own hints and my attempts to discern and imagine rightly. The resulting reconstruction is not something I propose to be believed, but only to be understood and hospitably entertained. If it is found to justify the facts, then it will in turn be justified by those facts. If not, then just as I have changed my mind about the adequacy of previous reconstructions, including ones of my own devising, so I am prepared to change again under the impact of better explanations, better justifications of the facts, more adequate critical imaginings and surmises.

Five Gospels is a work of historical reconstruction. As such, it is bound to be historically scientific, which means not that it is allowed to make only proposals that are certain, or proposals that conform to general scholarly opinion, but that its freedom to reimagine must be disciplined by a responsible consideration of the evidence and a sound and coherent way of thinking about its patterning. The results are necessarily provisional and tentative. It has been my book during the writing of it, but now it is no longer mine. Once published, it belongs to the interested public. As a member of the interested public, I will defend its strengths as long as they seem strong; but I will abandon its weaknesses as I am persuaded to do so by the better thinking of others. In the historical enterprise, it is foolish to be loyal to secondary sources, even if one happened to author them. Proper loyalty belongs to the evidence, and to the quality of public discussion about it. I acknowledge my gratitude to *Five Gospels* for what I have learned in the course of its coming to be. But it is no longer mine, and I wish it only all the success that it deserves as an attempt to make sense of the facts.

That is, of course, hardly the whole of the matter. *Five Gospels* is an attempt at historical reconstruction, but it is not a reconstruction of the Trojan War, or of the transformation of medieval Christian philosophy by the discovery of the Arab and Jewish sages, or of the stages by which the Philippines achieved independence. Those are momentous events, but they do not radiate the range of consequences normally attached to the matters with which this book deals. When one treads upon the historical ground of Christian origins, it rumbles with theological reverberations. I cannot possibly take them up in this book (though I intend to do so in another), but neither can I leave this subject without a few remarks along those lines.

I do not think that theological implications have any direct place in the work of historical reconstruction. One cannot fail to notice that to assert that this did take place and that did not, or that these things were said and those probably weren't, or that it was they and not he, automatically raises theological questions. But theological questions are not for the historian to decide, though the historian may offer to turn theologian and enter the fray under a different banner. I will do so, but not now. At the moment, I wish to make only three relevant points.

The first is that just as the historian as such must recognize theological issues as beyond the scope and competence of the historical task, so must it be said that theological issues as such may not fairly enter into historical work, except when the issue is the historical recovery of what theological ideas and presuppositions entered into the events of history through the minds and actions of those who held them. Ultimate theological truth or falsity is simply not to the point. No historical reconstruction can be fairly faulted for failing to support a given theological view or for giving reason to call one into question. If I have not pleased my reader theologically, I assure him or her that it was none of my undertaking to do so. If another reader likes the theological implications of what I have presented, that too must be understood as an accidental by-product, and no intent of my own. This is history; theology must take care of itself.

The second point is that the relationship between history and theology is in itself a theological question, not a historical one. The historian can, and often must, try to recapture what was thought to be the relationship betwen history and theology at that time, in that place, among those people; but history is not competent to decide what should be the proper relationship. Most of the actors on the stages I have described seem to have believed that theology and history are intimately bound together—that history is often the unfolding of theology in time and space, and that theology is to a great extent a faithful, and faith-filled, reading of history. Whether they were right in these beliefs is not for the historian to propose. Whether it is appropriate for theologians to follow them in these beliefs is not necessarily a permanently settled question.

For my third point, I wish to speak both as historian and as theologian, to speak both of what the rules of theological thought ought to be, and of what the past suggests are normally the consequences when these rules are not observed. Theology can depart from history, ignore it, appeal to a more perfect source of understanding, and find respectable ways of preserving on other grounds what history might seem to undermine. But theology is not free to remake history in the name of a higher cause or a more important goal. What actually happened is not for the theologian to decide. The theologian may offer ways of seeing implications that are beyond the historian's reach, or may argue for certain ways of valuing or disvaluing what took place, but when the theologian offers to say what the facts are and what were the events, this is no longer theology as such: it is history, and it must be undertaken according to history's rules of procedure. As theologian, I assert that I think it ought to be done that way. As historian, I opine that doing otherwise has usually led to tragic results, and not infrequently to disasters. The dialogue between theology and critical history has often been painful over the last few generations and will probably be no less painful over the next few. It is a pain that should not be avoided but honorably endured. The Christian tradition has always managed to sustain the hope that on the other side of pain may lie a peace beyond our easy imagining. There is much that we still must undergo. Let us proceed.

Notes

Introduction

1. C. H. Dodd, "The Framework of the Gospel Narrative," *Expository Times* 43 (1932):396; reprinted in *New Testament Studies* (Manchester: 1953), p. 1.
2. For overviews of this movement, see George Wesley Buchanan, "Current Synoptic Studies," *Religion in Life* 46 (1977):415-425; William R. Farmer, "Modern Developments of Griesbach's Hypothesis," *New Testament Studies* 23 (1977):275-295 and "The Present State of the Synoptic Problem," *Perkins Journal* 32 (1978):1-7; M.-E. Boismard, "The Two Source Theory at an Impasse," *New Testament Studies* 26 (1979):1-17; and H.-H. Stoldt, *Geschichte und Kritik der Markushypothese* (Göttingen: 1977), now available as *History and Criticism of the Marcan Hypothesis*, trans. D. L. Niewyk (Macon, Ga.: 1980).
3. Philip R. Lee et al., *Symposium on Consciousness* (London: 1974), p. 30.
4. Norman Perrin, *Rediscovering the Teaching of Jesus* (New York: 1976), p. 15 (unchanged from the original edition in 1967).
5. There are sound alternative ways of reading this verse that do not have this implication, but there are other texts that register a dramatic sense of difference rather than absolute identification—e.g., Rom 1:3-4.
6. Ellen Fremedon, "On Reading and Righting," *Ankewada* 4 (1976):55.
7. *Rediscovering*, p. 16.

Chapter 1

1. The second-century Anti-Marcionite prologue to Luke. The text may be found in Albert Huck, *Synopsis of the First Three Gospels*,

ed. F. L. Cross, 9th edition, ed. Hans Lietzmann (Oxford: 1963), p. viii.

2. There is a considerable amount of literature on John the Baptist. The following is a selection of some of the more helpful items (others will be cited in later notes) and some of the more divergent opinions: C. H. Kraeling, *John the Baptist* (New York: 1951); Walter Wink, *John the Baptist and the Gospel* (Ann Arbor, Mich.: University Microfilms, 1963)—note especially the survey of earlier studies on John the Baptist, pp. 4-74; M.-E. Boismard, "Les Traditions johanniques concernant le Baptiste," *Revue Biblique* 70 (1963):5-42; Charles H. H. Scobie, *John the Baptist* (Philadelphia: 1964); Walter Wink, *John the Baptist in the Gospel Tradition* (Cambridge, Mass.: 1968); John Reumann, "The Quest for the Historical Baptist," *Understanding the Sacred Text,* ed. Reumann (Valley Forge, Pa.: 1972), pp. 181-199; J. Becker, *Johannes der Täufer und Jesus von Nazareth* (Neukirchen-Vluyn: 1972); John H. Hughes, "John the Baptist: The Forerunner of God Himself," *Novum Testamentum* 14 (1972):191-218; Morton S. Enslin, "John and Jesus," *Zeitschrift für die Neutestamentliche Wissenschaft* 66 (1975):1-18; Ernst Bammel, "The Baptist in Early Christian Tradition," *New Testament Studies* 18 (1971):95-128; John P. Meier, "John the Baptist in Matthew's Gospel," *Journal of Biblical Literature* 99 (1980):383-405.
3. *The Antiquities of the Jews,* 18.116-119. A good basic discussion of this passage, and of disputed (and almost universally rejected) passages in the Slavonic version of Josephus's *Jewish War,* may be found in Scobie, *John the Baptist,* pp. 17-22.
4. Since the discovery of the library at Qumran, there have been various attempts to link John the Baptist with the Dead Sea Scrolls in general or with the Qumran community in particular. I am persuaded that no substantial connection can be established. See W. S. LaSor, *The Dead Sea Scrolls and the New Testament* (Grand Rapids, Mich.: 1972) and L. F. Badia, *The Qumran Baptism and John the Baptist's Baptism* (Lanham, Md.: 1980).
5. The gospel of the Hebrews was a title used in antiquity for what modern scholarship has differentiated into two or three separate gospels, of which only fragments survive. See the chapter by P. Vielhauer, "Jewish-Christian Gospels," in Edgar Hennecke, *New*

Testament Apocrypha, ed. Wilhelm Schneemelcher (trans. R. McL. Wilson), 1 (Philadelphia: 1963), pp. 117-165. The passage in question is there assigned to the gospel of the Nazareans, and is translated on pp. 146-147. For a survey of other sources bearing on John, but of doubtful historical usefulness, see Ernst Bammel, "The Baptist in Early Christian Tradition," *New Testament Studies* 18 (1971):95-128.

6. See E. P. Sanders, *Paul and Palestinian Judaism* (Philadelphia: 1977), pp. 147-182.
7. So claims Josephus (e.g., in *Antiquities* 18.15). Morton Smith, "Palestinian Judaism in the First Century," *Israel: Its Role in Civilization,* ed. Moshe Davis (New York: 1956), pp. 61-81, advises caution about these claims, on the ground that Josephus was attempting to promote the Pharisees to the Romans. But even if Josephus exaggerates, the balance of evidence suggests that he is essentially right.
8. *Antiquities* 18.118.
9. *Jewish War* 5.415.
10. Mishna *Hagigah* 2.7 and *Demai* 2.3 restrict contact with the religiously defective (*'am ha-aretz,* or "people of the land"), and *Aboth* 2.6 claims that Hillel, before the days of John the Baptist, used to say that "an *'am ha-aretz* cannot be saintly." The rabbinic antipathy to the *'am ha-aretz* may have been less pronounced in the time of John (see Aharon Oppenheimer, *The Am ha-Aretz* (Leiden: 1977), but the evidence of the Gospels and of early Rabbinic sayings suggests that it was already established then.
11. Psalm 118 is associated especially with the Feast of Tabernacles (see Mishna *Sukkah* 4.5 ff.), but as the last part of the Hallel (Pss 113-118), it was also sung at Passover (Mishna *Pesahim* 5.7, 9.3, 10.6-7), including a special instance at the conclusion of the Passover meal (*Pesahim* 10.7). It is not implausible that the Hallel, and therefore Ps 118, was sung by Passover pilgrims as they entered Jerusalem.
12. The received Hebrew text of Habakkuk 2:2-3 deals with a vision (*hazon*) and concludes by saying "it's really coming [i.e., to fulfillment]" (*bo yabo*). The Greek translation of the LXX, done well before John's mission, translates the Hebrew masculine noun *hazon* by the Greek feminine noun *horasis,* which is quite right—but in the last statement, the Greek text shifts to the

masculine to say that what is coming is *erchomenos,* i.e., no longer the vision itself but some "he." This suggests that the Greek translator already had some special expectation of a masculine Coming One; and certainly the translation encouraged readers to think in such terms.

13. R. H. Charles, *The Apocrypha and Pseudepigrapha of the Old Testament* 2 (Oxford: 1913), p. 135. Another instance of a judicial ordeal in a river may be found in 7th-century Babylon: see W. G. Lambert, "Nebuchadnezzar King of Justice," *Iraq* 27 (1965):1-11.
14. See, for instance, Mt 13:39-43, 25:31, Mk 13:27, Rev 12-20. Michael, as the special protector of Israel (Dan 10:13,21, 12:1—cf. 1 Enoch 20:5), will avenge Israel on its enemies at the end of the world, according to *The Assumption of Moses* 10:2 (cf. Rev 12:7ff.). Angels were readily representable in human form, with human clothing (e.g., Dan 10:5, Rev 15:6); the angel in Dan 10:5 is in fact first identified simply as "a man" (*ish*; LXX *anēr*—cf. Jn 10:30).
15. A deft survey of the development of the Messianic idea may be found in Joseph A. Fitzmyer, *Essays on the Semitic Background of the New Testament* (London: 1971), pp. 113-126; a more comprehensive treatment is S. Mowinckel, *He That Cometh* (Oxford: 1959)—see also Joachim Becker's *Messianic Expectation in the Old Testament* (Philadelphia: 1977). Instances of non-Messianic eschatology include Malachi, Sirach (Ecclesiasticus), Wisdom, *The Assumption of Moses, The Book of the Secrets of Enoch,* and various portions of composite books.
16. *Life,* 11-12.
17. Manual of Discipline, 8.1.
18. See H. Strack and P. Billerbeck, *Kommentar* 1 (Munich: 1922), p. 597.
19. The Hebrew text will support the way it is usually translated, "the angel of the covenant, *whom* you are longing for"; but I think the alternative translation more apt. There is no other record of a longed-for covenant *angel* in the Scriptures or in other surviving documents; and I think it not unlikely that there is a connection between this text of Malachi and the "new covenant" promised in Jeremiah 31:31-34 (cf. Ezekiel 36:24-30), which could readily be understood as "the covenant *which* you are longing

for," the angel being the messenger who brings or promulgates it. The group that produced the Damascus Document saw itself as entering into a new covenant, but does not align it with Malachi's eschatological prophecy.

20. Babylonian Talmud, *Baba Bathra* 14B is the earliest source for the arrangement, and although this text was set down long after the first century, and scarcely proves that this ordering was already conventional then, the text nevertheless "cannot be later than the end of the second century C.E., and most likely reflects a much earlier tradition" (Nahum M. Sarna, "The Order of the Books," *Studies in Jewish Bibliography, History and Literature in Honor of I. Edward Kiev,* ed. Charles Berlin [New York: 1971], p. 528).
21. 1 Mac 9:27 clearly assumes that prophecy had ceased before the 2nd century B.C. *Aboth* 1.1 makes the prophets as a group the predecessors of the rabbinic movement, and that movement eventually reaffirmed that Haggi, Zechariah, and Malachi were the last of the prophets. It is now generally conceded that the Book of Daniel is later than Malachi, but it pretends to be earlier and accordingly was in the days of John the Baptist thought to be earlier.
22. Justin Martyr, *Dialogue with Trypho* 8.4, 49.1. This is probably not Justin's invention, and the tradition is undoubtedly older than the dialogue; but there is no ground for thinking it a century older. The period between John the Baptist and Justin was one of the most actively creative in the history of Jewish thought: many such amalgamations of previously distinct ideas took place in the course of it. It is of course possible that the compilers of the gospel traditions knew some such combined version, and meant John's baptism of Jesus to be seen as Elijah's anointing of the Messiah; but I think this very doubtful, since only Mt and Mk have John baptize Jesus, and neither draws attention to such a meaning. Mt 3:14-15 even works against it. See John P. Meier, "John the Baptist in Matthew's Gospel," *Journal of Biblical Literature* 99 (1980):383-405, and M. M. Faierstein, "Why Do the Scribes Say That Elijah Must Come First?" *Journal of Biblical Literature* 100 (1981):75-86.

Chapter 2

1. Jn 7:41-42 seems to me clearly to indicate, despite the efforts of some commentators to argue the contrary, that the narrator at that point supposed that Jesus was not born in Bethlehem: cf. Jn 7:27 and 1:46. The issue of Jesus' birthplace simply does not come up in the other Gospels during his public career. The Matthean and Lucan preludes are undoubtedly late and factitious accommodations to the same biases as those shown among the Jews reported in Jn 7:41-42, and are deeply inconsistent with one another: see Raymond E. Brown, *The Birth of the Messiah* (New York: 1977).
2. In the Fourth Gospel, Jesus has an extensive mission in Judea as well, early in his public career and before his work in Galilee. Jn 5:30-35 appears to play with the supposition that Jesus was sent by John, does his will, and is authenticated by him. This play is ultimately in order to claim a more important sender, will, and testimony—but its point of departure evidently presumes that it would not be difficult for Judeans to see Jesus as an extension of John the Baptist.
3. Jn 3:22,26 also represents Jesus as baptizing, but otherwise neither the Fourth Gospel nor the Synoptics make baptism a part of Jesus' work or of his gospel. Given the ready resumption of baptism by his followers after the conclusion of his public career, it is likely that the image of Jesus baptizing would have been more amply recorded had it been part of his major mission. The odd Jn texts to the contrary may be relics of an early participation by Jesus in the baptizing mission of John before John's imprisonment and Jesus' return to Galilee, or of a representation of the baptizing activities of early Christians as if they were the work of Jesus himself, or a conflation of the two.
4. For an introduction to the huge body of modern scholarship on Jesus' message, one may consult the sampling surveyed in Gustaf Aulen, *Jesus in Contemporary Historical Research* (Philadelphia: 1976), or the extensive bibliography by D. E. Aune, *Jesus and the Synoptic Gospels* (Madison: 1980), or the comprehensive survey by W. G. Kümmel, "Jesuforschung seit 1965," *Theologische Rundschau* 40 (1975):289-336; 41 (1976):197-258, 295-363; 43 (1978):105-161, 233-265; 45 (1980):40-84, 293-337.
5. A general survey of modern scholarship on the subject may be

found in Norman Perrin, *The Kingdom of God in the Teaching of Jesus* (London: 1963). See also the same author's *Jesus and the Language of the Kingdom* (Philadelphia: 1976), and J. Schlosser, *Le Règne de Dieu dans les dits de Jésus* (Paris: 1980).

6. Or YHVH, or YHWH, depending on which system one uses for transliterating Hebrew into Roman letters. Hebrew rarely wrote vowels in its earlier days, and the exact pronunciation of the divine name must remain uncertain. It is now well known that the reconstruction "Jehovah" is a blunder arising from a misinterpretation of annotations designed to avoid pronouncing the name at all by substituting *Adonai,* "Lord."
7. See Mt 12:28, 19:24, 21:31, 21:43, where the reading is "Dominion of God." None of the other Gospels uses Mt's circumlocution "Dominion of the heavens," and Mt elsewhere shows little hesitation about writing "God." Apparently, the euphemistic mannerism was, for Mt, more a convention for this phrase than a general principle. (Cf. the formula "the Lord's Prayer"—never "Jesus' Prayer.")
8. The relevant literature may be found in Norman Perrin, *Jesus and the Language of the Kingdom* (Philadelphia: 1976), pp. 16-32, and in Strack Billerbeck, vol. 1, pp. 173-184. The occurrence of the term in the Targums is duscussed in Bruce D. Chilton, "Regnum Dei Deus Est," *Scottish Journal of Theology* 31 (1978):261-270. Did John use the same expression? Mt 3:2 claims he did; Lk 16:16 suggests either that he did or that he was at any rate preaching the same thing. The balance of probability seems to me about even and the matter is not in any way crucial.
9. For overall background to the linking of these two commandments as the epitome of the Law, see Klaus Berger, *Die Gesetzauslegung Jesu* (Neukirchen-Vluyn: 1972), pp. 136-165.
10. The basic history is given by Norman Perrin, *The Kingdom of God,* especially chapters 4 and 5.
11. The text may be found in R. H. Charles, *The Apocrypha and Pseudepigrapha of the Old Testament* 2 (Oxford: 1913), pp. 647-651, and in various other collections of intertestamental material.
12. Here I must give regrettably short shrift to two controversial issues in the scholarly discussion of the parables: the problem of deciding which parables come from Jesus himself, and the

problem of their interpretation. I tend to be less doubtful about authenticity and less radical in interpretation than the most recent new waves of criticism; and while I acknowledge that various of the parables show signs of post-Easter concerns and understandings, I find the general pattern of basic tendencies suggestive of a coherent underlying gospel, different from that of the early Church, which I suppose to be the gospel of Jesus. I have touched on these matters in the Introduction; for the history of parables-study and an ample bibliography, see W. S. Kissinger, *The Parables of Jesus: A History of Interpretation and Bibliography* (Metuchen, N.J.: 1979).

13. The literature on "the Son of Man problem" is vast and still growing. For surveys and further references, one may consult A. J. B. Higgins, "Son of Man *Forschung* since *The Teaching of Jesus*," *New Testament Essays*, ed. Higgins (Manchester: 1959), pp. 119-135; Matthew Black, "The Son of Man Problem in Recent Research," *Bulletin of the John Rylands Library* 45 (1963):305-318; I. H. Marshall, "The Synoptic Son of Man Sayings in Recent Discussion," *New Testament Studies* 12 (1966):327-351; G. Haufe, "Das Menschensohn-Probleme in der gegenwartigen wissenschaftlichen Diskussion," *Evangelische Theologie* 26 (1966):130-153; Carsten Colpe in *TDNT* 8, pp. 400-477; and the survey article, with further bibliography, by Paul Ciholas, "Son of Man in the Synoptic Gospels," *Biblical Theology Bulletin* 11 (1981):17-20. T. W. Manson, *The Teaching of Jesus* (Cambridge: 1935), pp. 211-236 and C. D. F. Moule, *The Origin of Christology* (Cambridge: 1977), pp. 11-22 offer interpretations that I find especially congenial.

14. This is a currently disputed issue, especially on the basis of the recent contributions by Geza Vermes, "The Use of *Bar Nash/Bar Nasha* in Jewish Aramaic," in Matthew Black, *An Aramaic Approach* 3rd ed. (Oxford: 1967), pp. 310-328, and "The Present State of the 'Son of Man' Debate," *Journal of Jewish Studies* 29 (1978):123-134. But I do not see that any of Vermes' texts establishes that "son of man" was used as a direct self-reference: as Frederick Houk Borsch pointed out in the *Son of Man in Myth and History* (Philadelphia: 1967), p. 23, there is another way of reading them, one which seems to me more plausible. See also Joseph A. Fitzmyer, "The New Testament Title 'Son of Man'

Philologically Considered," *A Wandering Aramean* (Missoula: 1979), pp. 143-160, and J. W. Bowker "The Son of Man," *Journal of Theological Studies* 28 (1977):1-30.

15. 1 Mac 2:59-60 uses parts of it as a special rallying point. Josephus attests to its continuing popularity in his own day in *Ant* 10.267.
16. See 1 Mac 1 and 2 Mac 4-6.
17. See H. H. Rowley, "The Herodians," *Journal of Theological Studies* 41 (1940):14-27, and Jean le Moyne, *Les Sadducéens* (Paris: 1972), pp. 340-343.
18. John C. Meagher, *Clumsy Construction in Mark's Gospel* (Toronto: 1979), pp. 82-142.
19. An unbiased reading of Ps 80:14-19 will show an interesting and perhaps significant parallel: the petitioning people of Israel are represented collectively as a vine and finally as "we" and "us." In between the parallel constructions that suggest identical meanings, there are references to the *Son*, then to the vine again, then to the man at God's right hand, then to the son of man who has been authorized by God—and then to "us, we." It is possible that the Psalm turns from its central preoccupation to glance at the King as son, man, son of man; it is frequently read that way. But it seems to me at least equally plausible (and to some others, downright obvious) that son, man, and son of man are, like the parabolic vine, references to the collectivity of petitioning Israel.
20. The basic formulation of this view was by Phillipp Vielhauer, "Gottesreich und Menschensohn," *Festschrift für Günther Dehn*, ed. W. Schneemelcher (Neukirchen: 1957), pp. 51-79. He and others have developed it further since then, but have been only partially persuasive—see the surveys cited in note 13 of this chapter.
21. See Gerhard Delling, "Die Bezeichnung 'Söhne Gottes' in der jüdischen Literatur der hellenistisch—römischen Zeit," *God's Christ and His People,* ed. Jacob Jervell and Wayne A. Meeks (Oslo: 1977), pp. 18-28.
22. See Eduard Lohse in *TDNT* 8, pp. 360-362: "There is no clear instance to support the view that in pre-Christian times Judaism used the title 'son of God' for the Messiah"—but although the term was not standard, "Israel . . . employed 'son of God'. . . when quoting the Messianic promises." See also the Qumran texts 4Q Flor I.11 and 4Q Dan Apoc, quoted in Martin Hengel, *The Son*

of God (Philadelphia: 1975), pp. 44-45.

23. See especially Joachim Jeremias, *The Prayers of Jesus* (London: 1967), pp. 11-65 and 108-112, and *New Testament Theology* 1 (New York: 1971), pp. 36-37. For a contrasting view, G. Schrenk, *TDNT* 5, 945-1067. It is often proposed that Jesus' way of calling God "Father" establishes a claim to a peculiar and exalted form of sonship in his case. This seems to me to founder on the general early Christian use of the same form of address. His use of "my Father" is intensive, but hardly exclusive, whether or not he ever used the first person plural in such a construction.
24. See George Foot Moore, *Judaism in the First Centuries of the Christian Era* (Cambridge, Mass: 1927-30); L. Baeck, *The Pharisees* (New York: 1957); Louis Finkelstein, *The Pharisees* (Philadelphia: 1962); Jacob Neusner, *The Rabbinic Traditions about the Pharisees before 70* (Leiden: 1971); John Bowker, *Jesus and the Pharisees* (Cambridge: 1973); Asher Finkel, *The Pharisees and the Teacher of Nazareth* (Leiden: 1974).

Chapter 3

1. The translated text of the *Didache* is available in various collections bearing the title *The Apostolic Fathers*. For a more comprehensive treatment, see Jean Paul Audet, *La Didache* (Paris: 1958).
2. The title was added quite early, but was not part of the original work.
3. There has been a great deal of study devoted to sifting the evidence Luke presents in Acts. Much of it is conveniently catalogued in A. J. Mattill, *A Classified Bibliography of Literature on the Acts of the Apostles* (Leiden: 1966), which may be supplemented and updated through the bibliographical survey articles by E. Grasser, "Acta-Forschung seit 1960," *Theologische Rundschau* 41 (1976):141-194, 259-290, and 42 (1977):1-68. For a fine survey of the literature, see W. Gasque, *A History of the Criticism of the Acts of the Apostles* (Tübingen: 1975). There are several excellent commentaries on Acts; the most comprehensive and penetrating is perhaps Ernst Haenchen, *Die Apostelgeschichte* (Göttingen: 1956; 7th revised edition, 1977), translated as *The Acts of the Apostles* (Oxford: 1971). Although unfinished and relatively old, the monumental commentary by K. Lake and

H. Cadbury in F. J. Foakes Jackson and K. Lake, eds., *The Beginnings of Christianity* (London: 1933, reprinted Grand Rapids: 1979) is still useful. Others include H. Conzelmann, *Die Apostelgeschichte* (Tübingen: 2nd ed. 1972), C. S. C. Williams, *A Commentary on the Acts of the Apostles* (London: 1957), F. F. Bruce, *Commentary on the Book of the Acts* (3rd ed. London: 1962), O. Bauernfeind, *Kommentar und Studien zur Apostelgeschichte* (Tübingen: 1980), J. Munck, *The Acts of the Apostles* (Garden City: 1967), and I. H. Marshall, *The Acts of the Apostles* (Grand Rapids: 1980).

4. A survey of recent studies of Luke's favorite ideas and biasing tendencies may be found in F. Buvon, *Luc le théologien: Vingt-cinq ans de recherches* (Paris: 1978).
5. Just how early is a matter of dispute: there is a tendency in current scholarship to be skeptical about tracing the Twelve back to Jesus, or even back to early Synoptic tradition—but see E. Best, "Mark's Use of the Twelve," *Zeitschrift für die Neutestamentliche Wissenschaft* 69 (1978):11-35. See also next note.
6. For more thorough treatment of the complications of these questions, see G. Klein, *Die Zwölf Apostel: Ursprung und Gestalt einer Idee* (Göttingen: 1961) and Walter Schmithals, *The Office of Apostle in the Early Church* (Nashville: 1969).
7. See the judicious treatment of this issue by S. G. Wilson, *The Gentiles and the Gentile Mission in Luke Acts* (Cambridge: 1973).
8. There is great controversy about the nature and extent of Luke's sources, and about the ways in which he made use of them, as the commentaries attest. Jacques Dupont, *The Sources of Acts* (London: 1964), surveys the various attempts to isolate and describe the materials at Luke's disposal, and since then there has been considerable additional discussion, especially about the speeches in Acts. Just where Luke is using sources or authentic traditions and just where he is inventing from his own imagination is still a moot issue, though it is generally conceded that he did both. After considering various arguments that attempt to demonstrate that speeches in Acts are Luke's own invention, I have come to the provisional conclusion that Luke probably never simply quotes from a documentary source, but probably invented none of the speeches from whole cloth. Hence they contain Lucan turns of expression and occasionally conform to

known Lucan biases, but nevertheless differ considerably from one another and manifest ideas that are quite plausibly drawn from early tradition and highly unlikely to be Lucan—an obvious example being the negative attitude toward the Temple displayed in Stephen's speech in Acts 7, in stark contrast with Luke's own rather romantic regard for it (see F. D. Weinert, "The Meaning of the Temple in Luke-Acts," *Biblical Theology Bulletin* 11 [1981]:85-89). A less obvious example, but one that conveniently allows checking, is Luke's representation of Paul's preaching. Luke apparently did not know Paul's epistles (attempts to establish the contrary have failed), and there is good reason to suppose that Luke did not know Paul himself (see Haenchen, *Acts,* pp. 112-116), but Luke did know something about Paul's theology. Acts 13:39, where Paul tells his audience in Pisidian Antioch that faith in Jesus will justify them where the Law of Moses could not, is not only typical Paul but essentially *peculiar* to Paul—for this absolute use of the verb "justify" (*dikaioō*) occurs in the New Testament only in the writings of Paul and in works derived from Paul's gospel. Luke puts it in no other mouth but his (cf. his association of "grace" [*charis*] and the title "Son of God" with Paul's preaching and with no one else: here too he is on target). For a broader discussion of the problem, see especially Ulrich Wilckens, *Die Missionsreden der Apostelgeschichte* (Neukirchen: 1961) along with M. Wilcox, "A Foreword to the Study of the Speeches in Acts," *Christianity, Judaism, and Other Greco-Roman Cults,* ed. J. Neusner, pt. 1 (Leiden: 1975), pp. 206-225, and W. Ward Gasque, "The Book of Acts and History," *Unity and Diversity in New Testament Theology,* ed. R. A. Guelich (Grand Rapids, Mich.: 1978), pp. 54-72. For reasons that I will put forward shortly, I am less confident in the historical reliability of the situations in which Luke places the speeches, and in some cases I think he has wrongly assigned the speaker.

9. Luke's abrupt movements in and out of the first person plural in the latter chapters of Acts is literarily inconsistent and remains a mystery. Some (e.g., Haenchen) have argued that these "we-sections" are entirely artificial; others suppose that they represent Luke's own memories; still others presume that Luke is using and quoting a source. For an entry into the general

discussion of the matter, see S. Dockx, "Luc a-t-il été le compagnon d'apostolat de Paul?," *Nouvelle Revue Théologique* 103 (1981):385-400, and Vernon K. Robbins, "By Land and Sea: The We-Passages and Ancient Sea Voyages," *Perspectives on Luke-Acts,* ed. C. Talbert (Danville, Va.: 1978), pp. 215-242.

10. On the lack of Scriptural basis for Messianism, see Joachim Becker, *Messianic Expectation in the Old Testament* (Philadelphia: 1977). It is generally agreed that the widespread (but not universal) Jewish Messianic expectation at this time was projected into the Scriptures rather than derived from them. The most thoughtful and thorough treatment of the subject is S. Mowinckel, *He That Cometh* (Oxford: 1959).
11. For more ample discussion of the backgrounds of Stephen's speech, see (in addition to the commentaries) J. Kilgallen, *The Stephen Speech* (Rome: 1976), C. H. H. Scobie, "The Use of Source Material in the Speeches of Acts II and VII," *New Testament Studies* 25 (1979):399-421, and E. Richard, "Acts 7: An Investigation of the Samaritan Evidence," *Catholic Biblical Quarterly* 39 (1977):190-208.
12. The identity of the Hellenists (and Hebrews) is a much disputed point. The Hellenists have been variously identified as pagan Greeks, non-Christian Diaspora Jews, Greek-speaking Jewish-Christians, and other combinations. The most common assumption is that "Hellenist" designated the language they spoke. I suspect that this is the way Luke understood the term; but it seems to me overwhelmingly more likely that the original thrust of the term was religious and cultural, whether or not a language difference accompanied the more essential division. Martin Hengel, "The Hellenists and their Expulsion from Jerusalem," *Acts and the History of Earliest Christianity* (Philadelphia: 1980), pp. 71-80, considers the meaning of "Hellenists" to be primarily linguistic but the group's significance to be primarily a matter of its religious differences. The latter seems indisputable, and I am puzzled that it does not more frequently influence the primary interpretation of the names. See E. Ferguson, "The Hellenists in the Book of Acts," *Restoration Quarterly* 12 (1969):159-180 and L. Gaston, *No Stone on Another: The Significance of the Fall of Jerusalem in the Synoptic Gospels* (Leiden: 1970), pp. 154-161. It should be noted that Acts does not unequivocally say that

Stephen or any other member of the Seven belonged to the Hellenist group, and some scholars have offered alternative identifications with Samaritans, even with the Hebrews. It is possible to raise the question, but again I think it overwhelmingly probable that the Seven were the Hellenist leaders.

13. Paul's denial that Judean Christians would know his face, and his insistence that he did not "go up" to Jerusalem but "returned" to Damascus, would clearly lead us to suppose (if we had Galatians but not Acts) that Damascus was his home base, not Jerusalem, at the time of conversion. Moreover, he is at pains in Galatians to deny certain rumors about his movements that he knows to be in circulation—hence these clues are the more likely to be deliberate denials of the information on which Luke eventually relied (probably innocently). The notion of a commission to capture Christians in Damascus and bring them to Jerusalem for punishment is intrinsically unlikely, and is probably Luke's invention—a device to explain how this persecutor of the Hellenist Christians wound up in Damascus. Haenchen's commentary discusses the relevant texts incisively.
14. Especially puzzling is the set of inconsistencies about the relationship between baptism and the gift of the Spirit. Acts 2:38 assumes that the Spirit is received as a consequence of baptism, but the conversion of the Samaritans in Acts 8:12-17 entails a baptism that does not bring the Spirit (which is bestowed separately through the laying-on of hands), and the conversion of Cornelius and his people in Acts 10:44-48 shows the gift of the Spirit being given without baptism, the baptism then being added as a final seal of belonging. To compound the confusion, Acts 19:1-6 reports disciples who have been baptized but have never heard of the Holy Spirit, which is then invoked upon them by Paul. I will not try to do more than to suggest that these disjunctions may be rooted in a difference of early customs, one group having reinstituted the baptism of John in Jesus' name and another group not baptizing in water but only, as befit the new order, in Holy Spirit. If there was such a disjunction in the practices of the Hebrews and Hellenists at first, the two seem to have been joined before very long, and Luke's stories characteristically give the Hebrews the superior position in the course of sorting out the disjunction.

15. The Epistle of James does not undertake to explain what the future work of Jesus will be, and obviously assumes much of the gospel on whose preaching it is based. If the stand it takes is in opposition to (its musunderstood version of) Paul, it must have been written rather late, and thus at a distance from the earliest Hebrew gospel, since this motif does not appear in the earlier Pauline Epistles. But it is not necessary to assume that it is Paul's doctrine that is in question: the position it attacks may possibly have been promoted by early Christian Hellenists as by Jewish Hellenists before them. Philo analogously argues that the Law should be practised, in opposition to other sophisticated Jews who evidently treat it as instruction but not as literal prescription (*De Migratione*, 89.93).
16. This verse is difficult and its translation disputed. The AV reads, "Do ye think that the scripture saith in vain, The spirit that dwelleth in us lusteth to envy?" which seems to me to catch the sense aptly. The NEB understands it similarly, rendering the final phrase "turns towards envious desires." But the verse is frequently read as if the subject of the key verb were (implicitly) *God* rather than (explicitly) *spirit* (thus RSV) and is sometimes read as if *spirit* meant *Holy Spirit* (thus JB). Such readings depend upon unwarranted assumptions that go against the grain of the context, structure, and vocabulary of the text, all of which argue for its being a pejorative statement about the human spirit. (The "scripture" ostensibly quoted is unidentifiable.) For details of the problem and the arguments against the RSV and JB translations, see the commentaries by E. M. Sidebottom, James B. Anderson, and especially Sophie Laws (*A Commentary on the Epistle of James* [London: 1980], pp. 174-179).

Chapter 4

1. A. H. McNeile, *An Introduction to the Study of the New Testament,* 2nd ed., revised by C. S. C. Williams, (Oxford: 1953), p. 306. Cf. the flat opening assertion of the corresponding section of Kümmel's *Introduction to the New Testament*: "II and III John have the same author" (14th Revised edition [Nashville, Tenn.: 1966], p. 315).

2. See T. W. Manson's note in *Journal of Theological Studies* 48 (1947):32-33. (The Harnack proposal was made in *Zur Revision der Prinzipien der neutestamentlichen Textkritik,* pp. 61-65.)
3. James Moffatt, in *An Introduction to the Literature of the New Testament* (New York: 1917), pp. 478-479 (following Lightfoot in *Biblical Essays*) claims that the reference of the Muratorian canon is to 2 and 3 John, 1 John having already been quoted. But this argument founders on the statements of the text, which says that two epistles of John are accepted, not two additional epistles. It may be noted that the canon's earlier reference is in the plural, to the epistles of John (although the quotation is from 1 John alone); and that Revelation is likewise mentioned early in the text yet subsequently catalogued in its place toward the end of the list. Only special pleading can evade the evident meaning: the Church accepted only two Johannine epistles.
4. I suppose that the formula "received in the Church" (*in catholica habentur*) implies a rejection of 3 John rather than an ignorance of it. A similar statement had just preceded, with reference to unacceptable Pauline forgeries: "There is current also [an epistle] to the Laodiceans, another to the Alexandrians, forged in Paul's name for the sect of Marcion, and several others, which cannot be received in the catholic church; for it will not do to mix gall with honey." The statement just after the reference to the Johannine epistles likewise distinguishes between acceptable and unacceptable candidates. "Also of the revelations we accept only those of John and Peter, which [latter] some of our people do not want to read in the church" (Edgar Hennecke, *New Testament Apocrypha,* [Philadelphia: 1963], pp. 44-45).
5. In some places, 2 John was also excluded: according to Eusebius (*Hist.,* VI,25), Origen reported that some doubted the authenticity of both. Neither made its way into the Peshitta, nor into the Syrian Church up to the fifth century. It is possible that both were rejected as forgeries in earliest times, and that 3 John was recognized to be a forgery of a particularly pernicious tendency. It may thus have acquired a bad reputation that followed it to the West and impeded its reception even when the reasons for its ill repute had been lost, while the evidently orthodox 2 John, not so badly reputed, gradually won acceptance. But even if the immediate cause of doubt had been the suspicion of unauthen-

ticity rather than of heterodoxy, some taint of the latter is plausibly the ultimate reason for the slower admission of 3 John.

6. For a more detailed argument in defence of the proposition that John 1:14 originally read "the Word became Spirit and dwelt in us," see John C. Meagher, "John 1:14 and the New Temple," *Journal of Biblical Literature* 88 (1969):57-68.
7. Raymond E. Brown, writing of the words of 6:51-58, observes that "they are really out of place anywhere during the ministry except at the Last Supper. Even such a usually conservative critic as Lagrange has recognized this, and he has been followed by many scholars who otherwise show no facile tendency to dismantle the Johannine discourses" (*The Gospel According to John,* 1 [Garden City, N.Y.: 1966], p. 287).
8. It is not clear whether the reference to the witness of the blood (1 John 5:6,8) is original or a later addition (i.e., earlier than the now generally rejected verse 5:7 but later than the main body of the epistle), nor is it entirely clear just what it means. It has evident kinship with the water and blood from Jesus' side in John and could, depending on its meaning and purpose, derive either from original Johannine thought or from the hand of the later anti-Docetist emender.
9. The usual interpretation, in Kittel's *TDNT* as well as in standard commentaries, sees references to angels in verse 8. I think that reading extremely ill-founded, and have elsewhere argued the superiority of the interpretation I use here (*The Way of the Word,* pp. 171-172).
10. For a very thorough survey of the values of this and other verbs of seeing in pagan, Jewish, and Christian antiquity, see the article by Wilhelm Michaelis in Kittel's *TDNT,* 5, pp. 315-382.
11. For Philo's general use of verbs of seeing, see article by Michaelis in *TDNT* 5, pp. 334-338. His specific interpretation of "Israel" as "a man seeing God" may be found in various places: *De Abrahama* 12.57; *De Confusione Linguarum* 20.92; *De Fuga et Inventione* 38.208; *De Mutatione Nominum* 12.82; *De Somniis* II, 26.173; *De Posteritate Caini* 92; *Legatio ad Gaium* 4. For the meaning of Philo's idea of seeing God, see Harry Austryn Wolfson, *Philo,* 2 (Cambridge, Mass.: 1948), pp. 82-92: Wolfson concludes that Philo speaks of an indirect knowledge of God and thus of a metaphorical vision only.

12. The Fourth Gospel is especially emphatic about its assertive teachings on the Holy Spirit, and this emphasis may reflect another point of Johannine corrective struggle with the gospel of Demetrios. It is also worth noting that Jude's opponents are characterized as not having the Spirit (19).
13. With reference to Epiphanius' assertion that the followers of Cerinthus accepted only Matthew's gospel, Gustave Bardy observed that "il paraît certain que c'est Epiphane tout seul qui a imaginé la prédilection des Cérinthiens pour l'Évangile de Matthieu, car ni Irenée, ni Hippolyte, ni Pseudo-Tertullien n'en parlent, et Filastrius ne fait que traduire . . . la formule d'Épiphane. L'évêque de Salamine a été amené à cette théorie parce que dans sa pensée, Ébion et Cérinthe sont plus ou moins confondus, et qu'Ébion est présenté par lui comme un doublet de Cérinthe" ("Cérinthe," *Revue Biblique* 30 [1920]:368). Epiphanius may have invented the Cerinthian partiality to Matthew, but very likely inherited the tendency to confuse Cerinthus with the fictionally eponymous Ebion from which that invention was derived. Bardy's dismissal of Irenaeus' characterization of Cerinthus is on extremely flimsy and arbitrary grounds, and his acceptance of the later Judaizing image of Cerinthus is to my mind incautious and inadequately appreciative of the documentable confusion with Ebion. If Irenaeus is right—and of all the ancient witnesses, he has the greatest likelihood of being right—Cerinthus is very unlikely to have had Judaizing tendencies, since the authority of the Law is completely undermined by the Cerinthian doctrine reported by Irenaeus. I suspect that the eventual reputation of Cerinthus as Judaizer is a blunder as ironic as the eventual reputation of Diotrephes as a heretic.
14. See Bardy, "Cérinthe," pp. 354-361.
15. Bardy, "Cérinthe," p. 358.

Chapter 5

1. These and other questions are discussed in detail in major commentaries on the Fourth Gospel, of which some of the more recent and comprehensive are those of R. Bultmann, *The Gospel of John* (Philadelphia: 1971), R. E. Brown, *The Gospel According to John*, 2 vols. (Garden City: 1966-1970), R. Schnackenburg, *Das Jo-*

hannesevangelium (Freiburg: 1967-1977), M.-E. Boismard and A. Lamouille, *L'Évangile de Jean* (Paris: 1977), and C. K. Barrett, *The Gospel According to St. John* (Philadelphia: 1978). E. Malatesta, *St. John's Gospel: 1920-1965* (Rome: 1967) offers an extremely helpful and comprehensive bibliography for the period specified, and may be supplemented by the series of bibliographical surveys by Hartwig Thyen, "Aus der Literatur zum Johannesevangelium," *Theologische Rundschau* 39 (1974):1-69, 222-252, 289-330, 42 (1977):211-270, 43 (1978):328-359, 44 (1979):97-134, and (by Jürgen Becker) 47 (1982):279-301.

2. Surveys of scholarship on these matters may be found in D. Moody Smith, "The Sources of the Gospel of John: An Assessment of the Present State of the Problem," *New Testament Studies* 10 (1964):336-351; Raymond E. Brown, *The Gospel According to John* 1 (Garden City: 1966), pp. xxiv-xl; R. Kysar, "The Source Analysis of the Fourth Gospel: A Growing Consensus?," *Novum Testamentum* 15 (1973):134-152; and, along with surveys of other scholarly concerns, R. Kysar, *The Fourth Evangelist and His Gospel* (Minneapolis: 1975). D. A. Carson, "Current Source Criticism of the Fourth Gospel," *Journal of Biblical Literature* 97 (1978):411-429, calls for a "probing agnosticism " on the subject. My conjectural reconstruction is intended as a probe in that spirit.
3. For attempts to reconstruct the milieu of the Fourth Gospel's origins, see O. Cullmann, *The Johannine Circle* (London: 1976); R. Kysar, "Community and Gospel: Vectors in Fourth Gospel Criticism," *Interpretation* 31 (1977):355-366; A. J. Mattill, Jr., "Johannine Communities Behind the Fourth Gospel: Georg Richter's Analysis," *Theological Studies* 38 (1977):294-315; R. A. Culpepper, *The Johannine School* (Missoula: 1975); and Raymond E. Brown, *The Community of the Beloved Disciple* (New York: 1979). Two important features of the Fourth Gospel's formative milieu that will be neglected in this chapter are its relation to the Samaritans and the progressive alienation of the Johannine community from the Jewish Synagogues. For the former, see Charles H. H. Scobie, "The Origins and Development of Samaritan Christianity," *New Testament Studies* 19 (1973):390-414, and J. Bowman, *The Samaritan Problem* (Pittsburgh: 1975),

and for the latter, J. L. Martyn, *History and Theology in the Fourth Gospel* 2nd ed. (Nashville: 1979).

4. Lk 13:34 suggests that he had attempted to win Jerusalem to the gospel on previous occasions; all three Synoptic Gospels imply friendly contacts in Jerusalem in the provision of a Passover meal.
5. Wayne A. Meeks, "Galilee and Judea in the Fourth Gospel," *Journal of Biblical Literature* 85 (1966):159-169 argues against a Judean background for the Fourth Gospel, but on grounds that do not appreciate the difference made by postulating a *Hellenist* Judean background. His contention that the Galileans are generally represented as the believers and the Judeans as the unbelievers has considerable currency in the contemporary Fourth Gospel criticism, but I suggest that (a) a concern with the unbelief found in Judea is quite proper to a Judean account, (b) many of the key instances of belief are found among the Judeans (e.g., Nicodemus, Mary, Martha, Nathaniel), and (c) significant unbelief (though less hostility) is shown in Galilee as well (e.g., Jn 7:5, 4:44).
6. There appear to have been some displacements in the text with respect to these movements (e.g., many commentators suggest a transposition of chapters 5 and 6), but that does not affect the main conclusion.
7. It is generally recognized that Synoptic *traditions* were used in the composition of the Fourth Gospel, but, with a few exceptions, it is normally conceded that the Synoptic *Gospels* as such were not used.
8. Skepticism about the potential historical reliability of the Fourth Gospel has been dramatically reduced by recent scholarship, especially in the light of archaeological confirmation of details previously dismissed as inventions. See especially C. H. Dodd, *Historical Tradition in the Fourth Gospel* (Cambridge: 1963).
9. The intriguing problem of the Beloved Disciple has begotten a range of responses attempting to identify a specific historical individual and another range of symbolic interpretations: see J. Colson, *L'Enigme du disciple, que Jésus aimait* (Paris: 1969); T. Lorenzen, *Der Lieblingsjünger im Johannesevangelium* (Stuttgart: 1971); D. J. Hawkins, "The Function of the Beloved Disciple Motif in the Johannine Redaction," *Laval théologigue et philo-*

sophique 33 (1977):135-150; and J. O'Grady, "The Role of the Beloved Disciple," *Biblical Theology Bulletin* 9 (1979):58-65. I offer no speculation on the identity of the Beloved Disciple, but suppose that the editorial claim about the importance of his or her witness indicates that the Fourth Gospel is rooted in memories, however distant, of genuine witness. That does not mean, of course, that the earliest written form of the Fourth Gospel did not incorporate material drawn from other sources as well. I have not attempted to resolve how the witness of the Beloved Disciple relates to, say, the conjectured signs-source (see R. T. Fortna, *The Gospel of Signs* [Cambridge: 1970]: they could be identical, entirely discrete, or partially overlapping. For my purposes, the matter need not be resolved, as it makes relatively little difference to the foundation of the gospel of the Ultimate.

10. See the commentaries on Jn 1:51. It may be noted that the Fourth Gospel is much clearer than the Synoptics about Jesus' negative attitudes towards the Jerusalem Temple, which I take to be a further indication of its Hellenist origins.
11. The final version of the Fourth Gospel, unlike the Synoptic Gospels, identifies Jesus with the glorified and heavenly Son of Man. I believe that this identification was introduced at the level of development that I call the gospel of the Ultimate, and that at the earlier stage of composition, the gosepl of the Beloved Disciple, the motif of the Son of Man was present and intimately associated with Jesus but not identified absolutely with him. The description of the Son of Man motif in this paragraph is intended to show that there is a clear continuity between what was finally written in the Fourth Gospel and what had originally been the gospel of Jesus. Just how the gospel of Jesus was reinterpreted in the gospel of the Beloved Disciple (before the latter was reinterpreted again in the gospel of the Ultimate) is uncertain; but even in the final version, the traces of the original remain. See Francis J. Maloney, *The Johannine Son of Man* (Rome: 1976) and Eugen Ruckstuhl, "Die johanneische Menschensohn-forschung 1957-1969," *Theologische Berichte* 1 (Zürich-Einsiedeln: 1972), pp. 171-284, for the current discussion of the final state and for information on the individual texts.
12. For this interpretation of "Israel," see note 11 of the previous chapter. I presume that this sort of metaphorical reading was

not peculiar to Philo, and therefore do not suppose that he was its source for the Fourth Gospel.

13. I take Paul to be characterizing a moderate view of the Law as Wisdom, but much more radical versions were available: Philo shows that some of his contemporaries had almost totally abandoned the literal meaning and the practice of commandments concerning the Sabbath, circumcision, and the Temple.
14. The Gospels' emphasis on physical evidence in resurrection appearances—touching, eating, even palpable wounds—is clearly for the purpose of reassurance that the witnesses saw the risen Jesus, not an illusion or a ghost. It seems more likely that the reassurance is given to the later readers than to the early believers. Paul says nothing about such physical evidence in 1 Cor 15: it is quite possible that some of the witnesses, including himself, neither received nor required crude physical guarantees, but accepted a special revelation given through the Spirit (cf. Acts 7:55, "But being full of holy spirit, peering into heaven, he saw God's glory and Jesus standing at God's right") as the full disclosure of exaltation and glory. If so, for such witnesses resurrection would not be the main event but a rather incidental implication; and a Gospel written from such a perspective would not necessarily have an account of the resurrection at all, only of the encounter with the exalted Jesus.
15. This too, of course, is a conjecture. The original stimulus was the "Ecclesiastical Redactor" put forth in Bultmann's commentary; though it is by no means universally accepted, it seems to me clear that only by means of some such correctional theory can we make adequate sense of the evidence (although there are various ways of doing so: the motives, scope, and nature of the correction are arguable matters even if one has accepted the basic supposition of a corrective revision).